PERGAMON INTERNATIONAL LIBRARY
of Science, Technology, Engineering and Social Studies
The 1000-volume original paperback library in aid of education,
industrial training and the enjoyment of leisure
Publisher: Robert Maxwell, M.C.

Global Planning and Resource Management

Pergamon Titles of Related Interest

Haq   DIALOGUE FOR A NEW ORDER
Laszlo   REGIONALISM AND THE NEW WORLD ORDER
Meagher   AN INTERNATIONAL REDISTRIBUTION OF WEALTH
          AND POWER
King   THE STATE OF THE PLANET

Related Journals*

EVALUATION AND PROGRAM PLANNING
GEOFORUM
INTERNATIONAL JOURNAL OF INTERCULTURAL RELATIONS
LONG RANGE PLANNING
REGIONAL STUDIES
TECHNOLOGY IN SOCIETY
URBAN SYSTEMS
WORLD DEVELOPMENT
PROGRESS IN PLANNING

*Free specimen copies available upon request.

PERGAMON POLICY STUDIES ON INTERNATIONAL DEVELOPMENT

Global Planning and Resource Management

Toward International Decision Making in a Divided World

Edited by
Antony J. Dolman

Published in cooperation with
Foundation Reshaping the
International Order (RIO)

Pergamon Press
NEW YORK • OXFORD • TORONTO • SYDNEY • PARIS • FRANKFURT

Pergamon Press Offices:

U.S.A.	Pergamon Press Inc., Maxwell House, Fairview Park, Elmsford, New York 10523, U.S.A.
U.K.	Pergamon Press Ltd., Headington Hill Hall, Oxford OX3 0BW, England
CANADA	Pergamon of Canada, Ltd., Suite 104, 150 Consumers Road, Willowdale, Ontario M2J 1P9, Canada
AUSTRALIA	Pergamon Press (Aust.) Pty. Ltd., P.O. Box 544, Potts Point, NSW 2011, Australia
FRANCE	Pergamon Press SARL, 24 rue des Ecoles, 75240 Paris, Cedex 05, France
FEDERAL REPUBLIC OF GERMANY	Pergamon Press GmbH, Hammerweg 6, Postfach 1305, 6242 Kronberg/Taunus, Federal Republic of Germany

Library of Congress Cataloging in Publication Data
Main entry under title:

Global planning and resource management.

   (Pergamon policy studies on international development)
   Report of an on-going project of the Foundation
Reshaping the International Order.
   Includes index.
   1. International economic relations—Addresses,
essays, lectures. I. Dolman, Antony J. II. Founda-
tion Reshaping the International Order. III. Series.
HF1411.G646 1980   337   80-19081
ISBN 0-08-026309-7
ISBN 0-08-026320-8 (pbk.)

Printed in the United States of America

There is nothing more difficult to carry out,
nor more doubtful of success, nor more dangerous
to handle, than to initiate a new order of things.
For the reformer has enemies in all who profit by
the old order, and only luke-warm defenders in all
those who would profit by the new order. The luke-
warmness arises partly from fear of their adversar-
ies who have the law in their favor; and partly from
the incredulity of mankind, who do not truly believe
in anything new until they have had actual experience
of it.

Machiavelli
The Prince, 1513

Contents

Contents

Acknowledgments

The editor wishes to express his gratitude to all those who worked hard to make this publication possible.

Firstly, to those who, despite their excruciating schedules, were able to accept the RIO Foundation's invitation to prepare the position papers which make up this book: Silviu Brucan, Harlan Cleveland, Richard Falk, Johan Galtung, Johan Kaufmann, Stel Kefalas, Elisabeth Mann Borgese, Arvid Pardo and Christopher Pinto. To these and to Bert Röling, who allowed us to reprint a conference paper on a subject of great relevance to our investigations, he extends his grateful thanks.

Secondly, to those who bravely confronted a very tight publishing deadline to prepare the manuscript. Thanks are especially due to Peet Gerritsma who typed by far the largest part of the final manuscript under conditions which were sometimes far from ideal and to Jan van Ettinger who somehow managed to find the time to supervise and control its production. The assistance of Anneke Mohr and Maria Derwort Lievaart in making sure that the deadline could be met is also acknowledged.

Last but by no means least, the RIO Foundation gratefully acknowledges the support received from the Ministry for Foreign Affairs, Sweden for funding the project of which this volume is part. While indebted to the Swedish government, the Foundation is alone responsible for the conclusions drawn from the document's papers.

Introduction
Antony J. Dolman

The papers contained in this volume have, with a single exception, been prepared as part of the RIO Foundation's project *RIO - A 'Second Round'*. This project, started in 1978, sets out to identify possible ways in which global planning and resource management capabilities could be strengthened and to examine the various problems which could frustrate efforts which might be made by the international community in this direction. The project's main report will be published under the title *Managing the World's Resources*. (1)

The essential background to the project is provided by the *RIO Report*. (2) First published in October 1976, it reflects the thinking of a distinguished group of 21 specialists with widely varying background who, under the leadership of Jan Tinbergen, set out "to translate into politically feasible first steps the courses of action which the existing international community might choose to take in the direction of a more human and equitable order". (3) So far translated into eleven languages, the report has sold close to 200,000 copies.

Although the *RIO Report* has much to say about problems of national development, it is on the international order that the report obviously focuses. It suggests that there are at least ten areas in which effective and equitable international responses need to be formulated if progress in the direction of a fairer distribution of resources and opportunity is to be ensured. (4) The Report contains medium- and long-range proposals with varying degrees of specificity for each of these areas, about 100 proposals in all.

Conscious of the fact that such an extensive 'agenda' might serve to paralyse rather than to promote discussion of what needs to be done, the RIO Group examined ways of combining many of the proposals made into 'packages for comprehensive negotiation'. The Group felt that such packages, despite their

1

Madison Avenue overtones, possessed a number of important and
distinct advantages. (5) Firstly, packages can be usefully employed not only to demonstrate but also to utilize the trans-
sectoral linkages between proposals. Recognition of what the
Report calls "chain-reactions" and "ripple-effects" makes it
possible to present proposals in a more integrated fashion.
Secondly, packages have a tactical usefulness in that they can
serve as a means for balancing the divergent interests of rich
and poor countries. They provide a framework for devising po-
sitive-sum games. And thirdly, packages can facilitate the process of negotiation. Consideration of groups of proposals
rather than isolated initiatives increases the chances of comprehensive outcomes and the likelihood that results will have
a wider degree of acceptance.

The *RIO Report* contains proposals for three 'packages for
comprehensive negotiation'. The first of these seeks to redress
gross inequities in the distribution of wealth and opportunity
through a "global compact", aimed at eradicating the worst manifestations of poverty and satisfying the basic material needs
of the world's "poor majority" in the course of a single decade.
The second package groups together various proposals which
would help come to terms with the serious disruptions in the
international economic system and ensure more harmonious global
growth. The third and final package aims at putting into place
some important elements of a system of global planning and resource management.

The RIO Group considered its proposals for 'packages' as
being one of the most important ideas contained in the *RIO Report*. (6) It was only natural, therefore, that the RIO Foundation, when it came to draw up its first work program in 1977,
should choose to focus part of its attention on trying to elaborate one of the packages. But which one?

The idea of elaborating the first package - the "global
compact" on poverty - was soon rejected. It was felt that the
basic problem it addressed would receive more than adequate
attention both within and outside the intergovernmental system
as a result of the efforts to fashion an international development strategy for the 1980s. It was also feared that proposals aimed at the eradication of poverty and the satisfaction
of needs were in danger of being cooptated by entrenched and
vested interests which would present them as an alternative to
the structural changes being demanded by the developing countries as part of their efforts to build a New International
Economic Order. Our assumptions and our fears, as it turned
out, were not unrealistic. (7)

The idea of elaborating the second package aimed at ensuring the harmonious growth of the world economic system was
also rejected. At the time of drawing up the Foundation's work
program there appeared every indication that this area of concern would be adequately covered by the Brandt Commission, to

say nothing of an array of other studies then in the pipeline.
(8) Whether we were right in this assumption is a matter of interpretation and choice rather than of fact.

That left the third package: the strengthening of global
planning and resource management capabilities. An area of undoubted importance; indeed, of contextual significance to the
other packages. It is a package which is intimately linked to
the logic of the NIEO: what is a more equitable international
order if it is not one which ensures fair access to the world's
material and non-material resources and one which substitutes
planning mechanisms for market mechanisms in those areas and
for those commodities which, for various reasons, fail to respond to the 'hidden hand'. Since the RIO Foundation was established for the purpose of "promoting a widening and deepening
dialogue on the creation of a more equitable international
order" it was both natural and appropriate for it to set out
to elaborate the third package. This became the project which
has resulted in this publication. Through it and the project's
main report, the Foundation seeks to contribute to the 'second round' of debate on the institutions and mechanisms required to extend equality of opportunity between nations. Hence
the project's title, *RIO - A 'Second Round'*.

It was realized from the outset that the problems which
would beset the project would be formidable indeed. The field
of investigation is littered with booby traps of every description. There are problems resulting from the very size of the
area. The subject of global planning and resource management
is so broad that there are obvious dangers of falling into the
emptiest of generalizations and, on the other hand, of building
analytical walls around areas which are so small that contextual problems are completely lost sight of.

The subject is also one which easily lends itself to
flights of fancy and stary-eyed prescription. Indeed, the very
terms 'global planning' and 'international resource management',
with their connotations of 'idealism', are enough to bring a
twisted smile to the faces of those who deify the market. Certainly, analyses of global problems are bound to be colored by
value premises and ideological orientation. When made explicit
there is nothing wrong with that. But when the canvas is global
planning, the analyst must withstand the almost irresistible
temptation to paint pastoral utopias in shades of supranatio-
nalism and brotherly love.

Then there are the problems of theory. He who sets out to
examine ways in which planning and management capabilities at
the global level can be strengthened will soon discover that
there is no formally constituted and internally consistent
theory upon which he can draw. No matter how he deliniates the
boundaries of his investigation, his approach will need to
blend concepts and theories drawn from such areas as international relations, international organization and international

economics, all of which are themselves the subject of raging
academic controversies as to what is the 'right' and the
'wrong' theory. The approach selected is thus almost bound to
be eclectic, choices being conditioned by ideological prefe-
rences and by concepts of 'political feasibility'.

The analyst is usually the prisoner of his own background
and he carries the intellectual baggage of his own professional discipline. However much he advocates the need for transdisciplinary approaches to the study of complex phenomena, he
inevitably wears monodisciplinary spectacles which condition
his view, not only of how problems should be tackled, but also,
and more importantly, of which problems should be tackled. The
analytical dilemma has been succinctly stated by Abraham Kaplan: "I call it the Law of the Instrument and it can be formulated as follows: Give a small boy a hammer and he will find
that everything he ecounters needs pounding. It comes as no
particular surprise to discover that a scientist formulates
problems in a way which requires for the solution just those
techniques in which he himself is skilled". (9)

The social sciences are notorious for projects which be-
gin with a set of questions and end, not with answers, but with
another set of questions which are more 'relevant'. (10) We
began our investigation with such a list of basic questions.
What, for example, are the 'objective forces' which divide
the world's nations and continuously frustrate attempts to
strengthen planning and management mechanisms? What lessons
can be learnt from past attempts to fashion planning and management institutions and how relevant are these lessons in today's world? How effective is the United Nations as a planning
and management body and how, if at all, could it be made more
effective? Can transnational enterprises be afforded a positive
role in the reshaping of the international order or are corporate structures and the transnationalization of production
likely to prove immutable obstacles to the fairer sharing of
the world's resources? How can the legal basis of attempts to
build planning and management institutions be strengthened?
Are there new concepts which have a paradigmatic significance
or which could contribute to a political breakthrough? And
what will be the role and influence of 'power' in all of this?
As we complete our investigations, we still believe these questions to be of paramount importance. We have also learnt - as
indeed we knew we would - there are no 'easy' answers to them.

Given the problems confronting us it was decided to commission a number of 'position papers' from distinguished specialists - papers which could serve to help us formulate ten-
tative answers to the questions we considered important and
which would help strengthen the project's conceptual and analytical underpinnings. Nine persons agreed to prepare papers for
us: Silviu Brucan, Harlan Cleveland, Richard Falk, Johan Galtung, Johan Kaufmann, 'Stel' Kefalas, Elisabeth Mann Borgese,

Arvid Pardo and Christopher Pinto. In addition, Bert Röling
allowed us to use and reprint a conference paper prepared by
him on a subject of central importance to our study. The papers
have proved of great value to the project and they are repro-
duced here in the hope - and expectation - that others will
find them of no less interest.

The papers are presented in two groups. The first group
is essentially concerned with the institutional dimension of
attempts to shape a fairer world and to strengthen planning and
management capabilities; it contains the papers of Silviu Brucan, Harlan Cleveland, Richard Falk and Johan Kaufmann. Papers
in the second group focus more on specific concepts and strategies; here are to be found the papers of Johan Galtung, Stel
Kefalas, Elisabeth Mann Borgese, Arvid Pardo, Christopher Pinto
and Bert Röling. The division into two main parts is recognized
as being far from perfect. It is seen as a compromise between
a simple alphabetical listing of papers on the one hand and the
forced categorization of papers under an array of arbitray
headings on the other.

In the remainder of this introduction I will attempt to
summarize the papers and, having done so, point to what appear
to me some of the more interesting areas of agreement and disagreement between them.

                        THE POSITION PAPERS

Silviu Brucan was asked to elaborate his ideas concerning
a 'world institution', a supranational body vested with real
power to make and to enforce planning and management decisions
at the global level. (11) He was also asked to include in his
analysis an assessment of the deficiencies of the United Nations system and to explain his reasons for believing that the
U.N. will never be able to evolve into the 'world institution'
he deems necessary. The resulting paper is both stimulating
and provocative.

Brucan prefaces his paper with a brief sketch of the
trends and developments which seem destined to shape tomorrow's
world. He refers specifically to the untrammelled growth of modern technology, the struggle of the developing countries for
economic liberation, the collapse of capitalist market principles, and the assault of the transnational corporation upon the
nation-state system - trends which he believes "have all pushed
international anarchy to the point of no return". The collapse
of the old order, growing tensions between an increasing number
of nations, continuing super-power rivalries, a lengthening a-
genda of increasingly pressing global problems and - arrayed
above everything - the prospect of nuclear conflagration, forces Brucan to conclude that the last two decades of this century

may well go down as the "most critical and explosive period"
of human history.

The survival problems confronting mankind are much too
big for the United Nations. Already, Brucan argues, this organization has proved itself "inadequate and powerless". Founded
as a peace and security organization and as a development authority, it has failed on both fronts. Brucan argues that we
must view this failure and present crises in terms of changing
geo-political realities and power relations. The problem thus
becomes one of "the management of power" for, Brucan notes,
"we live in a world in which power is ubiquitous". Although
the United Nations has evolved as the international power
structure has changed, it still bears the indelible imprint
of the power realities which prevailed 35 years ago. Today's
power relations and conflicts are necessarily reflected in the
structure and workings of the organization.

Analyses of the dynamic of power should focus on the
"crucial conflict" between trends toward increasing decentralization and centralization: between, on the one hand, the
spread of national sovereignties and concomitant demands for
participation and equity and, on the other, the emergence of
a world system shaped by the integrating force of modern technology. This world system is a modern phenomenon and it has
given us world problems, world crisis, and world politics.

This new world system is, Brucan argues, of fundamental
importance. It means that no nation, however powerful, can escape world crisis. The OECD countries, for example, cannot hope
to resolve their problems by "planning in a closed circuit".
And because the capitalist mode of production was and remains
predominant in the world economy, the socialist nations are
ensnared in the world system, forming a sub-system that "cannot
run deeper than the system of which it is part". This new globalism has made the world power structure much more complex. It
ensures that the world can no longer be run by two super-powers
even though they are allowed to retain a monopoly of basic decisions on war and peace. In short, the world system gives rise
to a global power game which creates its own logic, a logic
which transcends traditional ideological considerations.

A world system does not necessarily give us a world order,
which Brucan defines as "a pattern of power relations among
states capable of ensuring the functioning of various international activities according to a set of rules, written and unwritten". The complexities of the world system and today's an-
archic pattern of relations among nations provide no guarantees
for the efficient functioning of international activities; on
the contrary, if left unchecked, they constitute a perfect re-
cipe for increasing disorder, chaos and, ultimately, nuclear
war with all its desparate and terrifying implications.

The answer to the fundamental conflict between the characteristics and demands of a supercomplex world system on the one

hand and a system of international decision-making based upon
the primacy of the nation-state on the other cannot be found
in the application of past experience. There is no past experience which is relevant. The answer, Brucan tells us, must be
found in the creation, over time, of a world authority vested
with real power to plan and manage the affairs of the international community. A world system demands a world institution:
the demand comes from the system as a whole rather than from
its constituent parts. The principal task of this institution
must thus be to regulate the smooth functioning of the system
as a whole, rather than to seek to accommodate the contending
interests of its parts, as the United Nations has traditionally sought to do.

Brucan goes on to outline his model for understanding and
forecasting world political developments and he presents the
logic underlying his belief that, "sooner or later", a world
authority with real power will need to be created. He argues
that it is the pressure of modern technology acting upon relations between nations and upon class relations which ultimately produces social change. In this interplay of forces, it is
the power of technology which is the main driving force. It
will lead, Brucan argues, to a progressively shrinking world
and, eventually, "in the very distant future", to an integrated world system whose "self-regulating motion will no longer
be interrupted or held back by the decisions of (today's dominant) nation-states". As a Marxist, Brucan sees this process
of integration as a dialectic between the forces that make for
conflict and division and those that make for cooperation and
consensus. Differences and cleavages both within and between
societies will constitute "formidable obstacles" to the process, which will inevitably be marked by "progress and regression, advances and setbacks". As it proceeds in stages, integration may first take concrete form at the regional level.
It will eventually result in the formulation of larger political units and the gradual dissolution of national power. Brucan's future world order is thus a dualistic order in which
nation-states and international institutions both exercise
power, the latter playing an increasingly active role in the
solution of problems of global dimensions.

The world authority is seen to have a cause-effect relationship with this dialectical process. On the one hand, the
growing complexity makes it necessary; on the other, it is required to guard over the process and, more specifically, over
situations of conflict which could give rise to a nuclear war.
For this reason, the process of building-up the world authority could be established prior to the formation of the new political units.

Concerning the architecture of the world authority, Brucan
is not precise, although it would be unfair to expect precision. He does maintain, however, that the world authority is

not analogous to 'world government' and is fundamentally distinct from the United Nations in conception and structure, competence and character. The world authority, Brucan explains, "is designed for a different historical stage".

In discussing the preconditions for the creation of a world authority, Brucan stresses that the gradual shift in power to the institution can only take place on a voluntary basis. This thus requires that nations, rich and poor, perceive it to be in their interest to transfer some of their rights and prerogatives to the world authority. There will of course be legitimate fears and suspicions, but these can be allayed by ensuring that the authority is democratic with a fair system of representation and distribution of power in the governing body. To this end, the world authority would have its own police force, tribunals and dispute settlement procedures.

The gradual transfer of power requires that the industrialized countries see the world authority "as the best and safest way of avoiding nuclear disaster" and the developing countries view it "as the only way of actually getting a better and more equitable world order". And here Brucan poses us a number of chicken and egg problems. Firstly, he notes that the world authority would be a democratic body concerned with large-scale conflicts involving super-power intervention. But as he notes earlier, democratic bodies are inappropriate for the conduct of power politics, the USSR and US having already chosen to remove their discussions on nuclear disarmament from the framework of the United Nations which, they evidently believe, has become too egalitarian and democratic for super-power politics. And secondly, whereas Brucan argues that the world authority can only come about after a long process of equalization of states, he also notes that the world authority is required to bring about this equalization. To lable this an inconsistency in his argument, however, would be to misunderstand his interpretation of the dialetic of change. But it would seem reasonable to conclude that if the process of supranational integration is to be preceeded historically by a period of the equalization of states, then the world authority is a long way off. One is left wondering whether the global problems so vividly described by Silviu Brucan give us this much time.

Certainly, he acknowledges that his concept of a world authority is "far ahead of present political and ideological realities" and that its very idea will encounter formidable opposition on all continents. But who would argue with Silviu Brucan when he contends that "paradoxically, but understandably, those who need it most fear it most".

We asked *Harlan Cleveland* to give us the benefit of his enormous experience by evaluating the efforts so far made to

institutionalize a system of global planning and resource management and to draw relevant lessons from this experience.
His paper combines retrospection with prospection and goes to
show, if indeed we needed reminding, that his views in many
areas are well ahead of US 'establishment' thinking.

Throughout his paper, Cleveland warns us of the dangers
of extrapolation. Even though extrapolation may furnish us with
"comfort in the midst of confusion", attempts to fashion world
orders through the extrapolation of the nation-state system
and by using national government as a model for world governance is bound to prove a futile exercise. The evidence, Cleveland argues, is now overwhelming that national governments
everywhere - in the West, the East and the South - are in a
state of crisis and "demonstrably unable to cope". Although
political leaders continue to "keep up a brave front", it is
now patently obvious that the traditional institutions of national sovereignty, defined by boundaries which were once relevant but which have become artificial, are unable to deal
with the interdisciplinary, interdepartmental and interprofessional problems - "cut across problems" - with which they
are now confronted.

Power, Cleveland argues, "is leaking out of national
governments into the hands of the many". It is leaking from the
top, for there are functions which only international institutions can perform; it is leaking from the bottom, under the
pressure of demands for greater participation; and it is leaking from the sides, to nongovernmental organizations of various
kinds".

The inadequacy of national government as a model for world
governance is clearly shown by the experience of the League of
Nations and the United Nations. Although clearly sympathetic to
these previous attempts to build a world order, Cleveland concludes that they have carried us no more than "ten per cent of
the way" toward a global system of peaceful change. The main
weakness of both the League and the U.N. has been that the conception was universal and the institutions unitary when in fact
the real world was pluralistic. The models assumed, like the
national government model assumes, that someone "has to be in
charge of the taxing, the planning and the managing". But in a
pluralistic community there is not, nor can there easily be.

In seeking to institutionalize a planning and management
capability at the global level, it is thus essential that we
avoid replicating the formulae which have proved so inadequate
at the national level. The starting point must be the realization that "something new is going to be needed". The challenge
is to use the crisis of national governance as a historic opportunity for engineering breakthroughs in the development of
international institutions.

Like Silviu Brucan, Harlan Cleveland points to the crucial-
ly important role played by modern science and technology in

shaping the world system. He argues that these have been behind growing global complexities and behind attempts - usually
piecemeal and fragmented attempts - to devise new international institutions. Each new scientific discovery, each technological innovation, has seemed to demand its own institutional
response, its own set of institutional arrangements to contain,
channel and control it. Cleveland illustrates how our answer
has usually been to wrap our new institutions around discrete
developing technologies. Scientific and technological invention, he concludes, "has become the mother of necessity";
strategies to strengthen global planning and management capabilities will, if they are to succeed, need to be cognizant of
what Cleveland terms "the technolgical imperative".

Moving to the field of prescription, Cleveland suggests
that the failures of national governance provide important
clues as to the most important requirements for new international institutions. They should provide for planning which is
neither rigid, vertical, authoritarian, bureaucratic, simplistic, quantitative - "in a word technocratic" - but which should
rather be seen as "plural improvisation on an agreed sense of
direction". They should focus on the middle-range, where problems of fundamental importance are piling up and must now be
faced. They should foster transdisciplinary approaches where
specialists realize that "you have to *think* about the situation as a whole if you are going to *act* relevantly on any part
of it". They must be based upon the realization that, in an
interdependent world, there are few clear dividing lines between 'domestic' and 'foreign' issues. And they must involve
non-governmental people and organizations who are less constrained and often more imaginative in their approaches to today's and tomorrow's problems.

Which problems should these new institutions address?
Cleveland argues that "there is no shortage of naturally international functions". He mentions four areas where they are especially required: to manage problems which can only be managed in a global context (climate, the oceans, outer space, protection of the ozone layer, and so on); to ensure that the
outer limits imposed on mankind's activities by the natural environment are not transgressed; to ensure that the basic material needs of everyone are met (which may demand the introduction of a 'poverty floor' and an 'affluence ceiling'); and to
facilitate the process of "planetary bargaining" between nation-states on issues which are not exclusively international
"but which also reach deep into traditional domestic arenas".
Cleveland gives ten examples of where "systems are waiting to
be born".

Will such new institutions emerge? All is not gloom. Cleveland sees a number of promising trends and "life-signs". He
notes that there is a growing recognition that the human predicament is a shared predicament, that, for example, science

and technology have brought mankind "close to the ultimate in military weaponry and close to the margins of biospheric damage". That there is a growing recognition that human needs can be met. That there is an awareness of the need for new procedures for cooperation; that, for example, consensus decision-making is preferable to voting procedures. That new kinds of international institutions are emerging with executive powers, such as "extranational organizations" like the European Community. And that, in all of this, there is growing recognition of the "priceless ingredient of pluralistic governance", that in a shared predicament "bargains can be struck which advance the interests of all".

Indeed, there is evidence of growing support for the main argument advanced by Cleveland: that in a pluralistic system, planning must be seen as a process of "improvisation on a general sense of direction" in which each faction "has to think hard about strategies for dealing with the whole predicament in order to act relevantly on any part of it". Harlan Cleveland concludes by reiterating the 'message' of his paper: that in devising the needed processes of innovation it is essential that we ensure that the international institutions which may emerge do not "follow the double helix of the nation-state".

Richard Falk we asked to write on the process of building up an effective institutional presence at the international level, a presence which would strengthen global planning and resource management capabilities. As could be expected, his paper combines analytical clarity with a commitment to normative change.

Falk begins his paper with a review of past attempts at global reform. The stimulus for such reform, he contends, has been the experience of two mutually destructive world wars, with the widespread fear that even worse tragedies could follow. This has twice led to the creation of general purpose international institutions - the League of Nations and the United Nations - operating on the basis of a very general constitutional document. Although established as the chrysalis for world government, both the League and the U.N. served mainly as extensions of the system of nation-states: they were not conceived as alternatives to it.

Efforts to build comprehensive international organizations have been supplemented by more modest attempts to create special purpose international institutions to deal with special problems on the basis of technical specialization, e.g. ILO,ITU, WHO and FAO. Both these approaches - the general purpose and the functionalist approach - have, Falk argues, been "derivates of and dependent upon statist logic and geopolotical constraints". Regional organizations have similarly been based upon statist considerations. As a result, the international institutions created to date have not produced any transformation

of the international order; their present and potential role
has been one of systems-maintenance. Falk is thus forced to
conclude that "the international institutional presence in the
present world system is marginal to the state system, and is
often a derivation from it that has little or no independence.
Its general role is to make the system function more smoothly,
as well as to make some cosmetic concessions to those who argue
that a more structured/centralized form of international order
is needed at this historical time to avoid large warfare and
to facilitate a level of international cooperation needed for
economic growth and stability".

Falk goes on to refer to the growing recognition and general agreement that the institutional presence at the international level should be strengthened, although this agreement
masks fundamental differences concerning whether an institutional build-up is required for purposes of systems-maintenance,
systems-reform, or systems-transformation. He looks at some of
the proposals which have been made in recent years to strength-
en the institutional presence. He is critical of the Trilateral
Commission approach with its emphasis on "managing interdependence" and of the "planetary bargaining" approach, advocated
by Harlan Cleveland, since both, Falk contends, leave structural issues and dominant power relations untouched. He is similarly critical of blueprints for grand designs; the advocacy
of world government must, given today's world, be "dismissed
as foolish and sterile", lacking both elite and popular support. Falk's assessment of recent proposals for institutional
reform is that they have in fact constituted little more than
exercises in "imperial geopolitics" and "sterile utopianism".

He goes on to outline guidelines for a positive approach
to global reform, an approach based upon the attainment of a
"preferred world" conditioned by an agreed set of world order
values and by a conception of the process of transition from
"now" to "then". His approach is predicated on two essential
starting-points: a commitment to normative change (to change
associated with values); and a commitment to political relevance (a sensitivity to issues of feasibility). Several other
elements condition his analysis; an overriding concern with
minimum order, especially with respect to super-power rivalries; an image of feasibility in a span of 10-100 years, and
thus unrestricted by political expediency; and a conception
of feasibility that is not shaped by the normative receptivities of existing governmental leaders.

Falk notes that a concern for political feasibility requires that analyses proceed outwards from the nation-state
and should thus reflect the diversity of national situations
around the world. At the same time, the approach should have
a "shared normative framework" which gives a coherent direction
to the process of transformation and the building of a new
world order that is both beneficial and sustainable. This im-

plies, Falk notes, a "tension between pluralism of interpretation and universalism of aspiration".

Drawing upon the work of the World Order Models Project
in which he has been very closely involved, Falk argues that
five values should be afforded central importance in constructing the normative framework which could lead to a preferred
world: peace, economic well-being, social and political justice,
ecological balance, and humane governance. These values may be
mutually reinforcing or they may be in conflict. The tension
among them and the ways of resolving it will, Falk contends,
be features of strategies of transition toward a preferred
world, or a system of world order in which the five values are
simultaneously realized. Falk believes that the preferred world
could take a variety of shapes: the most appropriate of the alternatives cannot be reliably predetermined, nor, he believes,
can its emergence be anticipated within the next 50 years or
so.

Falk goes on to discuss questions of institutional design.
He suggests that the five world order values adopted have no institutional implications *per se*, although humane governance
implies an attempt to minimize bureaucracy. This further suggests an emphasis on the decentralization of existing concentrations of institutional authority, on the separation of authority from power, and a softening of the sovereign-state system rather than a hardening of the global institutional network. The idea of humane governance also carries the idea of
participation and thus the need for institutions which facilitate participation. Falk goes on to present and discuss four
"images of humane governance" - a soft world state, a small
state world, a regionalist world, and a functionalist world -
which, he believes, could be consistent with the idea of a preferred world.

With respect to the transition to a preferred world, Falk
suggests that institutional reform should be assessed as to
whether it "appears to enhance prospects of structural transformation under approved value auspices or embodies approved
values in the present working of the world political system".
He concludes by noting that the place of institutions in the
process of global reform is likely to remain "necessarily illusive". But illusive or not, the institutional dimension is of
fundamental importance since "it provides the most viable and
stable indication of how life is to be organized in an alternate international political system".

In seeking to give concrete form to this dimension, the
essential task will be to ensure that our institutional prescriptions combine desirability with feasibility and are free of
both "premature specification" and of "covert imperialism". If
Richard Falk's paper has a single message, then this would be
it.

Johan Kaufmann was asked to take a critical look at the
functioning of the United Nations system. The *RIO Report* suggests that the U.N., despite its undoubted inadequacies, remains the only real machinery with the potential for building
a fairer world. The Report expresses the hope that major changes will be made in the structure of the organization over the
next decade thereby enabling it not only to play a more force-
ful role in world political affairs but also to evolve into a
World Development Authority capable of managing the socio-economic affairs of the international community. (12) Johan Kaufmann was requested to assess the capacity of the U.N. and its
family of agencies to evolve into the development authority envisaged by the *RIO Report* and to make suggestions for the necessary transitional strategies. His paper leaves no doubt as
to the uniqueness of his knowledge of and experience with the
United Nations.

Kaufmann argues that the capacity of the U.N. to evolve
into a genuine world development authority is determined by
three main sets of conditions: the willingness of governments
to transfer essential prerogatives and functions to it; changes
in the structure of the U.N. which enable it to perform more
effectively; and the evolution of world economic and technological conditions toward real interdependence, thus creating the
preconditions for the U.N. system to assume tasks related to
the management of the socio-economic affairs of the international community. The third of these conditions Kaufmann assumes
is now fulfilled and it is upon the first two conditions that
his paper focuses.

With respect to the transfer of functions, Kaufmann suggests that at least four basic requirements need to be met before governments can be expected to transfer their authority
to supranational bodies. The first requirement is that problems
should be global, thereby demanding world-wide treatment. This
requires that problems be made 'transparent'. The method usually used for obtaining this transparency is the preparation of
a report by a group of qualified specialists. But even the best
possible report - Kaufmann specifies the criteria which a report should meet - is in itself no guarantee for further action.

The second requirement is the obvious one that all governments should benefit from the transfer of power. Benefits, however, are notoriously difficult to measure and assessments of
them may differ according to the time-frame used. Kaufmann suggests that a useful start could be made by introducing more rigorous methods of evaluating benefits: cost-benefit analysis
when the results can be quantified and expressed in monetary
terms; and cost-effectiveness analysis where one is forced to
deal with intangibles.

The third requirement is that there must be a measure of
agreement on the objectives set and the means to be used to attain them. Kaufmann notes that progress on this front is some-

times hampered by misunderstandings and confusion concerning
concepts and definitions, the interminable discussion surround-
ing the expression 'New International Economic Order' being a
case in point. He suggests that the creation of a special ad
hoc Committee on Concepts and Definitions, composed of scholars
and practitioners could be useful in this respect. Although attempts at definition making would not overcome fundamental problems, it would, Kaufmann believes, "prevent some difficulties
and much time-consuming and sterile discussion".

The fourth requirement is that governments must have confidence in international institutions and in each other. So far
seriously neglected as a field of study, Kaufmann argues that
the "confidence factor" may, in the first and last instance,
"be the deciding factor in determining progress towards international cooperation and the acceptability of supranational organs..." He sees a real need for studies which provide "insight
into the psychology of nations and of their leaders". He argues
that states, like individuals, "can be analyzed in terms of abnormal psychological behavior" and that it might be possible to
identify states which are schizophrenic, which have a "persecution complex" or a "big power complex". He believes that this
could prove a valuable avenue of investigation and calls for
interdisciplinary case studies of specific countries.

Kaufmann furthermore notes that the question of government confidence in international secretariats has also received
little attention. Although it is often assumed that secretariats of intergovernmental organizations are above politics, they
are in fact "constanly pushed and pulled by various pressures".
He argues that some of the imbalances in secretariats could be
overcome by more rigorous staff recruitment procedures and goes
on to outline a possible approach.

Turning now to the structure of the United Nations, Kaufmann argues that it is too strongly divided along vertical
lines. The existence of an array of separate agencies as fully
autonomous units can be expected to interfere with the effective functioning of any world development authority, as and
when established. This problem cannot be overcome by the bland
suggestion that the specialized agencies should be disbanded or
otherwise done away with for experience has shown that the a-
gencies are "sacrosanct": they can be expected to resist all
attempts which might be made in this direction and would no
doubt forge some unholy alliances in the process. The way out,
Kaufmann believes, must be found by engineering a proper relationship between the world development authority and the agencies. Such a relationship could be one in which the development
authority issues directives with the specialized agencies retaining a great deal of autonomy in matters of secondary importance and in the case of technical questions.

Kaufmann goes on to present us with a model for restructuring the specialized agencies. It calls for the formation of

"clusters of agencies" around four substantive areas: basic
production sectors (industry, agriculture, resources); trade
and monetary problems; infrastructural sectors (health, education, intellectual property, telecommunications); and operational development assistance. The clustering of agencies in
these four areas would require that some agencies be merged
and others transformed and it would require that each area have
its own single advisory or legislative council for purposes of
central guidance and control.

Kaufmann suggests that the reclustering of the specialized
agencies would necessarily preceed the effective functioning of
the world development authority. He suggests that the Administrative Committee on Coordination (which includes the heads of
the specialized agencies) should be furnished with the task of
ensuring the smooth transformation of the clusters into the development authority. He goes on to outline other proposals designed to improve coordination within the U.N. system.

Kaufmann argues that a more effective U.N. structure will
need to be complemented by improved negotiation methods. He
suggests that in this respect special attention should be given
to problems associated with speech-making, negotiations between groups, the timing of the process of change, the use of
escape clauses, and obtaining agreement on long-term policies
and commitments. He goes on to formulate proposals (transitional measures) in each of these areas, including, with respect
to the latter, the possibility of all nations negotiating,
within the framework of the U.N., a long-term commitment policy which can be used to guide the process of change.

Kaufmann concludes his paper with a warning and a proposal. It would be foolish, he argues, to assume that because
something needs to be done by mankind "to master the awesome
challenges confronting it" that it will necessarily "happen by
itself". The forces arrayed against change are powerful and
deeply entrenched. Because of this, he suggests that television
and the mass media could be used to show to the enemies of
change the advantages which could be derived from the sensible
husbandry of planetary resources. The success of this message,
Kaufmann believes, will depend upon showing that a restructured
and substantially strengthened U.N. system is not synonymous
with 'world central planning'.

Johan Galtung opens Part II, devoted to the formulation
of relevant concepts and strategies. Johan Galtung was asked
to write on the question of power or, more specifically, how
the international power structure can be expected to influence
the process of institution-building and attempts which might
be made to develop a planning and management capability. His
paper is, as usual, stimulating and illuminating.

Galtung begins his paper by stressing the importance of
power analysis by noting that, in studies on global reform, it

is often conspicuous through its absence. He defines power analysis as the "analysis of social systems in terms of power in
balance and imbalance" and adds that it is impossible to say
anything sensible about power, or about the ways in which it
can be used to promote world order values, without recourse to
some typologies of power. Galtung goes on to present us with
such a typology.

He begins by taking positive and negative sanctions as
his point of departure and by interpreting social processes in
terms of a dialogue, a dialogue which can take place either
within an actor (internal) or between actors (external). Internal sanctions he then collapses into three types of power, or
"power channels": ideological power, concerned with the definition of standards and which can be used by the actor to evaluate behavior; remunerative power, concerned with the admini-
stration of 'bads'. In other words, the material out of which
power is made has three components: standards of right and
wrong, 'goods' and 'bads'.

Galtung now turns to the different ways in which this
power material is transmitted. Here he points to an actor-oriented approach and a structure-oriented approach (emphasizing
that the problem is not one of choosing one in preference to
the other but of realizing that they are two different modes
of operation and that, in practice, the dividing line between
them can seldom be sharply drawn). In the actor-oriented perspective, the exercise of power is deliberate and intended and
it is transmitted in discrete quanta in the form of either
'goods'(reward), 'bads'(punishment) or as ideological communi-
cation(moralizing). In the structure-oriented perspective the
exercise of power is neither deliberate, conscious or premeditated nor does it come in discrete quanta. Rather 'goods' and
'bads' flow automatically and continuously - "like a water
faucet left open" - from the structures in operation. Structure oriented power Galtung defines "as the normal exercise of
power, the famous nine-tenths of the iceberg". It tends to be
much less dramatic than actor-oriented power and it is much
less visible; "it is so much a part of society that it passes
unnoticed by many".

Galtung chooses to call actor-oriented power *resource
power*, where the powerful have an excess of resources ('goods',
'bads' and standards) and structure oriented power he calls
positional power, where power is derived from a certain position in a social structure. An understanding of resource power
calls for an analysis of the main institutions responsible for
the production and distribution of 'goods' and 'bads'(viz. the
economic and military sectors) and a knowledge of the extent
to which the actor's standards serve as a model for others. The
analysis of positional power should focus on such questions as
the extent to which structures result in conditioning, marginalization, fragmentation, segmentation and specialization, the

subject of Galtung's seminal work *A Structural Theory of Imperialism*.

Galtung's typology of power thus so far defines three
types of power (ideological, remunerative and punitive) and
two modes of exercising power (resource power and positional
power). It illustrates, Galtung contends, "one brutal fact
about social systems", that "power begets power". For one type
of power can be converted into another type - punitive power
can become remunerative power for example - and one mode of
power can be converted into another.

'Topdogs' are those generally high on all types of power;
they are in the center of the structure and they command all
kinds of resources. 'Underdogs', on the other hand, are low on
all types of power; they are at the periphery of the structure
and they command few resources. Galtung argues that whereas
actors will tend to strive for a full configuration of power -
at becoming "perfectly powerful" - there may well be power, and
considerable power, in an incomplete configuration.

The same types and modes of power can be found in both
formal and informal systems or, stated in other terms, in territorial systems of bilateral relations and non-territorial
systems of multilateral organizations.

Galtung moves on to the question of countervailing power,
the other element that must equally belong to any "fully fledged theory of power". He begins by making an essential distinction between "power-over-others" and "power-over-oneself";
these he presents as the two main types of countervailing power.
"Power-over-others" requires that the underdog builds up the
same types and modes of power as the topdog until a balance is
achieved. This desire to catch up, however, implies acceptance
by the underdog of the topdog as a model. And this is the main
limitation of a "power-over-others" strategy of countervailing
power. For even if the underdog were to develop the same ability to administer 'goods' and 'bads', the topdog, because it had
served as a model, would retain its ideological power.

Galtung's starting point for the "power-over-others" strategy of countervailing power is the concept of a power receiver. Power has to be received to work. For ideological power to
work, there has to be an element of submissiveness; for remunerative power there has to be an element of dependency; and
the effective transmission of punitive power requires that the
receiver be fearful of that power. And, as Galtung notes, "is
this not precisely the 'portrait of the underdog' -, submissive,
dependent and fearful". The underdog not only lacks resources
and has a peripheral position; he is also characterized by an
attitude or a psychological make-up. The conclusion, Galtung
maintains, is obvious: a less receptive attitude is one characterized by self-respect, self-sufficiency and fearlesness,
where less attention is paid to the topdogs. This new attitude
he sees as the very essence of autonomy and self-reliance. Gal-

tung notes that this attitude does not come about easily. Indeed, it may well require a "mental declaration of independence" and a "fight against oneself". It demands knowledge of how
and where the ideological power of the topdog is built into
the underdog, in the form of what Galtung calls "power bridgeheads".

Viewed in these terms, self-reliance should be seen as
a power strategy rather than as a purely economic strategy.
And translated into politics of today, it would have dissociation and delinking from the world power structure as a major
component.

Galtung goes on to define six basic forms of countervailing power as responses to the six basic forms of power identified earlier. By introducing balance-building and autonomy-
building as different approaches to the development of countervailing power, he ends up with a typology with twelve types of
countervailing power.

Galtung next turns to the question of power strategies.
The starting point, he reiterates, must be to realize that the
basic resources for change - in the cultural, economic and military spheres - are with oneself and that "to gain control
over them is where everything starts". Once such control is
achieved one can prepare "for attacks on the structure of power" and "start playing the other party's game, penetrating the
topdog". In this context, Galtung advocates the idea of a Third
World "counter-deterrence" and the building-up of Third World
structures for the purposes of ideological transmission. A concern for one's own situation implies a concern for the position
of those in a similar situation, which in turn suggests that
importance should be accorded to the development of horizontal
links and to strategies of collective self-reliance. Galtung
also observes that delinking need not apply to all fields of
interaction, but only to those of critical importance.

The order in which things are done in strategies of countervailing power is stressed as being of considerable importance. Galtung presents us with a recommended strategy of countervailing power which, in combining over time autonomy and balance-building approaches to the development of resource and positional power, would ensure that both resources and positions
would in future be more equally distributed than at present.
He notes, however, that the typology of countervailing power
could be used to develop many other strategies with varying degree of articulation and specificity. But whatever the combination of elements, the process of self-reliance should include
"autonomy, decoupling and recoupling strategies".

Galtung concludes his paper by discussing the implication
of power for global planning and resource management and the
institutions responsible for them. He begins by stating what
he believes to be the obvious conclusion to be drawn from the
preceding: that "if change is wanted, very little can be ob-

tained through negotiation with the holders of power". Given
existing systems and structures, the results of such negotiations can be considered "an almost foregone conclusion. The
cards are too well stacked in favor of the haves". Clearly,
then, conferences of the North-South type have major limitations and less time should be devoted to them.

What then is required? As far as the formal system of organizations is concerned, Galtung argues that the developing
countries should create autonomous Third World organizations
in fields of importance for the distribution of ideology, and
of 'goods' and 'bads'. He sees, for example, an obvious need
for a Third World Secretariat which would be concerned with
both autonomy-building and balance-building and he goes on to
specify its most important tasks. As far as the informal power
system is concerned, Galtung argues that the emphasis must be
placed upon the gradual development of horizontal, bilateral
relations to replace or counter the vertical ones generated in
various forms by 500 years of colonialism.

In terms of strategies, action with respect to the informal system may prove the most important, the formal system the
more feasible. The key, Galtung suggests, would seem to be
"small steps in the former, big steps in the latter". The essential point, however, is to identify and exploit the many
"cracks", "points of attack" and "levers" in the power structure which, at first sight, appears so monolithic. There are
"many opportunities" Galtung concludes "for those who want to
make use of them".

'Stel' Kefalas was asked to write on the possible role and responsibilities of multinational corporations (MNCs) in the process of shaping a more equitable international order and of
strengthening global planning and management capabilities. His
paper is clear in its answers, comprehensive in its treatment,
moderate in its opinions, and fascinating in its presentation.

Kefalas looks first at the evolution of the MNC, identi-
fying different stages in its unprecedented growth. He argues
that although MNCs have "exhibited a remarkable ability to mobilize resources over much of the globe and to create wealth"
they have begun to show signs of "tumorous overgrowth". An important part of the cure for this disease, he argues, must be
the realization by managers that the policies and procedures
adopted in the past "provide absolutely no guarantee" for survival and growth in the future. He argues the need for a "re-
conceptualization of the role of the MNC in the process of
transition from undifferentiated to organic growth" and goes
on to provide one.

Kefalas suggests that there are three basic ways of looking at MNCs: an optimist's view ("what's good for the MNC is
good for you" - "the prevailing opinion of the contemporary executive"); a pessimist's view (which sees the MNC as "one of

the most dangerous beasts since the Hydra"); and what he calls
a "meliorist view" which, being located between optimism and
pessimism, "affirms that the world can be made better by human
effort". The meliorist view does not attempt to bring together
the best of both worlds in a giant compromise but rather attempts to create a new framework on the basis of "recognition
and acceptance of the evolutionary changes which have taken
place over the last quarter of a century regarding the relationships between man and man and man and nature".

The meliorist believes that the MNC is "a potentially useful instrument" which "must play a definite role in the orchestration of the new world order". Whether it is able to play
this role is seen to depend not only on the creation of institutions which can control and channel the activities of MNCs in
socially desirable directions but also, and more importantly,
on changes affecting "policies, strategies, objectives and operations principles" within the enterprises themselves. In other
words,in the attitudes and perceptions of MNC managers. Kefalas
argues that these managers must be convinced of the need for
change and that more can be achieved by appealing directly to
them than by attempting to by-pass them or, ultimately, to coerce them.

Most MNC managers, Kefalas contends, work today with an
obsolete model. In this model - which he calls "the surrogate
model" - the manager tends to see the enterprise as a "closed
system capable of generating changes in its environment while
maintaining complete immunity from any demands emanating from
the changes it generated". In this distorted view, the manager
sees others as misguided and slow and views the world as divided by ideologies and legal system which are in need of MNC manipulation. The manager falsely believes that the enterprise
"can grow indefinitely along a path of undifferentiated growth
characterized by replications of some 'ideal' form of organization".

This model, Kefalas argues, has been rendered obsolete by
some fundamental changes in the environment of the enterprise.
He specifically refers to changing perceptions of globalism,
abundance, development and growth. In all these fields there
are "new world realities" and discontinuities which together
demand new managerial philosophies and practices and the transformation of the MNC.

Kefalas goes on to outline the framework of a new model -
a meliorist model. He prefaces his presentation of the model
with five premises on MNCs and the process of transformation,
acknowledging that these premises can be considered as consti-
tuting an "optimistic vision" of what may be possible. His vision assumes the pursuit by mankind of a number of fundamental
goals (world security, increased food production, stabilized
world population, sustainable economic growth, equal opportunities for development, and monetary stability) and that the

MNC can be instrumental in the achievement of these goals. The
view presented thus requires that the MNC be "recognized as a
full-fledged partner in the new world order design" and that
the MNC "engage in a process of 'self-assessment' for the purpose of bringing its philosophies, policies and operating procedures in line with the new world realities in an interdependent world of diverse but unified societies".

Kefalas proceeds to outline four philosophical principles
which should constitute the "pillars of a new managerial ethos".
The first requires that the MNC manager in designing organizational strategies endeavor to utilize the enterprise's collective intelligence to detect and use 'learning potentials' in
developing countries. The second principle is to recognize that
organic systems are wholes with irreducible properties and that
the holistic forces in the MNC environment can be expected to
strengthen rather than weaken in the years ahead. The third
principle is to realize that, as the traditional antagonisms
between nations fade, organizational structures and corporate
strategies should be cooperative in nature. And fourthly, MNCs
must abandon the exponential growth mentality and instead cultivate an intellectual commitment to organic growth and adaptation to the systemic requirements and dictates of a finite ecosystem.

Kefalas goes on to formulate the ten operational principles
of the new model. These principles are designed to serve as
practical guidelines for MNC managers in "long range planning
and day-to-day operations". They cover the need to accept a low-
rate of return on investment; the need for labor-intensive and
generally small-scale production processes and technologies;
the need for ecologically sound strategies; resource conservation and the need to evaluate production factors in non-monetary terms; the need to enlarge geographical and physical horizons
to include the Third World; the need to 'think-small' in developing country operations; the readiness to accept new ownership
arrangements; the readiness to be 'unpackaged' in developing
country operations; the need to promote rural development and
upward mobility in the organizational hierarchy; and, last but
not least, the need to expand the definition of ethics to include the social and political environment.

Is the acceptance of these principles by MNCs a pious hope?
Kefalas does not think so. Although he recognizes that "hard
core evidence" of a shift away from the surrogate to the meliorist model is still "very meagre", he believes that considerable
evidence exists in the form of public statements made by high-
ranking executives of some of the largest U.S. MNCs to suggest
that a true "change of heart" is taking place in corporate
boardrooms. It would be foolish, Kefalas contends, to dismiss
these statements as pure rhetoric or "cosmetic colorings".

Kefalas believes, moreover, that "once the philosophical
principles of cooperation and organic growth have become part

of the corporate philosophy of an MNC then it would not be too
long before the principles of a low rate of return, environmental quality, and so on would become standard operating procedures of a corporation". Most of us can only hope that this
would be so. We may be left wondering, however, whether the
1980s - which will no doubt bring many 'new world realities' -
will give corporate boardrooms the time to voluntarily embrace
the philosophical principles presented and thus to choose their
own roads to "a new managerial ethos".

   Elisabeth Mann Borgese was asked to review the possibilities of applying some of the innovative concepts and ideas concerning planning and management developed for the world's oceans to land based development and to problems associated with
decision-making at the international level. Given the leading
role she has played in elaborating the concept of the 'common
heritage of mankind' we were naturally keen to obtain her views
on whether this concept could contribute to a breakthrough in
the stalemated relations between rich and poor countries. Her
answers to the questions posed are quite unambiguous.
   Mann Borgese begins her paper by briefly reviewing the
work of the ongoing Law of the Sea Conference. She stresses
that, given their vast potential, no attempt to fashion a more
equitable international order can afford to exclude the oceans.
Indeed, the new order for the oceans may well serve as both a
model and a test case for a new international order in general.
It would follow that the Law of the Sea Conference has a significance far greater than the oceans themselves.
   Reviewing the history of the concept of the 'common heritage of mankind', she notes that its adoption by the United Nations General Assembly in 1970 "as a norm of international law
marked the beginning of a revolution in international relations". For the concept, she contends "has the potential to
transform the relationship between poor and rich countries. It
must and will become the basis of the New International Economic Order....". Moreover, the fact that the concept is able to
draw upon support from very divergent sources - she quotes examples from the Law of the Sea, the Law of Outer Space, Catholic thinking, and Third World aspirations - leads her to suggest
that the concept "is here to stay, and to expand".
   What are the main attributes of this revolutionary concept?
Mann Borgese defines them as non-appropriability (the common
heritage cannot be owned); shared management prerogatives; benefit sharing by mankind as a whole; use for peaceful purposes
only; and conservation for future generations. The concept thus
carries with it real promise for coming to terms with the ever
growing disparities in wealth and opportunity between rich and
poor countries as well as strong disarmament and environmental
implications.
   The common heritage concept was originally applicable to

non-living resources of the ocean floor beyond the limits of
national jurisdiction. At the time of the 'launching' of the
concept in 1967 this 'Area' could be said to extend to the 200
meter isobath offshore and to include, in addition to the polymetallic modules of the abyssal ocean floor, the vast hydro-
carbon resources of the outer continental margin. Since that
time, the 'Area' has undergone a process of shrinkage owing to
increasingly excessive claims to national jurisdiction by
coastal states.

Although she greatly regrets the territorial reduction of
the areas beyond national jurisdiction, Mann Borgese argues
that losses may be compensated by a functional expansion of
this 'Area'. In other words, she argues that there should exist
a functional area beyond the limits of national jurisdiction
which may provide for the management of any resources, technologies, or a system of production on which the international
community, by treaty or other international instrument, may
agree upon. Mann Borgese argues that there are today different
imperatives to extend the concept of the common heritage from
the international area to areas under national jurisdiction.

The resources of outer space and celestial bodies, Mann
Borgese contends, are bidding for the status of common heritage.
More than that, the products of space technology (such as the
information gathered by satellites on earth resources, climate
pollution, military activities) should also fall into that same
category. Antarctica, governed by an obsolete treaty which ex-
pires in 1991, should similarly be subject to a common heritage
regime. It can also be shown, she argues, that resources cannot
be separated from technology and that the common heritage regime must therefore comprise the whole production system, including resources and technology.

Mann Borgese seeks to allay possible fears and misunderstandings with respect to the relationship between the common
heritage concept and national sovereignty over natural resources. They are not, she argues, in conflict. Rather, the
common heritage principle "transcends the principle of national
sovereignty.... by transforming the concept of sovereignty,
considering it functional rather than territorial, and adding
a new dimensiton; that of participation". Under a common heritage regime, resources in areas under national jurisdiction may
be used and managed under national law but not owned or exploited for national gain.

Mann Borgese goes on to deal with the international machinery which should embody the common heritage system. She argues
that the system proposed by the United Nations Conference on
the Law of the Sea is conceptually defective in that it attempts
to create a dualistic system in which the International Seabed
Authority - the only example to date of an international resource management system and which is "without precedent in the
history of international organization" - would be forced to

compete with consortia of industrial enterprises from a handful of rich countries rather than cooperating with private
industry in a unitary system.

She goes on to present an alternative model for the production system, a model which already enjoys the support of a
number of developed and developing countries. It is based upon
structured cooperation between the private sector and the international management system, following the pattern, well accepted in industry, of equity joint ventures. Under this approach, any private company would have access to the Area under the condition that it forms a new Enterprise, to which the
International Seabed Authority would contribute at least half
the capital and appoint at least half the members of its board.
Product and profit would be divided in proportion to investment.

Mann Borgese argues that the proposed unified system
"would solve some of the thorniest problems still before the
Conference". It would, she contends, establish a model which
could be generalized to cover other international resource management systems and it would, for the first time, bring multinationals "into a structured relationship with the international community", paving the way for some sort of public international chartering for multinationals. "No other approach", she
argues, "would provide such broad participation of developing
countries in the management of the resources, and such broad
financial participation by the Authority". At the time of writing, the proposal for a dual production system is under consideration by the Conference.

Turning to the subject of the international institutional
machinery required for effective and equitable resource management, Mann Borgese outlines a management system for the oceans.
This system, which is centralized at the level of policy-making
and decentralized at the operational level, she characterizes
as "a functional federation of international basic organizations". It is a module system and she suggests that the most
sensible approach to the developmet of a global resource management capability might be the building, over time, of such
module systems - or "world economic communities" - for the
basic fields of the oceans, outer space, energy, food, mineral
resources, science and technology, and international trade. The
whole modular system, she suggests, could be drawn together in
a restructured ECOSOC, which might be composed of delegations
from the various conferences or assemblies.

Too ambitious an approach? Mann Borgese is forced to conclude "that this might be looking a bit too far - and too logically - into the future. History", she suggests, "will fumble
along its own way: far less logical, far less straight forward".
But if Elisabeth Mann Borgese's paper has a single 'message' it
would be that concepts and ideas are taking root and it is impossible to turn back the clock. As she notes at the beginning

of her paper "We are not concerned here with the problem of
timing". Sooner or later, some of the revolutionary concepts
will find a practical application and they will start transforming the relationships between nations. There will be setbacks and disappointments. No effort, however, should be considered wasted. For the more advanced the solution elaborated
by present efforts, the more advanced will be the starting
point of those called upon to carry on the fight after the disruptions we may have to suffer.

Arvid Pardo was asked to suggest ways in which attempts
to shape a more equitable international order could be more
effectively supported by the force of international law and,
more particularly, to elaborate a proposal contained in the
RIO Report for a 'framework treaty'. (13) This request was motivated by the belief that the new international order and the
planning and management mechanisms required to bring about and
sustain it must, if they are to be more than instruments of
convenience, be incorporated and laid down in legal rules and
standards which govern the behavior of states, international
organizations, transnational corporations and other subjects
of law. Arvid Pardo's paper must be considered an important
contribution to the discussion on how this can best be brought
about.
　　Pardo shares the conviction that efforts to build a more
just world must, if they are to amount to anything, be backed
by the force of international law. The problem is what law.
Although he acknowledges the potential inherent in international law, Pardo is forced to conclude that, given legal developments in recent decades, neither customary law, international
conventions nor U.N. resolutions are likely to lead to comprehensive arrangements which would effectively govern the economic relationships between nations. Nor are these sources of international law likely to give concrete shape to the ideas and
principles contained in the Declaration and Plan of Action on
the Establishment of a New International Economic Order and in
the Charter of Economic Rights and Duties of States which Pardo
sees as containing the building blocks for the construction of
a more equitable international order.
　　Pardo argues that the way out of the present dilemma could
be found in the negotiation of a "framework treaty", involving
all nations, in the West, East and South, which are committed
to the process of peaceful change. The provisions of the treaty
could in turn be developed, he suggests, when a greater degree
of international consensus has been achieved, into more detailed treaties and action programs in the economic and social
fields.
　　Pardo argues that, in drawing up the provisions of the
framework treaty, it would neither be necessary nor desirable
to start with a fresh sheet of paper. The treaty could, he sug-

gests, be modeled in part on the Charter of Economic Rights and
Duties of States. He also recognizes that the negotiation of
the treaty could be used as a delaying and diversionary tactic
by the industrial nations for he stresses that attempts to
draft a framework treaty should be designed in such a manner as
"not to interfere in any way" with continuing North-South negotiations.

What exactly would the framework treaty set out to do?
Pardo is quite precise. It would seek to lay down the ground
rules for international cooperation and the guiding principles
to be adopted by nation-states in the building of the new order. It would constitute an umbrella treaty which would specify
the principles and mechanisms to be used in the negotiation of
agreements for specific problems or sets of problems. The treaty would thus be concerned with procedural rather than substantive issues; it would lay down the procedures and principles on
the basis of which substantive issues could be subsequently and
progressively negotiated.

The framework treaty would not, therefore - and Pardo
stresses this point so as to prevent possible misunderstandings
- constitute an attempt to legislate a new world order in a
single stroke. Rather, its "basic purpose would be to make an
unmistakable initial step toward international economic - and
social - solidarity, and hence toward a world order based on
cooperation rather than competition between States". It would,
Pardo contends, serve as the legal foundation for the NIEO:
"it would represent a binding commitment to peaceful structural
change and to the elaboration of a law of nations that serves
the interests of all peoples, poor as well as rich".

The core of the treaty, Pardo suggests, should contain
provisions on three major subjects. Firstly, the procedures to
be used in the progressive negotiation of substantive issues.
Secondly, the establishemnt of a flexible but also comprehensive, compulsory and binding system for the settlement of disputes arising from the interpretation or application of the
treaty. And thirdly, the treaty could contain provisions acceptable to states on matters directly affecting international
economic relations and which are not mentioned in the Charter
of Economic Rights and Duties of States. Arguing that "science
and technology are the keys to the future of poor countries",
Pardo singles out the need for a provision covering the access
of the developing countries to the scientific and technological
heritage and the development of indigenous strengths and capabilities. He also suggests that the framework treaty could
very usefully serve to give legal status to the concept of the
'common heritage of mankind', the treaty extending this status
to ocean space, outer space and celestial bodies and thereby
introducing into international practice a measure of the effective cooperation required to bring about a New International
Economic Order. (14)

Arvid Pardo finds it fitting to conclude his paper with
a warning. The negotiation of a framework treaty and the creation of a new world order, he observes, is dependent upon the
existence of peace in the world and the readiness of all nations, in the North and South and East and West, to cooperate
in the building of that order. He witnesses, however, a deterioration in the international political climate, a deterioration which has undoubtedly accelerated in the period following the completion of his paper. This deterioration does not
augur well. A further worsening of the international atmosphere,
he believes, will not only mean that there can be no framework
treaty; it will also sound the death knell for the new international order.

Christopher Pinto's paper is also concerned with questions
of international law. He was requested to give us his views on
the problems of fashioning an institutional regime for the 'international commons' - defined to include ocean space beyond
national jurisdiction, outer space and the Antarctic continent
- a regime which was guided by and could draw upon the support
of the force of international law. His paper precisely answers
our request and its contents are both stimulating and original.
Pinto begins by noting that although the technique for the
development of legal principles in the case of the oceans, outer space and Antarctica has been substantially different, there
is now widespread agreement on the nature and character of the
three domains. It is generally recognized that these areas and
their resources must not be wasted or selfishly exploited to
the detriment of the interests of the world community and that
they must be treated as the property of all mankind, to be co-
operatively managed according to the principles that would secure from them the greatest benefit for the greatest number
over the longest period of time. In other words, the areas are
a resource and should be used and managed for the benefit of
all mankind. They are, Pinto contends, international public
property.
Pinto goes on to discuss the formation of legal principle
under modern customary international law. He argues that there
are principles in a wide range of U.N. General Assembly decisions, resolutions and other texts which can be used to fashion
the architecture of an equitable regime for international public property. There are decisions and resolutions pertaining
to the deep seabed, outer space and Antarctica which declare
that these areas and their resources have an international social or public character. The principles contained in these
decisions and resolutions, Pinto contends, have been the subject of extensive discussion and negotiation by the international community and are couched in reasonably precise and mandatory terms. Because they have been accepted by the vast majority of states, the principles must be recognized as reflecting

rules of customary international law, an obligation reinforced
by the state's membership of the United Nations. And once accepted as a uniform practice, customary law is legally binding.
There are, therefore, Pinto argues, sufficient legal grounds
for assuming that, if gone about correctly, the regime for
international public property can be backed by the force of international law.

Of the concepts which could be used to shape a regime for
international public property, Pinto suggests that the 'common
heritage of mankind', as developed under the Third U.N. Conference on the Law of the Sea, is "the most mature, and the most
fertile for deriving legal principle expressive and protective
of the community's social interest in the use and exploitation
of an area and its resources". Through the idea of 'inheritance' which it conveys, the concept suggests, Pinto argues, the
notion of rights in property commonly held.

But what exactly would be the nature of those rights?
This question leads Pinto to review which of the concepts of
Roman law could be considered the most appropriate legal ante-
cedent for the common heritage of mankind. The concepts of
res nullius and *res communis omnium* are rejected as being defi-
cient in one or several respects. The more neglected concept of
res publicae is presented as one which most closely approximat-
es the meaning ascribed to the common heritage of mankind. According to this concept that which was *res publicae* was not,
in its original form, capable of individual ownership but was
rather permanently subject to the collective ownership of the
community. Things considered *res publicae* had to be transformed or converted in one way or another before they could become
the object of individual ownership. Pinto notes that in this
process of transformation, the state served "as the agent of
the people or the public...(and) kept careful control, to ensure that through it the potential for use by every other person was not impaired, or if impaired, was appropriately compensated for through taxation of one kind or another".

Pinto thus summarizes his argument as follows: "..when an
area and its resources have been declared by the community to
be 'the common heritage of mankind', or to have a comparable
status, whatever the precise term used, they assume the character of things *in patrimonio populi*'; they become international
public property, and collective rights of ownership must be
recognized in every state of the community and their nationals,
as well as in other groups of mankind such as peoples who have
not yet exercised their rights of self-determination. The fact
of collective ownerhsip is thereby recognized as a part of customary international law".

Drawing upon various documents accepted by the international community, notably the Revised Informal Composite Negotiating Text (the draft treaty) prepared within the framework of
the Conference on the Law of the Sea, and on the clear trend

of the negotiations at the Conference, Pinto goes on to set
out the principles of a regime applicable to international
public property. These principles, which he presents in the
form of an embryonic treaty, are grouped under the following
headings: general principles, principles of resource management policy, the development authority (responsible for managing all activities in the area covered by the treaty), operational principles, compliance and damage liability, reservations, and amendment and revision.

Pinto's presentation of these principles accounts for
about one-third of the length of his paper. It must be considered an original contribution to the growing debate on the
regime required for the 'global commons' and an exercise which
could be valuably elaborated.

Bert Röling has contributed the final paper to this collection. Although not prepared for the project RIO A 'Second
Round', we have included it because of its relevance to the
problems addressed by the project. (15) It is clear that science and technology have been one of the prime motive forces behind growing global interdependencies: they have, in Miriam
Camps' words, "eroded the traditional insulators of time and
space". (16) The uncontrolled growth of modern science and
technology has also resulted in a complex array of problems of
truly global dimensions and given mankind, for the first time
in history, the real possibility of destroying itself and all
other forms of life. Clearly, if global planning and resource
management is to have any impact then it must include efforts
to come to grips with problems resulting from the growth of
scientific and technological capabilities. Bert Röling's paper
addresses exactly this question: the formulation of appropriate
international responses to the 'technological challenge'.

Röling begins by noting that the origins of today's technological predicament can be traced to the 'New Learning', to
the emergence of the natural sciences and their foundation in
empiricism, to a desire to learn about 'things'. Early pioneers
of the 'inductive method', like Francis Bacon, sought to use
their science to recapture the artless power and innocence
which Adam is supposed to have had before his expulsion from
the Garden of Eden. Perversely, it is this very tradition which
has given us, not artless power, but the dreadful power to
destroy all living things; not innocence, but the guilt which
must accompany the corrupting knowledge of such destructive
power.

Röling argues that technological developments in a number
of fields, such as armaments, nuclear energy, space activity,
environmental pollution, and 'genetic engineering', are truly
global in their implications and cry out for an effective international response. This response must aim at regulating the
development and use of technology - Röling suggests that little

can be done to hinder research - and, more specifically, at
maximizing possible benefits, minimizing negative impacts, and
at ensuring fair access to the technology, something which demands a participatory system of management. Because the technological developments are planetary in scale, it follows that
the only adequate response is a global one. And given the destructive power and negative side-effects of many of the technologies, it also follows that an effective response calls for
the creation of a supranantional body, representing all those
likely to be affected by the technology, vested with real
powers to take and to enforce decisions.

Röling discusses the problem of institutional design,
focusing on questions concerning the size of the organization,
its madate and its power. He discusses some of the legal problems associated with the formulation of an adequate institutional response, notes that there are many sources of international law upon which we can draw, and advises us not to underestimate the power of the law-making resolutions which emanate
from the United Nations.

The need for responses which are differentiated and flexible is stressed in the paper. Röling introduces a number of
basic distinctions which need to be recognized and thought
about when formulating a response: distinctions concerning the
type of technology (is it to be used for peaceful or destructive purposes); the role and responsibilities of intergovernmental and non-governmenal organizations; the tensions between
'public' and 'private' interest and between medium- and long-
term aims and concerns. He warns us of the danger of simple-
minded approaches since these can have counter-productive effects and illustrates this with examples drawn from past efforts to legislate arms control. He warns us, too, that in today's world there are no problems which are exclusively technical or functional; if the problems are not already 'political'
they can soon enough become politicized.

It is of course one thing to draw up strategies of change
and quite another to see that they are implemented. Röling observes that the international response to the problems posed
by technology has so far "been inadequate in every field". He
discusses the reasons why: super-power rivalries which have led
to warped interpretations of 'security', precipitated the arms
race and distorted the development of science and technology;
the nation-state system and the preoccupation with national
sovereignty "which sometimes exists more in theory than in practice" and which is continually obstructing attempts to build
the strong international organizations required to rise to the
"technological challenge"; the mutual mistrust and the fundamental differences which divide East and West, North and South; our
reluctance to face the facts when confronted with them and "the
deeply rooted tendency to adhere to all that is known and established"; the "adolescence of our technical culture" reflected

in our readiness to uncritically accept all that science and
technology can give us and in our failure to "apply moderation
and restriction".

A desperate situation but not yet hopeless. Röling sees
information and education as an important way out. The gap between what is required of us (derived from our understanding
of the 'thing' we seek to control) and what is possible (determined by 'public opinion') can only be bridged by knowledge
of the facts. Some of these facts are terrifying and - Röling
quotes Richard Falk - "are capable of their own sombre eloquence". Röling argues that "with more information, more knowledge about what is really at stake, more insights into the
madness of the present situation, something may emerge which
if not wisdom may be worthy of the word 'prudence'".

And this brings Röling back to where he started. With the
fundamental difference that if the natural sciences are the
cause of our predicament, it is the social sciences which offer hope for our salvation.

DISCUSSION

In this final section of the introduction I would like to
attempt to summarize some of the contents of the position
papers and, in doing so, point to areas of agreement and disagreement. It goes without saying that the summary has no pre-
tence as to completeness. Rather, the discussion draws selec-
tively upon the papers. I have also allowed myself considerable
latitude in presenting and interpreting their contents and I
have also surreptitiously blended them with views for which I
must assume full responsibility. I trust that the position
paper writers will neither begrudge me this liberty nor protest
the license.

The papers are virually unanimous in their judgment that
mankind has so far failed to develop a real institutional presence at the international level. Some writers view this failure compassionately and sympathetically, explaining it as being
in the scheme of historical things, others are more impatient
and aggressive in their criticism. Cleveland suggests that attempts at building world institutions have taken us no more
than "10 per cent of the way" along the road we must travel
and Falk similarly argues that the international institutional
presence has been marginal to the system of nation states it
has sought to influence and direct. Brucan argues that the
United Nations has proven "inadequate and powerless" and "neither functionally streamlined nor structurally built" to deal
with the complex array of problems that is building up.

The main function of the network of international institutions has been one of systems maintenance: it has largely

served to promote the smooth functioning of the world economic
system. The foundations of the system were laid at the end of
the Second World War - the IMF and the World Bank were established at Bretton Woods, New Hampshire in July 1944 - and the
period which immediately followed. The system was organized
as a commercial undertaking of major proportions: international economic affairs were 'normalized', Western European and
Japanese capitalism was rejuvenated, a basis was established
for the expansion of trade and investment, and the U.S. dollar
was enshrined as the chief means of international payment.
The whole purpose of the exercise was, in the words of a former U.S. Treasury Secretary, to provide for "a world in which
international trade and international investment (could) be
carried on by businessmen on business principles".(17)
     As a commercial undertaking, the system and its support-
ing network of institutions worked very effectively, bringing
unparalleled prosperity to its architects and beneficiaries.
Until the early 1970s. Since then, the props upon which the
system was built, notably the Bretton Woods institutions, have
collapsed in, for the rich countries, uncomfortably quick succession.
     During the post war period, the number of nation-states
tripled as the majority of mankind freed itself from foreign
suzerainty. The new nations, anxious to embark upon the process of social and economic development, were soon to discover
that the system of international institutions was generally
unresponsive to their pressing needs. There was, as always,
little space for the poor in the plans and institutions of the
rich. The consequence has been determined attempts by the developing countries to complement their political independence
with their economic emancipation, a part of a process which
Harlan Cleveland calls the "global fairness revolution".
     As a result of these and other trends and developments,
the world has become demonstrably more complex. The world's
nations are no longer a collection of giants and dwarfs. There
are a great many middle powers - in the South as well as the
North - and there are many additional levels of intercourse
and interaction than the purely political, economic and strategic. The world can no longer be run by the superpowers. Even
though they retain a monopoly on decisions of life and death,
they cannot, perversely enough, impose a world order. As Henry
Kissinger has remarked, in today's world "power no longer
translates into influence" (18) although it remains true that
"power impinges on weakness".(19)
     Today's international system is thus, as Brucan tells us,
a "supercomplex system" where old rivalries have been supplemented and compounded by new conflicts between the old and the
new, the strong and the weak, the rich and the poor. Because
our attempts to build international institutions have been modeled on the extension of the nation-state, it is inevitable

that these rivalries and conflicts be reflected in the world's
institutions. It follows that any 'predictions' about the future of international institutions imply assumptions about the
future of international politics, the exercise of power, and
the success of attempts to come to terms with the growing disparities in wealth and opportunity between the rich and poor
nations. For it would seem safe to assume that world institutions, given their nation-state origins and rationale, will
continue to reflect the variety and complexity of the world
with all its competing forces and antagonisms. It is thus also
safe to assume that, at least in the foreseeable future, international relations will continue to exert more influence on
international institutions than institutional changes will exert upon the conduct of world affairs.

    This leads several writers - notably Brucan, Cleveland
and Falk - to draw the conclusion that future attempts to develop an international institutional presence must start with
fresh premises. Attempts to develop this presence by replicating the nation-state system at the world level - by following
"the double helix of the nation-state" as Cleveland calls it -
are bound to end in disappointment and frustration. If national governance no longer works at the national level how can
we expect a system derived from it to work at the global level?
Today's problems are new and today's situation is unique. So
must be our responses. "The answer", Brucan tells us, "cannot
be found is any past experience". Cleveland would certainly
agree.

    In developing these new premises, it will be essential to
draw upon the growing recognition, documented in several papers
that 'something needs to be done' at the international level
and that this requires an institutional build-up. It may even
be possible to get basic agreement on the value premises which
should underpin our attempts to shape a more equitable order:
few would disagree with Falk's "world order values" or Kefalas'
"fundamental goals". It will be no less important to recognize,
however, as Röling observes, "that consensus is a fragile commodity which can easily evaporate in the process of translating
goals into strategies". And Falk reminds us that the apparent
consensus on the need for an institutional build-up masks fundamental differences among the world's nations as to whether
this is required for purposes of systems-maintenance, systems-
reform or systems-transformation.

    That the international order represented by the Bretton
Woods institutions is in many respects obsolete and virtually
unserviceable is no longer a question of serious debate. The
central question is what kind of 'new' order is to replace it.
The rich and poor nations need a new order for basically different reasons and for different purposes and their strategies,
even if guided by similar value premises and sharing fundamental goals, can be expected to differ in crucial respects. The

rich countries will naturally seek to rehabilitate Bretton
Woods institutions and to reformulate capitalist market principles, the source of much of their wealth. This reconstitu-
tion will inevitably seek to preserve existing patterns of
privilege and power and will include attempts to incorporate
Eastern Europe into the international exchange network and to
more effectively and completely integrate the developing countries, especially the newly industrializing countries, into
the international economic system which is dominated by the
rich, market-economy countries. (20) This integration will require that the poor countries absorb the overproduction in the
rich countries - a requirement condoned by Brucan but condemn-
ed by Galtung - and aim at safeguarding supplies of essential
raw materials. Because it will effectively maintain and conso-
lidate present unequal relationships, this strategy, it is contended, has little to offer many developing countries, especially the smallest and poorest among them. The international
capitalist system, even in reconstituted form, will not and
cannot bring universal prosperity.

Most Third World countries cannot be expected to welcome
such a strategy. Their only real choice would seem to be to
pursue, however difficult this will prove in practice, strategies of (collective) self-reliance aimed at overcoming some of
the worst forms of domination and dependence. Galtung goes
some way in defining the main elements of this 'counter strategy'. It must include much higher levels of South-South cooperation, which suggests a reorientation of trade, and selective
participation rather than complete integration in the international economic system.

This is not to suggest that international relations are
in or will enter a state of war or that there is no means short
of war for bringing cooperation about. There are objective
forces at work in several areas of international relations and
economics which, common sense suggests, must bring the world's
nations together to find solutions to common problems: no nation, for example, stands to gain from disruptions in the oxy-
gen or nitrogen cycle, from the spread of contagious diseases,
from chaos in the world's airways and on the world's airwaves,
and few from continuous monetary instability.

It does, however, very clearly suggest that it would be
realistic to expect as much conflict as consensus on the goals
and process of international cooperation and on the kinds of
planning and management institutions which may be required. In
other words, progress towards a system of global planning and
resource management of the kind envisaged in the *RIO Report*
will be slow indeed. In this context there will be little or
no space for deterministic blueprints which presuppose the ex-
istance of a commanding and shared vision of what the world
needs and should look like and for what Falk calls "sterile
and foolish exercises" in grand design of the world government

type. Rather, the emphasis must be on the progressive democratization of existing institutions and identification of those
areas in which international cooperation appears possible,
achieving some measure of consensus on the roles the institutions are to play and the power they are to exercise.

Clearly, there can be no hard and fast rules for the design of international institutions or of responses to international problems. It may be possible, however, to formulate
some overall guidelines which have a general relevance and
application. World institutions should, for example, focus on
the medium-term where problems are accumulating which must now
be faced. They should foster transdisciplinary approaches which
recognize that, as Cleveland puts it, "you have to think about
the situation as a whole if you are going to act relevantly
on any part of it". They should provide more opportunities for
effectively involving non-governmental organizations which,
because they are less constrained by the need to defend national interests and by the requirements of diplomacy, may be able
to bring a freshness and new purpose to stale deliberations.
And it may be possible and more appropriate to develop an institutional presence at the regional level rather than the
world level or on the basis of voluntary action by a group of
'pioneering' or 'like-minded' countries.

The terms of reference of the institutions to be vested
with planning and management functions should be firmly related to the problems they are expected to cope with. Whereas it
will not generally be possible to draw firm dividing lines
between 'political' and 'technical' problems, it may be possible in the early years of developing a global planning and
management capability to make basic distinctions between those
relationships and practices which, because they benefit a large
number of parties, can be institutionalized and those which
must, at least for the foreseeable future, remain inevitably
politicized.

It would also seem essential that the right level of management be found for the problems which can be addressed. In
some instances effective action may require that these problems
be 'pushed down' to the national level or below or 'pulled up'
to regional or global levels. The guiding principle in this
respect would appear to be the need to ensure that all those
who are affected by the decisions taken with respect to the
problems are able to participate in the making of those decisions. Probably no less important is the general need to move
away from conventional, hierarchical, unnecessarily centralized
institutional structures to more decentralized, horizontal arrangements so as to encourage flexibility and innovation and
to provide broader involvement in the processes initiated. It
will be essential, however, to ensure that such decentralized
structures contain provisions for a central intelligence system, i.e. a central forecasting and guidance body responsible

for monitoring the implementation of policies and plans, evaluating their effects, and reviewing interconnections. To be
effective this central guidance system will require a measure
of independence and its own authority and should relate to policy, planning, programs and instruments. Mann Borgese's paper
contains all kinds of clues as to how these functions could
best be articulated. Obviously, the planning undertaken by
this management system cannot be of the bureaucratic or 'master
plan' kind: it must rather seek to engage in what Jan Tinbergen
has called "indicative planning", planning which sets out to
sketch longer-term trends, indicating where policies are, could
or should be heading instead of aiming to coerce nations into
fulfilling specific plan objectives.(21)

It will also need to be continuously borne in mind that
lowest common denominator decision-making, while usually better
than no decision-making, traditionally leads to simple-minded
approaches to complex problems. Instead of congratulating ourselves that we have been able to find a 'line of least resistance' we would do well to remember that, as Röling tells us,
simple-minded approaches sometimes tend to be counter-productive and, as Mann Borgese observes, often mean that the difficulties which sooner or later will have to be faced have not
only been pushed further into the future but also probably made
very much more complicated as a result.

The approach to the development of a real planning and
management capability is thus bound to be piecemeal and fragmented, characterized, in Brucan's words, "by progress and regression, advances and setbacks". It will be a step-by-step
approach in which possible progress in one area is not made dependent upon progress in too many other areas.

Several writers present us with different models for organizing this step-by-step process. Kaufmann outlines an approach
for the progressive restructuring of the specialized agencies
of the U.N., an approach which calls for the formation of institutional "clusters" around major substantive areas. Under
this approach, each cluster would be equipped with its own advisory and legislative council for purposes of guidance and
control. Mann Borgese advocates a "modular" approach in which
institutional modules, or "world economic communities", would
be developed over time for each of the major complexes of
world problems. Each module would constitute "a functional con-
federation of basic organizations" in which decision-making
would be centralized at the level of policy-making and decentralized at the operational level. In similar vein, Cleveland
talks of "systems waiting to be born". In articulating the
step-by-step approach to the development of appropriate institutional responses, we can thus serve as architects of "clusters" and "modules" or as midwives to nascent world systems.

Whatever the role we afford ourselves it will be essential
to recognize that international institutions, as mirrors of the
world, are bound to reflect changing geo-political realities

and that the effectiveness of planning and management institutions is linked, first and foremost, to the willingness of
governments to conduct their affairs through them and not, in
the first instance, to the structure of the organization. Only
after an organization has been charged with a responsibility
does its capacity to perform satisfactorily become really important.

This raises the question of 'confidence'. Confidence implies mutual trust. This is without doubt one of the scarcest
commodities in international politics. The trust which nations
have in each other is low - perilously low - and it is not too
difficult to see why this is so. Mistrust of motives is rampant
not only between the 'worlds', between East and West and North
and South, but also within the 'worlds', within the North, the
East and the South. This lack of trust is strongly reflected in
the workings of international institutions. Neither the rich nor
the poor nations, for example, appear to have much confidence
in the United Nations: the poor countries see it as Western
dominated, undemocratic and unresponsive to their needs; the
rich countries fear the consequences of relinquishing power and
privilege, of sharing control with a 'tyrannical' majority,
bent on the overthrow of capitalism, and inclined to politicize
even the most 'straight-forward' of issues. Yet trust is the
cement which holds international organizations together. When
trust in an organization is high it can withstand considerable
strain and buffeting; when it is low, a seemingly innocuous incident can lead to irreparable damage to the organization's capacity to perform satisfactorily.

Kaufmann tells us that the 'confidence factor' may well be,
in the first and last instance, "the deciding factor in determining progress toward international cooperation and the acceptability of supranational organs". Perhaps more than at any other
time there is a very real need for governments, in the South as
well as the North, to affirm and demonstrate their commitment
to international cooperation, the process of peaceful change,
and to economic justice. Several papers suggest ways in which
such a commitment could be given concrete shape.Pardo suggests
the negotiation of a "framework treaty" which would encompass
agreement on the principles and procedures to be used in the
subsequent progressive negotiation of substantive issues. Kaufmann proposes the negotiation of a "global long-term commitment
policy" to provide a foundation upon which can be built a new
world order. Such approaches carry a number of very distinct
advantages. They may help, for example, to lay the legal basis
for a new international order and they may actually encourage
the governments of the industrialized democracies to go to
their people on a whole range of policy choices and "cut-across
problems" which could be discussed in a broad perspective. And
because such exercises would be concerned with the progressive
reordering of world relations, it would be difficult for the
centrally planned economies to exclude themselves from it.

There is one area which several of the papers present as
a natural contender for the much needed demonstration of commitment and declaration of confidence: the design and rapid
implementation of a regime for the global commons based upon
the concept of the common heritage of mankind. Cleveland's and
Falk's paper point to the need for fashioning a regime for the
commons; Mann Borgese's and Pinto's focus upon it. Mann Borgese argues that this concept has revolutionary implications and
has the potential of transforming the relationship between rich
and poor nations: it brings with it the opportunity of coming
to grips with the ever widening disparities in wealth and opportunity while at the same time furthering the causes of disarmament and environmental protection. The design of a regime
for the commons would also make it possible to apply some of
the important and innovative ideas developed as part of the
Third U.N. Conference on the Law of the Sea - arguably the most
important 'law-making' conference ever held and one in which,
according to Mann Borgese, solutions have been found which are
"without precedent in the history of international organization".

The global commons can be defined to include the oceans
beyond the limits of national jurisdiction, outer space and
the Antarctic continent. Although the development of legal
principle for each of these domains has followed different
routes, there is, as Pinto tells us, clear recognition by the
international community that they and their resources - and
thus, for example, the information derived from observation
satellites and remote sensing technologies - should be used
and managed for the benefit of all mankind, not exploited for
the purposes of national gain by the nations which possess the
technology which makes this possible.

Both Mann Borgese and Pinto agree on the importance of the
concept of the common heritage of mankind and that it has become an accepted norm of international law. They differ, however, on a number of very basic points. Mann Borgese stresses
that the common heritage cannot be appropriated; by nation-
states or by the international community. Pinto argues that the
common heritage should be viewed as international public property, i.e. in terms of a property relationship, not an individual
relationship but the collective ownership of the community.
Mann Borgese's position he finds "premature", too much in advance of what may be politically possible. "Recognition of a
right of property, albeit a collective or 'common' one", he argues, "is a traditional and well understood way of defining an
interest so as to protect it". For her part, Mann Borgese would
probably argue, as hinted earlier, that limited approaches, despite their apparent pragmatic foundations, may well lead to unnecessary complications at a later date, as it did following
the rejection by the international community of the 'Maltese
proposal' for a management system for the world's oceans.

Mann Borgese would probably also reject the expression
'global commons' with its connotation of something 'left over'
when all national boundaries have been drawn. She would argue
that, if its true potential is to be realized, the common heritage of mankind must also be applied to areas within national jurisdiction for it is within these areas, notably in the
exclusive economic zones, that the vast majority of accessible
and usable resources (hydrocarbons, minerals, fish stocks) are
to be found. (22) Limiting its application to areas which no
nation wants - or has yet to develop the technology to want
to have - is likely to yield meagre results. Her approach to
this dilemma is a very elegant one: to combat the territorial
shrinkage of the concept with its functional expansion, whereby resources in areas under national jurisdiction could be
used and managed under national law but not owned or exploited
for purposes of national gain. Such an approach would thus
make it possible to interweave national and international jurisdiction within a single tapestry of territorial space. Pinto would no doubt concur with the wisdom and desirability of
this approach but would probably argue that it is just too far
ahead of its time; too much in advance of what, even with much
good will on all sides, could be achieved at the world's negotiating tables.

Clearly, then, the application of the common heritage concept to ocean space, outer space and Atarctica raises all manner of conceptual and legal problems as well as the more obvious ones of privilege and vested interest. But urgent efforts
to resolve these problems could yield very substantial results
as well as hinder, if not prevent, a handful of nations staking
even larger claims in those domains which have already been
declared common heritage of mankind; claims which, if they become any larger, will constitute a permanent obstacle to the
fashioning of an equitable regime for the global commons. There
simply is not much time left. For the commons is one of those
areas where the benefits are to be safeguarded today. This cannot be postponed until tomorrow because by tomorrow the benefits may have been *de facto* appropriated by a small group of
nations.

And the potential benefits are very considerable. Not the
least of these is an important first step in institutionalizing
the principle which must guide attempts to fashion an equitable
system of global planning and resource management: that it is
access to resources rather than their distribution which counts
and that the world's resources belong to all the world's inhabitants on the basis of priority needs, not on the basis of
geographical accident or according to the ability to exploit
or to consume them. (23) Agreement would make it possible to
develop automaticity in the flow of benefits and funds to the
poor countries, a requirement about which there is a great deal
of consensus between rich and poor countries.(24) It would also

give real expression to the idea of solidarity with existing
and future generations and introduce the notion of conscious
planning and management practices for the benefit of all
rather than a privileged few. And if it were to do this, it
would contribute significantly to the much needed process of
confidence building.

With respect to confidence-building, Kaufmann's suggestions concerning the possible value of studies on the psychology of nations should be mentioned. Could nations be analyzed
in terms of normal or abnormal behavior? Do nations suffer
from the same neuroses and psychoses which plague individuals?
Does history confer upon nations 'delusions of grandeur' or
'inferiority complexes'? And if nations do have 'personalities'
are there those with paranormal faculties, with the gift of
clairvoyance or even of prophecy? Perhaps psychoanalysis and
'client-centered' therapies would make it easier for nations
to make the "mental declaration of independence" which Galtung
considers an indispensable step in the direction of true autonomy and self-reliance. An intriguing prospect.

At a more concrete level, many of the papers point to
another area in which an appropriate international response
has to be formulated if progress in the direction of a global
planning and management capability is to be made: the management of our technological future - the subject of Röling's
paper, and, indirectly, of that of Kefalas. Technology is now
recognized as one of the prime motive forces in the process of
development and change. Its influence is all pervasive. At the
global level its integrating force has led to a shrinking
world, a point stressed by Brucan, and to growing quantitative
and qualitative interdependencies. At the same time, it has
undoubtedly been one of the main forces which have driven the
rich and poor worlds further apart. (25)

In its national context technology is critical to development for four main reasons: it is a resource and the creator
of new resources; it is a powerful instrument of social control; it bears on the quality of decision-making to achieve
social change; and it constitutes a central arena wherein new
meanings must be created to counter alienation, the antithesis
of meaningful existence. (26) No wonder that some suggest that
planning in the area of technology may be more important for
national development than planning for investment. (27)

Technology is not neutral; it incorporates and reflects
value systems. It embodies deeply rooted assumptions about the
organization of knowledge, space and time, of human relations
and relations with nature. It not only reflects but also per-
petuates a set of structures. The development and transfer of
technology thus implies the development and transfer of structure, social and cognitive, within nations as well as between
nations. (28) Technology is both an agent of change and a des-
troyer of values. It can promote equality of income and oppor-

tunity or systematically deny it. It follows that technology
not only influences society but also that society imposes conditions on the choice and development of technology and on the
distribution of its benefits. It follows also that the desire
to exert influence over the future implies the ability to
exercise control over the growth and development of modern
science-based technology.

Cleveland shows in his paper that much institution-building in recent times can in fact be characterized as attempts to
wrap an international response around discrete technologies.
"Each new scientific discovery, each technological innovation",
he notes, "seems to require the invention of new international
arrangements to contain, channel and control it". In his paper,
Röling makes a clear distinction between technologies which
are to be used for destructive purposes and those which have
peaceful applications. Meeting the technological challenge,
he argues, calls for more than concerted efforts to come to
terms with destructive technologies, however desperately important and difficult that in itself will be. It also requires
recognition of the fact that much civil technology "may involve
insidious, although less obvious dangers" and thus require regulation. In this connection, he supports the idea that special
efforts should be made to regulate the development of technology in the fields of nuclear energy, cybernation, molecular biology, climate modification and - and this should be stressed -
the development of technologies required to exploit the global
commons (the oceans, outer space, and the polar regions).
Röling suggests that the least that should be done here is that
efforts be made to maximize benefits, minimize disadvantages,
and to ensure a fair distribution of advantages and disadvantages. Even if the development of specific technologies cannot
be stopped, it can sometimes be hindered and obstructed.

It may also prove a very useful exercise to attempt to
identify 'dual purpose' technologies or those with a potential
for both good and evil. Such technologies would appear to include nuclear energy technologies, environment modification
technologies, marine - notably antisubmarine warfare - technologies, laser technologies, aerospace and satellite technologies, and chemical and biological technologies. Progress in
this area would serve to simultaneously advance the causes of
development and disarmament. (29)

There is not too much disagreement among the papers about
what will eventually be required if a real planning and management capability is to be developed in the long-term. Substantive complexities, objective interdependencies and political
necessities call for collective problem-solving and the kinds
of guarantees which can only come, not from the exercise of sovereignty which, as Röling observes, "exists more in theory
than in practice", but from international institutions vested
with real power. This in turn, may entail the imposition of

limitations on the exercise of sovereignty and, eventually,
the transfer of some elements of sovereignty to international
institutions.

Already the developing countries are discovering that
strategies of (collective) self-reliance require not only the
fierce and fearless exercise of sovereign rights so as to help
redress present power imbalances but also the kind of territorial guarantees which can only be provided by international
agreements and thus the fora in which they are negotiated. (30)
Moreover, it is becoming increasingly obvious, to both rich
and poor countries alike, that sovereign rights and territorial
prerogatives are proving inadequate defenses against new and
dangerous threats. In today's world, national security can no
longer be viewed in exclusively military terms. There are new
and less obvious threats which stem, directly and indirectly,
from the rapidly changing relationship between mankind and
the world's natural systems and resources and which carry the
seeds of social unrest and hence political instability. It
might prove easier for some nations, for example, to counter
external aggression than to defend the health of their populations, the strength of their currencies or to ensure adequate
supplies of food, energy and raw materials. (31) In other
words, there are objective forces at work which demand that
nations reinterpret traditional notions of sovereignty.

The idea that all aspects of sovereignty can effectively be
exercised without a strong institutional presence is, at best,
an illusion and, at worst, a precondition for international
conflicts and tensions which could well push the world over the
nuclear precipice. The attainment of objectives in many fields
will inevitably be found to depend upon the forging of links
and coalitions of various kinds with nations which are similarly
situated - the notion that lies behind the concept of collective self-reliance. In the final analysis, the refusal to attempt to harmonize the exercise of sovereignties so as to deal
with the growing list of problems which defy national solution
- even when these solutions call for limitations on the exercise of sovereignty - must be viewed as an implicit decision
which serves to erode rather than strengthen national prerogatives. Failure to make such attempts will eventually harm the
interests of all nations and, given the present international
power structure, those of the smallest and weakest nations the
most. About one third of the world's sovereign states have populations which are smaller than those of Birmingham, Munich,
Naples and Prague and they typically lack the infrastructure
and resources required for rapid social and economic development. As Carlos Andrés Perez has observed, for such states
"survival ....is becoming impossible".(32) Strong international
institutions which truly represent the community of nations
help provide the countervailing power to the hegemony of the
rich nations and should thus be seen as the natural allies of

national institutions which aim at fostering self-reliance.

Ultimately, the creation of an equitable system of global planning and resource management will require that the territorial interpretation of national sovereignty gradually give way to a functional interpretation based upon jurisdiction over determined uses rather than over geographical space. Such an interpretation will bring so much closer the United Nations as a world development authority as described by Kaufmann and the world institution advocated by Brucan as well as make it possible to extend the application of the concept of the common heritage of mankind beyond the oceans, space and Antarctica to such new domains as mineral resources, science and technology, the means of production and other sources of wealth.

A long way off? Certainly. But as Mann Borgese rightly argues it is important to launch and to promote discussion of the ideas and concepts which may just have the power to pull the world from the hole into which it is sinking. Falk similarly warns us about time horizons. A "preferred world", whatever form it may take, will neither emerge nor can it be anticipated, he suggests, within the next fifty years or so.

And perhaps the long-term prescriptions are too rational. History has repeatedly shown us that mankind only adopts a rational approach to problems when it has exhausted all other possibilities. In today's world, a world which, to use Brucan's words, "is so small and so susceptible to destroying itself", the exhausting of all other possibilities could conceivably mean that there is no world left in which to be rational. And in this respect it is appropriate to remind ourselves of the main themes of Brucan's and Galtung's papers: that the issues which need to be addressed must be focused from the perspective of the management of power in international society and in terms of the dynamics of change in power relations. This perspective allows little space for the exercise of 'enlightened self-interest', for demonstrations of confidence and declarations of commitment of the types discussed above. Power structures, whilst not indestructible, are highly durable: they cannot be dissolved by the heat of academic debate, although they can be mined with ideas. As Galtung reminds us, power is not given up voluntarily; it has to be taken away - sometimes forcibly - from the power holders by the application of countervailing power. In this international arena, horizons are essentially short-term and national preoccupations and fears predominate. International cooperation is not shaped by appeals for 'solidarity' and by a readiness to incur real short-term losses for possible longer-term gains; it is something which is viewed through the distorted prisms of parochial mercantile, strategic and ideological interests. There is little space for 'gentlemen's agreements' let alone bold and binding initiatives. Galtung's paper has no space for such noble concepts as harmony, dialogue, partnership or global bargains, concepts central

to many of the other papers. His paper contends that fight and
struggle are the only ways of breaking out of crippling structures of dependence and domination, both internationally and
intranationally.

Yet ultimately the basic choice confronting all nations
is surely between chaos and cooperation, or, in Galtung's terms,
of coming together and finding ways to manage inevitable conflicts so as to avoid catastrophes, be they wars or extreme
misery. Nations will of course continue to act in what they
believe, however 'right' or 'wrong', to be their own self-interest and it is, as observed earlier, reasonable to assume
that the coming decades will go down in history as a period of
turmoil and struggle marked by change - conceivably violent
change - with farreaching consequences for political, social
and economic systems. The rich will continue to associate 'order' with existing patterns of privilege and power and will
fight for the maintenance of the institutions which have made
them prosperous even though they may no longer guarantee their
prosperity. The poor nations will continue their struggle for
another 'order' which extends real equality of opportunity. And
all the time the 'hawks' in the superpower military establishments will be pressing for 'shows of strength' and looking for
the opportunity to show just 'what they can do' (33). In this
atmosphere, international cooperation and international institutions will be subjected to unprecedented strains and have difficulty maintaining themselves, even though the need for them
will be greater than ever before.

As nations seek to exert their influence, exercise their
rights and act in their own self-interest, they will be continuously frustrated and defeated by substantive complexities.
Given the many levels of interaction among states, the growing
quantitative and qualitative interdependencies, the interpenetration of 'domestic' and 'foreign' issues, the conflicts and
tensions, and ever-changing geo-political realities, they will
have no rigorous ways of knowing what exactly constitutes 'self'
and what precisely is 'interest'. (34) And this is where international institutions will come in. For nations will no doubt
discover that international organizations, because they set the
arena, can affect which 'self' and which 'interest' ultimately
prevails.

Antony J. Dolman   May, 1980

NOTES AND REFERENCES

(1)   Antony J. Dolman and Elisabeth Mann Borgese, *Managing the World's Resources*, Pergamon Press (forthcoming).

(2)   Jan Tinbergen (coordinator), *Reshaping the International Order: A Report to the Club of Rome*, E.P. Dutton, New York, 1976.

(3)   Ibid, p. 4

(4)   The ten areas are the international monetary order, development financing, food production and distribution, industrialization and trade, energy and raw materials, science and technology, transnational corporations, human environment, arms reduction, and ocean management. Working groups, usually made up of persons from both the 'North' and 'South', were formed to analyze problems and to formulate proposals in each of these areas.

(5)   *RIO Report*, op.cit., chapter 19, pp. 176-187.

(6)   This view was generally shared by the 250 participants from nearly 60 countries who attended a meeting held in Algiers from 25-28 October at which the *RIO Report* was 'unveiled' to the international community. See the report of that meeting: *Towards a New International Order:An Appraisal of Prospects*, published by the governments of Algeria and the Netherlands in cooperation with the RIO Foundation, 1976.

(7)   For a review of the various types of proposals made in the past few years for increased capital transfers to the Third World, see Ronald E. Muller and David H. Moore, *A Description of a Preliminary Evaluation of Proposals for Global Stimulation*, UNIDO, Vienna, 1979.

(8)   Special mention needs to be made here of OECD's 'Interfutures' Project which resulted in *Facing the Future. Mastering the Probable and Managing the Unpredictable*, Paris, 1979; the various studies undertaken as part of the Council on Foreign Relations 1980s Project; and the United Nations' study on future economic growth prospects published as Wassily Leontief, et.al. *The Future of the World Economy*, Oxford University Press, New York, 1977. These and other important studies on the future of 'North-South' relations and the world economic system are reviewed in the project's final report.

(9)   Abraham Kaplan, *The Conduct of Inquiry:Methodology of Behavioral Science*, Chandler, San Francisco, 1964.

(10) The reasons for this are well described in P.E. Hammond (editor), *Sociologists at Work*, New York, 1964.

(11) As a member of the RIO Group, Brucan was instrumental in getting the proposal for a 'world organization' included in the *RIO Report*. The Report notes, op.cit.,p. 185: "To be able to plan, make decisions and enforce them, a world organization working on a truly democratic basis must be empowered by its members to do so....if it is really to reflect intedependencies

between nations and solidarity between peoples, (it) should ultimately aim at the pooling and sharing of all resources, material and non-material, including means of production, with a
view to ensuring effective planning and management of the world
economy and of global resource use in a way which would meet
the essential objectives of equity and efficiency".
(12) *RIO Report*, viz. p. 185.
(13) *RIO Report*, pp. 114-117.
(14) The *RIO Report*, suggests (p. 117) that in a future revision of the Charter consideration should be given to the inclu-
sion of the following provisions:

(a) All States shall facilitate access to technology and
scientific information;
(b) All States have the obligation to expand and liberalize
international trade;
(c) Ocean space and the atmosphere beyond precise limits of
national jurisdiction are the common heritage of all mankind:
as such they shall be administered exclusively for peaceful
purposes through international mechanisms with the participation of all States and their resources shall be exploited with
particular regard to the interests of poor countries;
(d) Developed countries have the duty to ensure that net flows
of real resources to poor countries shall not be less than the
targets established by the United Nations General Assembly;
(e) No State shall allow itself to be permanently and greatly
dependent on others for its basic food stuffs;
(f) All States shall encourage the rational utilization of
energy, with particular attention being given to non-renewable
resources, and develop new sources of non-conventional energy
which would particularly contribute to reinforcing the self-
sustained growth of the poorest countries;
(g) All States shall accept an international currency to be
created by an international authority;
(h) All States shall accept the evolution of a world organization with the necessary power to plan, to make decisions and
to enforce them.

It should be noted in this respect that the Charter, which was
adopted by the vast majority of states in the U.N. General
Assembly in December 1974, is subject to five-yearly revision.
The first opportunity for revision was thus the XXXIV session
held in 1979.
(15) The paper was originally published in Christopher Freeman,
Bert V.A. Röling, Alvin M. Weinberg and Herbert York, *Technological Innovation:A Socio-Political Problem,* Boerderijcahier
7701, Twente University of Technology, Enschede, 1977, pp. 83-
122.
(16) Miriam Camps, *The Management of Interdependence. A Preliminary View*, Council on Foreign Relations, New York, 1974,p.8.
(17) Henry Morganthau quoted in G. Kolko, *The Politics of War:*

48 Global Planning

The World and U.S. Foreing Policy 1943-1945, Random House, New
York, 1968, p. 257.
(18) Henry Kissinger, 'America and the world: Principle and
pragmatism', *Time*, 27 December 1975, pp. 43-45, at p. 44.
(19) Reinhold Niebuhr, 'Power and ideology in national and international affairs', in W.T.R. Fox (ed.), *Theoretical Aspects
of International Relations*, Notre Dame University Press, 1959,
p. 114. Niebuhr refers here specifically to the domination and
dependence resulting from the impingement of the rich countries
on the poor.
(20) This is in essence the strategy advocated by OECD's Interfutures Group. See *Facing the Future, Mastering the Probable
and Managing the Unpredictable*, Paris,1979. The group believes
that the OECD countries should give priority to ensuring that
the newly industrializing countries are effectively integrated
in the world economic system, arguing that these countries
"will have caught up with the industrial nations" by the end
of the century (p. 198). The NICs are seen as the "middle class
of an evolving world society" and of being of "fundamental importance for future equilibrium". (p. 400) The rich countries
should thus "accept them gradually as economical partners, on
an equal footing", and they should be afforded "a share in the
management of the world economy". (p. 281)
(21) See Jan Tinbergen, *Central Planning*, Yale University Press,
New Haven, Conn., 1964.
(22) A similar thesis has been advanced by Harlan Cleveland.
He has argued that the common heritage concept should be defined
to include resources traditionally under national jurisdiction
by virtue of geographic location. See Harlan Cleveland, 'Does
Everything Belong to Everybody', *Christian Science Monitor*,
December 19, 1978, p. 22.
(23) See Denis Goulet, *World Interdependence:Verbal Smokescreen
or New Ethic*, Development Paper 21, Overseas Development Council, Washington D.C. March, 1976; and Oscar Schachter, *Sharing
the World's Resources*, Columbia University Press, New York,
1977.
(24) This consensus is documented in Jorge Lozoya, Jaime Este-
vez and Rosario Green, *Alternative Views of the New International Economic Order. A Survey and Analysis of Major Academic
Research Projects*. Pergamon Press, New York - Oxford, 1979,
chapter 2.
(25) See on this, for example, Hans W. Singer and J.A. Ansari,
Rich and Poor Countries, Johns Hopkins Press, Baltimore, 1977.
They argue (p. 37) that "the fundamental advantage of the rich
countries is....not that they produce certain types of commodities, but rather that they are the home of modern technology
and the seats of the multinational coporations. It is because
of this that the rich industrial countries will be the chief
gainers from any type of commercial relationship with the Third
World - be it in the form of trade or investment". It is parti-

cularly interesting that Hans Singer should argue this way
for he was one of the first - together with Myrdal, Lewis and
Prebisch - to point to basic inequities in trading relationships between rich and poor countries.

(26) See Denis Goulet, *The Uncertain Promise:Value Conflicts
in Technology Transfer*, IDOC/North America, Inc., New York,
pp. 7-12.
(27) See I.S. Abdalla, 'Appropriate techniques and technological capacity in Third World countries' in *The Problems of
Technology Transfer Between Advanced and Developing Countries*,
chapter XII of the interim reports prepared as part of the
OECD's Interfutures Project, Paris, 1978.
(28) See Johan Galtung, *Development, Environment and Technolo-
gy:Towards a Technology for Self-Reliance*, UNCTAD, document
TD/B/C.6/23, June 1978.
(29) On 'dual-purpose' technologies, see Dick A. Leurdijk and
Elisabeth Mann Borgese, *Disarmament and Development,* Foundation Reshaping the International Order, Rotterdam, 1979,
Chapter 5.
(30) As the *RIO Report* observes (p. 83): "Nations whose citizens are affected by the external effects of decisions made in
another country in whose decision-making process they have no
part have in fact, for all practical purposes, lost their sovereignty. The protest made by the Australian and New Zealand
governments following the testing of French nuclear weapons
serves as a case in point. The Australian government contended
that the deposit of radioactive fallout on the territory of
Australia and its dispersion in its air-space without the
country's consent was a violation of Australia's sovereignty
over its territory".
(31) See Lester R. Brown, *Redefining National Security,* Worldwatch Paper 14, Worldwatch Institute, Washington, D.C., 1977;
and *The Global Economic Prospect:New Sources of Economic Stress*,
Worldwatch Paper 20, Worldwatch Institute, 1978.
(32) Carlos Andrés Perez, former President of Venezuela, inter-
viewed in *Time*, 3 November 1975.
(33) General McArthur sought permission to use nuclear weapons
in Manchuria. French generals requested U.S. carriers to launch
a nuclear strike at Dien Bien Phu. The world waited to see
whether they would be used in 1962 at Cuba. And General West-
moreland sought permission to use tactical nuclear weapons in
Vietnam.
(34) See on this Joseph S. Nye, 'Transnational and transgovern-
mental relations', in Geoffrey L. Goodwin and Andrew Linklater
(eds.), *New Dimensions of World Politics*, Croom Helm, London,
1975.

I

International Institutions and World Order: Past Efforts and Future Prospects

The progress of mankind is like the incoming
of a tide, which for any given moment is almost
as much of a retreat as an advance, but still
the tide moves on.

Sir A. Helps
Friends in Council

The World Authority:
An Exercise in
Political Forecasting
Silviu Brucan

INTRODUCTION

As we approach the closing decades of the twentieth century the task of building international institutions capable of
dealing effectively with the new problems of our epoch emerges
as one of the principal policy questions before mankind. The
unifying thrust of the scientific-technological revolution
clashing with social antagonisms and national divisions, the
struggle of a hundred nations or so against the mighty and
rich to decentralize power and redistribute wealth and knowledge, the deterioration of the capitalist market principles
that have so far kept the world economy functioning, and the
assault of transnational corporations upon the state-system,
have all pushed international anarchy to a point of no return.

The remaining two decades of this century may go down in
history as its most critical and explosive period. For never
before have so many social and political contradictions requiring structural changes converged in a world so small and
so susceptible to destroying itself. Against this background,
horrendous problems are piling up, threatening the air we
breath, the food we eat, the cities we live in, and, in the
final analysis, the very existence of the human species. The
world of the next decades will be a 'small world' in which the
per capita GNP of the developed nations will still be twelve
times that of the developing nations, even if the growth targets set by the United Nations are achieved. (1) The population
ratio of the two groups of nations, however, will show the reverse: one to five. Put these two sets of figures together and
imagine what may happen in a world in which it will take about
two hours to fly from Buenos Aires to New York, or from Lagos
to London; a world in which the Bolivian or the Pakistani will

see on television how people live in affluent societies; a
world where there will be no suburbia in which the rich can
insulate themselves from the poor. If present trends continue
unchecked, the world of the year 2000 will live and sleep with
a 'balance of terror' in the hands of the twenty or so ambitious nations which posess atomic weapons, not to mention ter-
rorist groups with small portable A bombs which they can use
for the purposes of blackmail or ransom. Pollution will imperil
the ecological balance, already so fragile, while problems of
food, water, and climate may become cirtical. As the pillars of
the old order crumble one after the other, the world of the
year 2000 will look like New York, Tokyo or Paris without traffic regulations and policemen to enforce them!

What kind of an institution could sucessfully cope with
problems of that magnitude and scope; problems without precedent in human experience? Certainly, the United Nations was
neither conceived nor is it equipped for such tasks. In this
paper it is assumed that a new type of international organization is required: a world institution vested with the authority to plan, to make decisions and to enforce them. What is more,
it is contended that the establishment of a New International
Economic Order, as sanctioned by U.N. resolutions,will *only*
materialize when an institutional framework which makes it possible is created.

Having thus set the scene for the debate, let me now
frankly point out that a World Authority, however ideal in conception and rational as a solution, is far ahead of present
political and ideological realities. The very idea of it is,
therefore, bound to encounter formidable opposition on all continents. Paradoxically, but understandably, those who need it
most fear it most.

Nevertheless, a World Authority, or something similar,
will have to be established sooner or later. The sooner, of
course, the better. This makes it imperative to first review
the performance of the United Nations and its evident constitutional limitations and, on that basis, to define the conditions
favorable to the emergence of a new type of institution, and
the prospects for its realization in our times.

                        THE UNITED NATIONS:
                     INADEQUATE AND POWERLESS

Thirty-three years after its founding, the United Nations
is a far cry indeed from the idyllic picture drawn up in its
early days. It was conceived as the international organization
that would usher in an era of peace and harmony and, as its
Charter proclaims, save succeeding generations from the scourges
of war. Between 1945 and 1975, however, there were no less than

119 wars - civil and international - involving the armed forces of 81 countries, some of them the respectable founders of
the organization established to guarantee peace. (2) Although
the thunder and tumult of the Cold War are things of the past,
the continuing clashes between contending groups of nations,
the harsh polemics of super-power rivalries, and, looming over
everything, the insane nuclear arms race, all serve to testify
to the fact that the warless world is not around the corner.

It seems logical to conclude that international organizations are not and cannot be isolated from the world they are
supposed to regulate: the power relations and conflicts which
exist in the world at large are necessarily reflected in the
structure and workings of the organization. Or, in plain language, the United Nations cannot be better than its members.

The issue may be properly focused from the perspective of
the management of power in international society. In international society there is no center of authority and power, like
the state in domestic societies. The resulting vacuum has been
filled over the ages by various schemes whereby great powers,
acting as coordinate managers of power, perform in the international sphere the order-keeping and integrative functions of
the state inside society - if possible through international
organizations.

The United Nations was created in the aftermath of World
War II and, as such, its structure and mechanisms bear the
imprint of the power realities of 1945. The Big Five of the
victorious coalition were given a privileged position in the
organization's governing structure as permanent members of the
Security Council. The argument of the Charter's drafters was
that the unanimity principle of the five (U.S., U.S.S.R.,
Britain, France and China) would limit their freedom of action
and thus guarantee the peace. Yet, the practical consequence
has been that the U.N. is unable to take effective action whenever one of the great powers is involved in a conflict, directly or indirectly. Hence, there are very few military outbreaks
where effective U.N. action becomes possible, for we live in a
small world in which power is ubiquitous.

Since power relations are never dormant, the evolution of
the United Nations has followed post-war shifts in the world-
wide distribution of power, though always one step later. After
all, international organizations are meta-bureaucracies and,
as such, are peculiarly resistant to change. For the first fifteen years, the United States, as the leader of both Western
and Latin American groups, controlled more than two-thirds of
the votes and could easily get its way. This coincided with the
Cold War period when the world looked bipolar, with the U.S.
and the U.S.S.R. as the protagonists of the two hostile camps.
By the end of the 1950s, a new political factor - the Third
World - began to assert its presence in the U.N. The Afro-Asian
group became the largest bloc and, gradually, with most Latin

American nations joining the Third World, the shift in the
composition of membership and in voting power became categori-
al.

In terms of power, then, the United Nations has come a
long way: from George Ball's "blunt truth that far more clearly than the League (of Nations), the U.N. was essentially conceived as a club of great powers". (3) to the present state of
affairs in which great powers bemoan the "tyranny of the majority". The least that can be said is that the 'minority' does
not seem to be exceedingly oppressed. In fact, in recent years,
issues involving the super-powers have been tacitly removed
from the framework of the U.N. The protagonists probably feel
that they are in a better position to handle their affairs
outside a setting that has become too egalitarian and democratic for power politics. With new forces joining the power game,
significant changes have been belatedly felt in the U.N. system. Since 1971, China has been fighting to overcome the status
of a runner-up, while Japan, a global economic power, is seeking a front-ranking position in the organization. To sum up the
point regarding the management of power, let us conclude that
with decentralization of the international system, the world
can no longer be run by great powers. In international organizations this situation is reflected in the gradual deterioration of the political and military blocs of the Cold War.

Apparently, the nuclear stalemate outside the U.N. has
been compounded by a political stalemate within the organization. On the one hand, major decisions, to be effective, require the agreement of the great powers which control the largest means of action; on the other hand, neither of the great
powers, nor any combination of them, are any longer in a position to force the U.N. to do something that negatively affects
the interests of the developing nations.

Inadequacies as a Peace-Keeping
Organization

As noted above, the maintenance of peace and security has
traditionally been viewed as the principal task of the United
Nations. Its record in this field, however, is, as we have
seen, far from satisfactory. In the period 1945-1965, 55 conflicts were referred to the U.N. Of these only 18 (or 33 per
cent) were settled wholly or in part on the basis of U.N. resolutions. The other conflicts were settled outside the U.N. or
reamain unsettled. (4) M.W. Zacher examined 57 international
disputes which occurred in the period 1946-1966 and found that
in 29 cases (52 per cent) no action whatever was taken by the
U.N. (5)

The legal prohibition of the use of force, as provided in
the U.N. Charter, has apparently a rather limited effect since

there are no tribunals and police to enforce the law. As for
the moral commitment implicit in the voluntary adherence by
Member States to the Charter, this has been no more effective
as a check on violence than have the legal constraints. Peacekeeping has only been possible in cases where no great power
is involved and where an emergency situation is perceived by
the superpowers as a harbinger of nuclear confrontation, as
illustrated by Cyprus and the Middle East. However, peacekeeping purports to control armed hostilities rather than to
settle the conflict. Since some forms of violence originate in
the very structure of international society (structural violence), (6) the elimination of violence presupposes an attack
upon its sources.

Inadequacies as a Development Organization

Development, in the celebrated dictum of Pope John XXIII,
is the name of peace today; one more reason for the U.N. to
play a central role in mapping and conducting the strategy of
development. However, the U.N. is not equipped to deal with
such a formidable task. While in the early 'sixties, the General Assembly began to play a positive role in the decolonization struggle, the economic and financial agencies did not dis-
play the same capacity for adaptation. Although the underdeveloped countries made strenuous efforts to secure the transfer
of capital from the rich countries through SUNFED, and thus to
avoid being left at the mercy of private and public donors,
capital transfers have remained well and truly under the control of the latter. The World Bank and the International Monetary Fund have displayed a special preference for the stimulation of private capital investment in Third World countries.
As for GATT, it is no exaggeration to say that the tariff arrangements in the post-war years have heavily favored the industrialized nations. (7)
    Such preferential policies are not hard to explain. At
the time of the Bretton Woods or the Havana conferences, from
which the World Bank, IMF, and, indirectly, GATT ensued, the
initiators and builders were the rich industrial nations.
Quite naturally, they created the institutions which they themselves required to regulate international trade and finance.
The Gold Exchange Standard institutionalized the supremacy of
the dollar. The Third World, as we understand it today, simply
did not exist and hence its interests were not taken into account.
    It must be admitted that the post-war economic order serv-
ed its creators well, particularly the United States. Between
1946 and 1969 the book value of U.S. direct foreign investment
rose from $7,200 million to $70,623 million. (8) U.S. multinational corporations expanded in Europe from 2,236 affiliates in

1950 to 8,611 in 1966; in Asia from 524 in 1950 to 1,599 in
1966; in Africa from 175 in 1950 to 683 in 1966. (9) As for
Latin America, even before the war it was the U.S. backyard.

In the early 'seventies, the Third World succeeded in
rallying its forces and saw to it that, in 1974, the Sixth
Special Session of the U.N. General Assembly adopted the historic resolution on the Establishment of a New International
Economic Order. In other words, it became clear that the Third
World is no longer prepared to accept a marginal status in the
U.N. and is determined to make full use of the available international machinery to further its interests. UNCTAD, as a
response to GATT's preferential policies, has marked institutional duality in the field of trade. The World Bank has begun
to move in support of development strategies, though the industrial nations are still in a position to decide over how
the Bank's funds are to be used. The proliferation of specialized agencies (UNDP, UNIDO, UNEP, etc.) has led to functional
overlapping and very often helpless confusion of responsibilities, evidence of the fact that there is no single body to
purposefully coordinate their activities.

While the First Development Decade (1960-69) fell short
of its goals, and the Second Decade, now nearing its end, has
been no more successful, the strategy adopted by the industrialized market economies to haul themselves out of stagnation
has been similarly a failure. The OECD Scenario for 1980, which
presupposes a determined effort by its members to overcome the
crisis, provided for an annual average rate of growth of 5.5
per cent per annum. However, the actual performance in 1976
and 1977 was much lower; inflation continues to rise and the
unemployment situation is getting worse rather than better.

There is but one inescapable conclusion from this failure:
that the industrialized nations alone cannot overcome the present economic and financial crises by planning in a closed
circuit. Indeed, the OECD countries are already saturated with
industrial products, and the ominous result of this strategy
thus far has been growing protectionist measures and the quar-
rel among the partners of the Trilateral Commission (particularly with Japan) over import quotas and trade imbalances, resulting in the decline of the dollar and increasing financial
instability.

In the meantime, three vast continents, plus the socialist
nations, eagerly await the industrial equipment of the developed countries. They together constitute a huge market, provided there is political will and cautious planning on a global
scale to avoid disorder and disruptive competition.

Surely, global planning and management is the kind of task
only a world institution can cope with. But as things stand
now, the U.N. is neither functionally streamlined nor structurally built to perform such a task. And since function in a system cannot be dissociated from its structure, change must ne-

cessarily affect both. It is only through constitutional
change that international organizations may become effective
in dealing with problems which transcend national territories,
interests and perceptions. The crux of the matter here is the
contradiction between the nature and scope of these problems
and the international system based on national sovereignty and,
implicitly, on decision-making power resting exclusively with
individual nation-states.

Is there a way of overcoming this contradiction? The answer cannot be found in past experience. We must therefore think
and act anew.

THE CASE OF A WORLD AUTHORITY

The discussion of a new international or world order has
so far been dominated by moral, religious, ideological and,
more lately, by juridicial and economic, principles or values.
Certainly, none of these criteria should be belittled or ne-
gated since they provide the motivation which must underlie
efforts to reshape the global order. What is still lacking,
however, is conceptual clarity and scientific groundwork, particularly with respect to bringing into focus the fulcrum of
politics which is and remains of decisive importance in sett-
ling the issue of world order.

A serious intellectual effort is required to fill this
gap. Below are listed various suggestions as to how to go about
it conceptually and historically. As for scientific analysis,
given the state of the art, one can claim no more than to combine verified knowledge with quantitative and statistical data,
whenever the latter are available.
(i) To start with, international organizations have never had
the authority to make decisions and enforce them for the very
simple reason that in an international state-system this is
the exclusive prerogative of nation-states. Throughout history,
international order (if we may call it as such) was maintained
rather precariously by the empires or great powers of the time
on the premise that each one enforced international decisions
(made chiefly by them) in its own zone of influence. This is
what makes some believe that: (a) the Concert of Europe, with
four or five powers running world affairs, provided the 'golden
age';(10) (b) the colonial system developed a mechanism for
preserving its stability and preventing 'primitive' people from
disrupting world order; (11) and (c) the postwar bipolar structure of power was a guarantee of peace and order in the world.
(12) Briefly, the fewer centers of power, the better for world
order.

Although all these models today appear reactionary and re-
trogade, they nevertheless reflect views on world order at va-

rious historical stages. Now, for the first time in history, we are talking about an international institution which is able to wield *power of its own*. In practical terms, this requires that a transfer of power - a partial and gradual one to be sure - must take place from nation-states to the world institution. It is this kind of institution, and only this one, which will be able to maintain world order under the changing conditions and relationship of forces.

By *world order* I refer to a pattern of power relations among states capable of ensuring the functioning of various international activities according to a set of rules, written and unwritten. Since the transfer of power to the World Authority will be gradual, it logically follows that in the transition period world order will be maintained by a *duality* of power: the *nation-state*, retaining most of its sovereign rights, and the *World Authority*, exercising power in international affairs to the extent of its delegated authority and competence.
(ii) What are the historical grounds for the initiation of a world institution of this type? Historically, the case for a World Authority rests on the emergence of a *world system*. This system is tending to supersede the present international state-system. Indeed, in the second half of the twentieth century the international system has began to function as a world-system in which information is ubiquitous and instantaneous, communication is universal, transportation is supersonic, and modern weaponry is planetary in both destructive and delivery capability. For the first time in history we can speak meaningfully of world politics, world market, world problems, and world crisis, and only now does the old dictum 'peace is indivisible' acquire a global meaning.

While in the past the global social system was the national society, and nation-states functioned as self-contained social systems whose decisions were determined from the inside (though not in isolation from the rest of the world), under present conditions the global social system is the world system, with its boundaries and structure of power, its limited resources governing national policies, its conflicts and problems requiring solutions at the world level. Through its interaction with the natural environment, it functions as a living organism with a life-span, an equilibrium, and recurring breaks in the continuity of its development. Suffice it to note that major powers, such as Britain and Italy, now have to calculate and draw up their budget according to the instructions of the International Monetary Fund, in order to see the difference.

Here I must point out that there are those who consider the origin of the world-system as going back to as early as the XVth century, on an exclusively European basis; (13) there are others who stress the role of the great powers (starting with Portugal) in creating the system. I suggest that the wa-

tershed of a global system encompassing the whole planet and
functioning with sufficient regularities as to impose certain
recognizable patterns of behavior on all its subsystems is related primarily to the scientific-technological revolution.
It is the revolution in communication and information, transportation and modern weaponry, that has changed the entire environment in which international politics is perceived, formulated, and conducted. It is this revolution that has made it
possible for a global sphere of multilevel interdependencies
to emerge and function with a unifying and integrating force.
I thus place the appearance of the world-system at the middle
of the twentieth century, when major breakthroughs in science
started to be applied on a large enough scale to become conse-
quential in world politics. Previously, large sections of the
world remained isolated and practically unaffected by central
capitalism, even by two world wars. At the time of Portugal's
overseas expansion, the Portuguese knew neither what nor where
the planet was, a condition hardly consonant with the notion
of world-wide domination.

The important point is that 'world-system' is the conceptualization best suited to handle the new world problems that
have arisen in recent decades. Needed in this regard is a
conceptual link between the world-system and the origin and
nature of these problems. Certainly, development, ecological
equilibrium, nuclear proliferation or scarce resources cannot
be adequately dealt with in the context of the 'world-system
of the 1500s or, for that matter, of the 1800s, for the very
reason that they were not world problems then. And they could
not be so because there was no world-system to account for
their global scope.

The integrating force of the world-system can be illustrated with many types of examples. Suffice it to mention the
effect of nuclear weapons on the strategies of the nuclear
powers, irrespective of their internal economic and political
regimes, and the fact that the prevailing world crisis affects
all nations without exception.

(iii) Globalism in the nuclear era has given the United States
and the Soviet Union a monopoly on basic decisions concerning
war and peace. Both superpowers have been driven by this vital
strategic goal to alienate some of their major allies; for example France in the case of the U.S. and China in the case of
the U.S.S.R., while reserving for themselves the possession
of strategic nuclear weapons. By the same token, China's ad-
vocay of a strong Western European defence build-up instead
of the European security system by all European socialist
countries serves as another example which demonstrates that
the global power game creates its *own logic*, transcending all
other considerations, including ideological ones.

(iv) All nations, however different internally, conduct their
international economic exchanges and financial transactions

according to the rules and practices of the world market. In
the world economy, the capitalist mode of production remains
predominant and it has shaped the formation and expansion of
the international system. Relations among socialist nations are
not independent of but rather subject to the motion of the
world system and hence to capitalist mechanisms and relationships.

The main theoretical point here is that a subsystem cannot
run deeper than the system of which it is part. Even if different in its inner structure, it must adjust to the exogenous
forces and motion of the world-system. Briefly, then, *the
world-system causes nation-states to make adaptive decisions
to its dynamic motion*, decisions which states would not take in
response to domestic influences only.

(v) Turning now to political relations and the way they crystallize in the world power structure, the first thing that
strikes the researcher is that they do not necessarily parallel
either the economic or the military state of affairs. There are
world powers in a preindustrial stage (e.g. China), and major
centers of power (e.g. Japan) without significant military
strength. Besides the global game referred to earlier, power is
today exercised on various lines, particularly economic and financial. Thus, huge power is concentrated in the industrialized
and rich nations, placing them in a strong position in many a-
reas of world politics. Owing to their economic strength, West
Germany and Japan are able to play an increasingly important
international role. At the other end of the spectrum, in the
Third World, we witness the rise of states, wielding new political weapons (read OPEC), determined to challenge the present
power structure. Small and medium-size powers are becoming more
active and influential, while the great powers are finding it
increasingly difficult to control even their 'client-states'.
In summary, we are witnessing a crucial conflict: the old thrust
toward centralization of power is now clashing with the drive to
decentralize power in the world-system.

(vi) The impact of the world-system upon its basic units, the
nation-states, is thus felt in all major areas of foreign policy, be they military, economic or political. And all the evidence suggests that the influence of external stimuli on the behavior of nation-states is likely to increase rather than decrease in the years ahead.

It is at this stage of history that the World Authority
becomes a relevant and credible institution. This time, the urgent call for such an institution comes from the whole rather
than its parts, from the world-system rather than from nation-
states; for the challenge is to regulate the functioning of the
supercomplex global system rather than to accommodate the contending interests of states, particularly the great and the
rich.

THE PRINCIPAL TASKS OF A
WORLD AUTHORITY

In the 'sixties, the central problem of world order was
assumed to be the avoidance of thermonuclear warfare. This focus of concern originated in the West and the editors of *The
Strategy of World Order* candidly admitted that although the
rest of mankind endures poverty and other terrible afflictions,
"the danger of nuclear war imperils the overall achievement of
the prosperous and fully developed countries in such a singular
fashion that it must inevitably dominate their political imagination".(14) Even Pope John XXIII, in his famous encyclical letter *Pacem in Terris* stated that "the present system of organization and the way its principle of authority operates on a world
basis no longer correspond to the objective requirements of the
universal common good" and suggested "a public authority,
having world-wide power and endowed with the proper means".(15)
    Given the experience of the past, the rest of the world
became suspicious of the unilateral emphasis placed on nuclear
war and of so lofty a pronouncement. The whole idea was discard-
ed as another rich man's concern, or as the desire of monopo-
lies to dominate the whole world. However, the Soviet proposals
made in the United Nations for general and complete disarmament
and the subsequent Soviet-U.S. agreement on the principles that
should guide such a disarmament program gave a new impetus to
the systematic study of world order. The warless world became
a central topic; models of supranational institutions and of
world government were hastily designed.
    Interestingly, Pope John's encyclical was not written as a
utopian or idealistic scheme but rather in the vein of a practical proposal for something attainable. Similarly, the Clark-
Sohn model for a warless world was viewed by the authors as a
'reasoned prediction': the plan for total and universal disarmament, including the institutions required to enforce disarmament, was to be drawn-up over a period of four to six years
(by 1965-67); the whole scheme was to be ratified by all (or
nearly all) governments and parliaments and come into force
some four to six years thereafter (by 1969-71). (16)
    The sixties were indeed happy years for day-dreamers and
well-wishers! The flurry of excitement, however, has now passed
into history, as have the disappointing results of the recent
U.N. Special Session on Disarmament. (17) It is perhaps now
appropriate to note that total and universal disarmament will
only come about when there is a World Authority which has the
power to bring it about and to enforce it. And, to this end,
liberal good-will, appeals to rationality, and scarce tactics
involving terrifying prospects of apocalypse will just not be
sufficient. Each of these has been tried time and again with
very poor results. Recent years have in fact witnessed a viru-

lent build-up of destructive capabilities: in addition to the
counterforce strategy and assured destruction capability of
the superpowers, cruise missiles, MX, Trident, Neutron bomb,
SS 20 and other nuclear weaponry, we have witnessed the determined efforts of France to build her *force de frappe*, the spectacular feats of China exploding her A and H bombs, and the
expansion of the arms race to the South, where the richer a-
mong the Third World elites have displayed a remarkable readiness to spend billions of dollars on modern weapons. All this
suggests that the (nuclear) arms race has gone out of control
and that the record of the U.N. in the field of disarmament
must be considered its most spectacular failure.

Obviously, the stupendous jump in the quantity, quality,
and cost of armaments has resulted in a decrease in the security of nations. There is but one logical conclusion: namely,
that there must be *objective forces* at work in the world that
are very little affected by rational arguments, that cannot be
frightened off by any of the modern bugaboo, and that are even
stronger than man's instinct for self-preservation. It is from
this angle that I intend to approach the problem of world order.

(i)   In the *World Order Models Project* (WOMP), (18) each author
was asked to start from a diagnosis of the contemporary world
order, make prognostications based on that diagnosis, state
his preferred future world order, and advance coherent and viable strategies of transition that could bring that future into
being. The models are intended to come to grips with four major
problems (war, poverty, social injustice, and environmental de-
cay) according to a set of values. The approach is *normative*,
in the sense that the world is viewed as it should be, not as
it is. WOMP is thus similar to Pope John's call and to the
Clark-Sohn model, though in this case war is no longer singled
out but rather lumped together with the afflictions which beset
mankind.

Indeed, if a stable peace through world order is to be
achieved, all of mankind must benefit from that order. At present, the rich and powerful nations refuse to give up nuclear
weapons and the threat of their use since they see them as instruments for protecting and expanding their privilege; and the
poor and underprivileged refuse to renounce political violence,
including terrorism, which they see as one of the few bargaining chips they have in their struggle for a better and more e-
quitable world. Obviously, the model of a new world order
should be built as a symmetric structure, striking a fair balance between the two main foci of concern.

Unlike those who look at the world as it should be, I
start from the state of the world as it is, try to identify the
objective forces at work in world politics, to see where they
are going to take us in the future and how man can influence
the course of events. Since we will be dealing with objective

forces - that is, forces which exist and act whether or not we
like or perceive them - I should probably emphasize my conviction that while man cannot create anew or eliminate such forces,
he can, nevertheless, once he is aware of their existence and
motion, regulate and modify them, and eventually channel them
in a worthwhile direction.
(ii) In Soviet theory, the traditional emphasis in dealing with
the causes of war has been on imperialism. (19) Lenin gave an
exhaustive class analysis of the social nature and character of
war under imperialism as well as its causes and purposes, reaching the conclusion that wars were inherent in the nature of imperialism and engendered by its aggressive character. Historical experience in recent decades, however, has made it abundant-
ly clear that radical transformations inside societies could
not fundamentally change the international system; nor could
they eliminate imperialism and its impact on war and peace.
Lenin was aware that the triumph of revolution in a country
like Russia did not imply radical change in the international
system. He believed that only when socialism triumphed "at least
in several advanced countries" was it "capable of exercising a
decisive influence upon world politics as a whole". (20) In
other words, the success of revolution in the weakest links of
the imperialist chains, to use Lenin's phrasing, could not possibly produce the qualitative transformation of relations among
nations that Marx had anticipated, as long as the citadels of
central capitalism, the Western powers, remained standing.

On the questions of war and peace, the restructuring of
class relations within societies is simply not enough; the *international* dimension is of decisive importance. And here, although a subsystem of nations has emerged which is dedicated
to the building of socialism and which has produced significant
shifts in the relationship of forces within the world system,
the structure of the system based on nation-states has remained
basically unaltered. And so has the pattern of behavior among
nations, among *all* nations, irrespective of their socio-economic system, resulting from discrepancies in size, wealth, and
level of development. As long as such discrepancies continue to
exist, *power* will remain an international factor in international politics, and so will its traditional instrument: the use
of force or the threat of it.

There is but one logical conclusion: the socialist nations
should be no less interested in a World Authority than the nations living under capitalism.

Surely, the concept of peaceful coexistence promoted by
the Soviet Union and other socialist countries is today an important principle in international relations - a principle that
has gained ground in the world as a whole. Viewed as part of
the class struggle in the international arena, peaceful coexistence implies that the competition between capitalism and socialism will not be fought out in bloody military wars, but will

take the form of peaceful contest, or, as Lenin said, of 'rivalry'. But peaceful coexistence is still an 'armed peace' and
like other noble principles is no guarantee whatever against
the outbreak of military hostilities, not even among socialist
nations. It is only a world institution 'with teeth' that can
provide such a guarantee.
(iii) In the West, the analysis of Sohn and Clark indicated that
the reluctance of the average person to make any drastic change
in his traditional pattern of behavior could be considered the
most important factor which works against disarmament and peace.
They then make mention of the habits, traditions and vested interests related to the units into which mankind has combined -
family, tribe, town, city, national state - and which are accustomed to assert or defend their interests, real or supposed,
by violence or the threat of it; a process which culminates in
an arms build up and, ultimately, in a world war. (21)
     Kenneth Waltz, in his inventory of the causes of war, men-
tions, in order of importance, firstly, the nature and behavior
of man, secondly, the political structure and social and economic conditions of individual states, and, thirdly, the state-
system itself. (22)
     Although there is something worth pondering in each of
these causes, the placing of man's individual behavior or human
nature at the top of the list of causes makes the whole peace
and disarmament exercise both futile and hopeless. For if four
billion people must first change their nature and behavior, we
may expect disarmament and peace once in a blue moon!
(iv) In fact, man does not live alone, nor does his behavior
develop in isolation. I start from the assumption that it is
the aggregation of men according to the two basic types of social relationship - *classes* and *ethnicity* (at present nations
and nationality) - that condition their behavior and thinking
whenever they entroll in a collective large-scale movement.
Consequently, my theoretical model for forecasting world political developments proceeds from the idea that *pressure of modern technology* acts upon relations among nations under their
two facets: *power politics*, which today takes the principal
form of superpower rivalry and dominance; and its response,
national self-assertion of the small and the poor, as well as
upon class relations, ultimately producing social change. The
clashes and combinations among the four variables result in
the dynamics of world politics.
     The pressure of modern technology is the main driving
force toward a smaller and shrinking world that eventually, in
a very distant future, will turn into an integrated world-system whose self-regulating motion will no longer be interrupted
or held back by decisions of nation-states. Yet, social cleavages inside societies as well as differences among nations place
formidable obstacles in the path of integration. Precisely because of social and national inequalities, with the conflicts

they produce, the drive of modern technology does not operate
as a one-directional sweep and onrush, but as a *dual and contradictory motion* generating a dialectical interplay between
the factors that make for conflict and division, and those that
make for cooperation and integration, with the latter winning
only ultimately. Hence, I expect the process of integration to
be marked by progress and regression, advances and setbacks,
and to proceed in stages, starting first on a *regional* basis.
(v)   Since the process of integration means the formation of
larger political units than nation-states, ultimately requiring
the dissolution of national power, it is assumed that a World
Authority may be initiated *before* the regional units; for the
World Authority to come into being a partial transfer of power
is enough, whereas the new regional units imply the dismantling
of the entire state-power of the nations involved.

I have dealt elsewhere in detail with the conditions and
rules of integration, particularly with regional unions. (23)
Here I should only point out that while *territorial contiguity*
has proved an enhancing condition for regional integration, it
is not enough of a catalyst for such a sensitive change, except
when combined with homogeneity of *social structure* and *ideology*
(e.g. NATO and EEC, Warsaw Treaty and CMEA). Therefore, the
process has to be viewed in the context of the international
subsystems organized on such a basis (the so-called three
worlds) which should be placed in our model on an intermediary
level, between the national systems and the world-system.

However, one must view this long historical process in the
perspective of the dual and contradictory motion that is at
work in world politics with its effect on the factors of conflict and those of integration. The setting up of a World Authority would help guarantee that the conflictual situations arising at various stages will not turn into large-scale violence
with a nuclear potential.
(vi) Even if total and complete disarmament is eventually
achieved, this will not eliminate conflicts originating in
class and national antagonisms. It is all the more incumbent to
have a World Authority, endowed with an international police
force and tribunals, not only to control disarmament and ensure
that rearmament does not take place, but also to control conflict so as to prevent it from turning into war. Social change
and revolutions have always been the focus of international conflicts with foreign powers intervening to influence the outcome;
recent events in Europe as well as in Africa, Asia and Latin
America have shown that such practices are fraught with great
dangers.

                            THE PREREQUISITES FOR A
                               WORLD AUTHORITY

     The most important prerequisite for supranational integra-
tion and for a World Authority is the elimination of the vast
disparities in wealth and power which characterize our world.
Without this, a legitimate question arises whenever supranational integration is suggested: will not the rich and mighty use
the coercive power at their command - military strength or economic sanctions - to force the poorer and weaker partners into
a larger unit which the powerful will control?
     The answer I would suggest is that, unlike the past, co-
ercive power is today ineffective and counterproductive in the
realization of a supranational unit. To make a nation possessing a strong will of self-assertion renounce its identity, with
the prospect of losing its language, territory, economy and
culture with all its deeply rooted symbols, and shift its loyal-
ty, expectations and political activity toward a new and larger
center of power is only possible on a *voluntary* basis. The decision to make such a shift is obviously a crucial decision,
conceivably one of life or death. It cannot be forced upon a
modern nation, peopled by increasingly educated, aware and sophisticated citizens. The validity of this law has been proven
whenever a process of integration has been initiated - in the
West or in the East. The notion that the new unit will offer
fair and equal opportunities to all the nations participating
in it is, therefore, an essential prerequisite for successful
integration. This effectively means that supranational integration in which the great disparities existing among nations
are gradually reduced to tolerable proportions.
     The principle is applicable to the World Authority, though
to a lesser extent. Here the transfer of power is limited and
nations maintain their identity and most of their sovereign
rights. Nevertheless, experience shows that in international
organizations disparities in power and wealth provide the powerful and rich nations with the opportunity of dominating them
and transforming them into agencies which serve primarily *their*
interests. This has implanted in the small and poor nations
suspicion and fear of such manipulation and misuse of international organizations. What is more, the new nations are particularly jealous of their recently acquired sovereignty and
eager to fully enjoy it. This is reinforced by the conviction
that national sovereignty is the last line of defense against
domination and exploitation by foreign powers. Yet, while the
great and developed nations look at the World Authority as the
best and safest way of avoiding a nuclear disaster, the small
and poor should look at it as the only way of actually getting
a better and more equitable world order. The fears and suspicions vis-à-vis the World Authority could be allayed by a fair

system of representation and distribution of power in the
governing body of the institution.
(i) In the years that have elapsed since 1974, when the U.N.
adopted the resolution on the Establishment of a New International Economic Order, it has become all too clear that no significant headway in the direction of a more equitable world
will ever be possible without global planning and management
so as to avoid disorder and disruptive competition. And such
planning is inconceivable without a World Authority. What is
more, even a partial, piecemeal agreement in North-South negotiations will come up against the issue of enforcement. Whether
it involves the 1 per cent concessional resource transfer target, the reduction of food-wastage in the industrialized countries and the organization of production of basic foodstuffs
in the Third World, or the linking of the prices of industrial
goods to those of raw materials, the question will arise: *who*
will ensure and *how* will it be ensured that all the parties involved observe the provisions of the agreement? The real choice
is between a World Authority and the laws of the market. And
by now everybody knows that the laws of the market systematically work in favor of the rich industrial nations. And as for
the privileged nations, they will be unable to come to terms
with the present crisis in the international economic and financial system without recourse to global planning. A World
Authority will thus become a *must*.
(ii) The World Authority is fundamentally distinct from the
United Nations in conception and structure, competence and
character. Actually, the World Authority is designed for a different historical stage. It is hard to imagine, therefore, that
the new world institution could come into being merely by a
revision of the U.N. Charter, however thorough and radical. The
U.N. could be instrumental, however, in the initiation phase
of the new institution, providing the proper forum for the discussion of its principles, organization and structure with the
participation of all the nations of the world. Moreover, the
wholly new world organization will probably have to make use
of the experienced staff and vast facilities of the U.N., once
the latter would cease to exist.
(iii)Finally, a clear distinction should be made between a
World Authority and World Government. World Government presupposes the dissolution of nation-states and the transfer of
their entire power to a single governing body designed to effectively control and manage the whole world. The World Authority, on the other hand, requires the maintenance of nation-
states with only a partial transfer of power to the new institution enabling it to operate on a world-wide scale with a
limited competence clearly defined in its constitution.
        Since world government has been advocated solely for the
purpose of eliminating war and, implicitly, for controlling
conflicts with a potential for violence, its installation is

perceived to mean the freezing of the social and national status quo; the rules made by the world government prohibiting
disorderly conduct and violence will prevent the underprivileged classes of society, the poor nations and oppressed ethnic
groups, from striving for a better life and a more equitable
world order.

Conversely, the World Authority would not interfere with
social and national movements and conflicts, which would continue to go on. Its field of concern would be large-scale violence involving foreign power intervention. It is these conflicts that would fall within the competence of the Authority
and with which it would be empowered to deal.

NOTES AND REFERENCES

(1)   Wassily Leontief et.al., *The Future of the World Economy*,
Oxford University Press, New York, 1977.
(2)   Frank Barnaby in the *Bulletin of Atomic Scientists*, vol.
32, no. 6, June, 1976.
(3)   George Ball, 'Slogans and realities', *Foreign Affairs*,
July, 1969, p. 625.
(4)   Ernest B. Haas, *Collective Security and the Future International System*, Denver, Col., 1968.
(5)   M.W. Zacher, *United Nations Involvement in Crisis and
Wars*, APSA, Los Angeles, 8-12 September 1970.
(6)   Johan Galtung, 'Violence, peace and peace research.',
Journal of Peace Research, vol. 6, no. 3, 1969, pp. 167-191.
(7)   See Jan Tinbergen (coordinator), *Reshaping the International Order: A Report to the Club of Rome*, E.P. Dutton, New York,
1976; and Volker Rittberger, 'International organization and
violence', *Journal of Peace Research*, no. 3, 1973.
(8)   Christopher Tungenhat, *The Multinationals*, Penguin Books,
Harmondsworth, 1974.
(9)   United Nations, *Multinational Corporations in World Development*, (U.N. Publication E.73.II.A.11), New York, 1973,p.143.
(10) E.H. Carr, *Nationalism and After*, Macmillan, London, 1945.
(11) TEMPO, *International Stability:Problems and Prospects*,
Santa Barbara, California, February, 1961, pp. 5-6.
(12) Kenneth Waltz, 'Stability of the bipolar world', *Daedalus*,
XCIII, Summer, 1964, pp. 881-909.
(13) Immanuel Wallerstein, *The Modern World-System*, Academic
Press, New York, 1974, vol. I, Introduction.
(14) Richard Falk and Saul H. Mendlovitz (eds.), *Strategy of
World Order*, World Law Fund, New York, 1966, Preface.
(15) 'Pacem in Terris', in *Strategy of World Order*, op.cit., pp.
117-118.
(16) Grenville Clark and Louis B. Sohn, *World Peace through
World Law*, Harvard University Press, Cambridge,Mass., 1962,

p.XLIII.
(17) Tenth Special Session of the U.N. General Assembly, held
in New York in June 1978. Its final document is contained in
resolution S-10/2, adopted by the 27th plenary meeting on
30 June.
(18) Richard A. Falk, *A Study of Future Worlds*, Free Press,
New York, 1975.
(19) See Y. Molchanov, 'The October Revolution and the question
of war and peace', *International Affairs* (Moscow), no. 11.1977.
(20) V.I. Lenin, *Collected Works*, Foreign Languages Publishing
House, Moscow, vol. 31, p. 148.
(21) Clark and Sohn, op.cit., p. XLIV.
(22) Kenneth Waltz, 'Political philosphy and the study of
international relations', in *Strategy of World Order*, op.cit.,
pp. 141-144.
(23) See Silviu Brucan, *The Dialectic of World Politics*, Free
Press, New York, 1978, pp. 79-112.

The Mutation of
World Institutions
Harlan Cleveland

...Within nations, there has been an evolution over time
of institutions and mechanisms which ensure greater planning and coordination of diverse economic activities
within the framework of overall national objectives. The
growth of progressive taxation systems, central banks and
planning commissions represent various elements in this
evolution. A similar evolution at the international level
is only a matter of time. Often, the evolution of international institutions has followed the same route taken
by national institutions, though with a time lag of several decades. One of the basic questions which today
faces the international community is whether it should
accelerate the process of this evolution and consciously
put in place the various elements of a system for global
planning and the management of resources.

The RIO Report, p. 184.

INTRODUCTION; THE DOUBLE HELIX OF THE NATION STATE

The temptation to extrapolate history is strong. It provides comfort in the midst of confusion to believe that you
know what destiny intends, so that you do not have to invent
anything new but merely hasten the advent of the familiar in
a new disguise.

The pull of analogy is strong, too, and the analogy of
the nation-state has pulled into its orbit most of the philo-
sophers of world order. The architects of the Roman Empire,
the Leninist world revolution, the League of Nations, Deutsch-
land Über Alles, Japan's East Asia Co-prosperity Sphere, the

United Nations and a hundred schemes for world government, all
focused on architecture, structure and authority, seeking arrangements by which a sovereign or committee of sovereigns
would tax, plan and manage a passive majority of peoples. In
each instance the beneficence of world order was to be assured:
its architects elected themselves to form the executive committee.

Fortunately for the destiny of mankind, if disturbing to
its planners and managers, the expectations and ambitions of
real-life men and women have in this century proved too various
and too vigorous for the static 'structures of peace' their
transient leaders established to contain them. The urgent rush
of science and technology, the mass migrations of people, the
rivalries of great powers, the ambitions of new nations, the
awakening of submerged races and classes, and the importunities
of plain people who came to consider their universal rights
more important than universal order and organized to struggle
for the blessings they felt were due them - in a word, the
global fairness revolution - outgrew each new set of institutions the way a baby outgrows its swaddling clothes or a teen-
ager its first two or three suits of civilized apparel.

The fallacy of the previous tries at world order was that
to ensure predictable order and peaceful change on a global
scale some one - an emperor, a Roman Senate, a ruling class, a
dominant race, a group of revolutionary cadres, a cabal of
great powers, a President, a Politburo, or if all else failed
a general - had to be in charge of the taxing, the planning
and the managing.

It was a quite natural assumption. The highest form of
order had been the nation-state, and the nation-state had assembled the power to govern by exercising the leadership of a
few at the expense of the many. Wouldn't government at world
level have to do the same? The extrapolation of history said
yes.

But while the latter day architects of world order have
been designing global institutions with the cultural raw materials of nationhood, the nation-state itself has been getting
older and more crotchety and less able to cope with an environment of accelerating change. As of 1979, national governments,
with all their progressive taxes, central banks and planning
commissions, are demonstrably unable to cope. Those of us who
presume to conceptualize a New International Order would do
well to be careful about extrapolating national government as
a model of world governance.

TWO TRIES AT WORLD ORDER:
THE LEAGUE OF NATIONS AND THE UNITED NATIONS

The founders of the League of Nations and the United Na-

tions, and most of the other advocates of governing institutions for One World, have in this century shared a common conception. Their 'world order' was peopled with universal institutions, administering and if possible enforcing universal
rights and duties, reflecting a near-universal political will
to band together to restrain and discipline outlaws and agres-
sors (in the image of Kaiser Wilhelm and Adolf Hitler), operating by the rule of law or at least of legalisms, making decisions through a parliamentary democracy in which sovereign
nations are substituted for sovereign individuals.

There was nourishment in all of these concepts, and they
have carried us part of the way toward a global system of
peaceful change. Perhaps ten percent of the way. They could
not carry us further because the governance of a world community presupposes a world community. And, as things turned out,
the *kinds* of institutions that emerged from these noble conceptions were inappropriate to the *kinds* of world community
that have begun to emerge in the last decades of the century.
The conceptions were universal, the institutions unitary; but
the emerging real-world community is pluralistic.

For the League to have succeeded would have required a
club of the 'like-minded', determined to dominate. Even at the
start it did not attract a still isolationist United States to
the club, and the members that did join soon found they had
neither the power or the will to deal with a growing band of
outlaws - first the Japanese militarists in Manchuria, then
the Italian Fascists in Ethiopia, then the German Nazis with
two-front ambitions in Europe. The doctrines of 'peace' were
frozen in a pattern of non-change, non-maneuver, non-negotia-
tion - and non-resistance until resistance was the only remaining option.

In those days, the global fairness revolution was still
dormant, kept in a soporific state by colonial rule, economic
dictation and naval superiority.

The institutions of world community made some progress
in projecting Western-style labor standards not expected to
apply to the East, developing a common language for talking
about the weather, and beginning to cooperate in tracking com-
municable disease. But most of humanity was effectively outside the pale of the like-minded. Latin America, the Africa
of blacks and Arabs, and continental Asia were quiescently dependent - whether they were formal colonies, or protectorates
like China and Siam and Ethiopia and most of the Wester Hemi-
sphere, or parts of a Commonwealth still meriting the adjective
British. And the Soviet Union was still struggling to be born
in Lenin's mold, preoccupied (despite Marxism's universal rhetoric) with infighting among the founding revolutionaries and
the reality of a profound internal revolution.

Then the whole League structure was washed away in the

tidal wave of a war which could not yet be technologically
global but managed to be effectively world-wide.

The United Nations was what the stop-Hitler coalition
called itself during World War II - the members asking each
other only what they were fighting against, not what they were
fighting for. Those United Nations decided in 1945 to organize
the postwar peace as well. They started with premises similar
to the League's: a universal order, enforced by universal institutions, reflecting universal rights and duties, demonstrating a universal will to band together against outlaws, operating by legalistic rules and pseudoparliamentary practice.

But the world after 1945 was much more fluid. Peace was
more obviously a function of change. And the dominant club
proved much readier to adapt to rising political ambitions and
rising economic expectations in the two-thirds of the world of
which they quite suddenly lost control.

One of the U.N. Charter's universal institutions, the
Trusteeship Council, presided over the astonishingly peaceful
decolonization of more than a billion people. The elite club
mandated to keep the general peace, the U.N.'s Security Council, has mounted a score of practical peacekeeping operations
- under a Charter so preoccupied with Hitler-style aggression
that it failed to provide for the kinds of peacekeeping in
which the United Nations has actually engaged.

Yet another universal organ, the U.N.'s General Assembly,
was conceived as a recording device for common national decisions, with some latent authority to raise revenues. In
practice it now makes no 'decisions' and even declined in the
1960s to enforce its Charter power to levy taxes on its members. Yet it has gone far beyond a forum for ideological debate, to set in motion far-reaching actions - an Emergency
Force in the Middle East, a new attitude toward population
control, a universal condemnation of *apartheid* in South Africa, treaties on the law of outer space and deliberate environmental change, a World Weather Watch, a shift in the political
definition of 'China', the creation of Israel, a dialogue (not
yet a negotiation) on a New International Economic Order, a
code of conduct for transnational business, a continuous (if
so far largely ineffective) conference on disarmament, and a
Universal Declaration on Human Rights which for the first time
fused 'political rights' (centered on the security of the person) with 'economic rights' (centered on the meeting of basic
human needs).

The General Assembly also turned on a series of world
conferences, beginning with Stockholm 1972, in such 'cut-
across' categories as the human environment, population, food,
the status of women, habitat, water, deserts, science and
technology for development, and declared 1979 the Year of the
Child. These 'town meetings of the world' should not be judged
by the carefully crafted 'action programs' they adopt just be-

fore the delegates have to leave for the airport. They are
best seen as problem-oriented sensitivity training on issues
that have been neglected by national governments and international agencies because they were too interdisciplinary, cul-
turally or politically too touchy, or merely too important for
political leaders to tackle.

There is a certain irony in the fact that national criticism of the bureaucratic sins of the U.N. - which are many,
and fully exposed - is at its height in the decade when the
U.N. system is breaking this new ground and pushing national
governments to look at the subjects they have done their best
to neglect.

THE TECHNOLOGICAL IMPERATIVE

In assessing the record of international cooperation since
1945, it is therefore best to examine, not what the architects
of world order said they wanted to construct, but the institutions that actually got built. During the generation since the
United Nations was conceived, we have been building peace in
parcels. The parcels are of functional sizes and shapes, because they have been, for the most part, designed to be wrap-
ped around discrete developing technologies.

President Franklin D. Roosevelt, preoccupied with post-
war planning even as he was managing a global war effort, was
mindful of the sour comment of John Maynard Keynes that the
failure of this century's first try at world order, at Versailles, was due to the lack of 'concrete ideas ...for clothing
with the flesh of life the commandments which (Woodrow Wilson)
had thundered from the White House". That is why Roosevelt
early developed the principle (which he practiced but was careful not to preach) that an ultimate pattern of peace must be
put together over a period of time out of its major fragments.
It was too much, he felt, to build a peace all at once, in a
single stroke of diplomacy, from such a ruin as World War II
might make of the world.

In the early years of postwar planning, therefore, the
planning was in bits and pieces, reaching into every specialized corner of the government. The dynamics of specialist enthusiasm would be used to provide motive power for building the
peace; the vehicles of peace would take the form of international organizations for special as well as general purposes, for
technical as well as political functions.

We can see now that it was clearly a good thing for the
pattern of peace to develop in a fragmented way. It was much
easier to reach international agreement in the relatively
'safe', relatively non-political arenas in which the U.N.'s
Specialized Agencies were set to work. Progress in one field

of endeavor could not be made to depend on simultaneous progress in all the others.

The unanswerable reason for creating each international
organization - each adding a fragment to the pluralistic pattern - has been the advance of science and technology. Whenever the scientists achieved a breakthrough in what can be
done by man for man, it suddenly seemed outrageous not to be
using for human purpose the new power that new knowledge
brought in its train.

Before we knew that mosquitoes carried malaria, and before we knew how to murder mosquitoes with DDT, nobody thought
about eradicating malaria from the face of the earth, because
it could not be done. Now that we know it can be done, we keep
trying to do it - even though DDT turned out to bring with it
new dangers, even though the mosquitoes proved more resistant
to our attempts to poison them than the scientists thought
when they proudly swept every anopheles from the island of
Sardinia just after World War II.

Before there was radio, we did not need to have a large
standing international conference to divide up the frequency
spectrum; now, the International Telecommunications Union's
World Administrative Radio Conference is just that. Before
there were airplanes flying across frontiers and oceans, we
did not need an International Civil Aviation Organization.
Today we have international agreements on aerial navigation
because the alternative would be mayhem compounded.

Before we could take synoptic pictures of the world's
weather, and sample from satellites the wind and temperature
and pollution and air-sea interactions all around the globe
(instead of operating from the earth's surface with only a
tenth of the necessary coverage), there was no basis for human
systems that tried to match in complexity the enormous sweep
of the real atmosphere in the real sky. But these new technologies, plus the fast computer to make possible large-scale
modeling and rapid combination of global data- fast enough to
be analyzed before the weather itself has come and gone - have
made a World Weather Watch suddenly feasible. From a standing
start in the early 1960s it was only a decade before such a
system was a working reality. We are now, in the late '70s, so
accustomed to watching the weather swirl across continents, on
the nightly satellite photographs we see on home television
sets, that we have almost forgotten how recently it was that
technology helped us realize the world is round.

Thus each new scientific discovery, each technological innovation, seems to require the invention of new international
arrangements to contain, channel, and control it. A precept of
American business is that necessity is the mother of invention.
But in the business of international institution-building, the
reverse is true as well: Invention is the mother of necessity.

Sometimes this technological imperative is in curious con-

trast to the alarums and excursions of political rivalry among
nations. Ever since the Bolshevik Revolution, the United States
and the Soviet Union have been working together in the hunting
of seals in the Bering Sea, simply because it makes sense to
do so, Cold War or no. Ever since the early 1930s the Turks
and the Russians have maintained an annual joint cattle market,
even while Stalin was claiming the very areas of Turkey where
the cattle are raised and sold.

Perhaps the clearest case of the technological imperative
is the extraordinary cooperation among the scientists who explore the frozen continent of Antarctica. Nations can cooperate
best, it seems, where the population is penguins who don't talk
back.

THE FAILURE OF NATIONAL ORDERS

If the existing architecture of world order has been
built by analogy with the modern nation-state, perhaps the clue
to building a New International Order that works is to make
sure we know why the several national orders are falling down
on the job of governance. The evidence is now overwhelming that
every national government is beyond its depth. This is certainly true of the industrial democracies, baffled by inflation,
unemployment, pollution, insecurity and youthful crime. It is
equally true of the Soviet system, unable to feed its people
and afraid to let them escape. It is true of the 'China model'
whose new leaders now speak openly about 'ten lost years' of
Cultural Revolution and political infighting. It is true in
most developing nations, unable to meet basic human needs or
avoid the worst mistakes of the early Industrial Revolution.
And it is true of the international organizations in which
governments form committees to blame each other for their impo-
tence, while international staffs try to work on world problems
that governments try to ignore.

Political leaders keep up a brave front, but their incapacity for decision-making becomes more and more feasible. Central economic planning, popularized around the world partly by
industrial democracies that do not practice it themselves, is
nearly everywhere in disarray. Transnational companies, weather-
ing the assaults of some sovereignties but welcomed by others,
have adapted their outlook, policies and practices to life in
an interdependent world far better than governments have. A
'new proletariat' streams across international frontiers in
enormous numbers. Ethnic and religious rivalries and subnational separatists threaten the integrity of long-established nations - South-Africa, Nigeria, Ethiopia, Jordan, Lebanon, the
United Kingdom and Canada are only the most current examples.

Part of the trouble is that the traditional institutions

of national sovereignty are badly designed for the kinds of problems they now face. They tend to be bounded by the artificial frontiers that survive from the history of rational thought
(physics, biology, economics, anthropology), from the history
of government activity in simpler times (mining, merchant marine, forestry, the regulation of commerce), and from the historic professions (law, medicine, engineering) - while the
real world agenda consists mostly of interdiciplinary, interdepartmental and interprofessional problems.

National government agencies are mostly still not organized to handle the problems that 'cut across' disciplines,
specialties and bureaucracies, to heighten awareness of the
interconnectedness of things, and to encourage integrative
training, staff work and decision-making. Instead, every
government is basically a collection of vertical ministries,
in which recommendations travel 'up' and orders travel 'down'.
But everyone (including the inhabitants of these paper pyra-
mids) knows that complex decisions that work are mostly the
product of lateral negotiation - what we call committee work
and the Japanese call consensus and the Communists call collective leadership.

A striking example of the resulting discontinuities is
currently on exhibit in the U.S. effort to get hold of its
energy problem. Before 1973 no part of the U.S. Government
(and no international organization, either) was responsible
for worrying about energy. The responsibilities for 'oil' and
'gas' and 'coal' were scattered around as parts of an unstudied
subject called 'energy', which includes sunshine, cloud formations, ocean movements, industrial technology, trade, monetary
stability, home insulation, housing patterns, transportation,
the mobility of populations and much more. We obscured the fact
that, in the end, the realm of 'energy' is politics and the
reach of 'energy' is global.

Before 1973 everyone knew what the 'policy' was: to help
make abundant supplies of energy available at the cheapest
prices to expand economic growth(for any purpose) and raise the
productivity of labor. For this, the institutional arrangements
were entirely adequate. But they were hopelessly unequipped to
deal with, or even to think clearly about, the crisis that
emerged after 1973. From this crisis dawned a consciousness
that energy was now going to be expensive, that very large international flows of investment capital would be thereby reversed, that the U.S. and its allies were dangerously dependent
on Arab oil, that oil might be a dwindling asset in a generation, that exploiting coal and nuclear fission as the main
short-term alternatives to oil raised scary environmental and
security problems, that we were wasting energy and not developing fast enough the longer-term alternatives we would all too
soon require. We quite suddenly realized that we could not
solve any of these puzzles without a wholly new dimension in

world-wide cooperation, including the invention, from scratch, of new international institutions.

LEARNING FROM THE LEAKAGE OF POWER

National governance, then, is not an attractive model for next steps in international relations. But the trouble national governments are in may provide useful clues about what to avoid in building world institutions:

● 'Planning' on a large scale cannot be so rigid, vertical, authoritarian, bureaucratic, simplistic, quantitative - in a word, technocratic - as it is in both the 'planned economies' and in the economies that declare themselves unplanned. For the international institution-builder, 'planning' should rather be seen as *plural improvisation on an agreed sense of direction*.

● Responsibility for governance at the national level has been almost a synonym for preoccupation with the very short-term. The institutions of world leadership will have to find ways of fixing their gaze on the middle distance, where problems of fundamental importance have to be faced now. (1)

● National governments are typically not skilled at interdisciplinary, interdepartmental and interprofessional problems. It would clearly be a mistake to build institutions at the world level which replicate in their organizational patterns the compartmentalization that has been at once the secret of success and the fatal flaw of 'modernization'. Instead of separatist clumps of lawyers, economists, scientists and other specialists, the coming era will require flexible task forces· of specialists who know that you have to *think* about the situation as a whole if you are going to *act* relevantly on any part of it.

● National governments are typically divided between 'domestic' and 'foreign affairs' functions. But the rapid growth of interdependence now makes it hard to find a policy question that is not both 'domestic' and 'international' in its impacts and implications. The international institutions of the future will have to be deliberately set up to cut across this increasingly fuzzy boundary, to arrange for negotiations (among nation-states, which will still be the most important building blocks of world order) that quite candidly treat 'domestic' decisions as the components of international bargains.

● National governments typically make a rigid distinction between 'government' and 'non-governmental' people and organizations. But those who are responsible for public-interest actions need continuous access to the best thinking of those who are not. And those who are privileged to think more freely because they are not burdened with responsibility must inform their thinking about the problems that face those who are. Be-

cause they are not 'responsible', non-governmental people are
sometimes better able than government people: (a) to work, a-
head of time, on problems that are important but not yet urgent
enough to command political attention; (b) to shake loose from
conceptual confines and mix up disciplinary methodologies; (c)
to think hard, write adventurously and speak freely about alternative futures and what they imply for public policy today;
(d) to generate discussion among people in contending groups,
different professional fields and separate sectors of society
who might not otherwise be talking to each other; and (e) to
organize 'dialogue' across national frontiers on issues not yet
ripe for more official 'negotiation'. (2)

Since the earlier successes of the nation-state were due
to its capacity to assemble power in the hands of a few, one
knows where to look for evidence of its latter-day incapacity
to govern. And sure enough, power is leaking out of national
governments into the hands of the many.

The leakage of power is in three directions at once. The
vessel of national government leaks from the bottom, as the
many get enough education to insist on participation in decisions affecting their newly understood rights and their dimly
understood destiny. The advocacy of openness, student protests,
consumer lobbies, public-interest law firms, the remarkable
role of Common Cause, the California tax revolt, and the tendency of local communities to use planning and zoning authority to mould their own futures, the evidence is piling up that,
in the United States at least, the long history of accretion
of power to Washington is beginning to be reversed.

Power leaks from the sides, too. Non-governmental enterprise is typically more enterprising - faster on its feet,
less constrained by national jurisdiction, and longer-range
in its planning than government agencies are. This is why
transnational business has managed to internalize so much of
international commerce (more than one-fifth of 'international
trade' is now the internal transaction of international companies). This is why a growing range of functions, even those
fully funded by the government, are farmed out to non-govern-
ment organizations - advanced research and development, legal
services to the poor, educational and cultural exchanges with
Asia, and the U.S. Post Office are only a few of many U.S.
examples. Some of the power has even leaked out to universities
research institutes, think tanks and policy analysis groups,
which each year provide a growing proportion of the strategic
thinking and long-range planning used by the government; this
trend is far advanced in the United States, but has also been
in evidence in Europe and Japan during the 1970s.

Government is also a bottle that leaks from the top. There
is now a rapidly growing list of functions that only credible
international institutions can perform. Since that creative
burst of institution-building after World War II, the require-

ment for international cooperation has been speeding up -
while the pace of social invention has been slowing down.

THE MAIN ELEMENTS OF A SYSTEM OF GLOBAL
PLANNING AND RESOURCE MANAGEMENT

There is no shortage of lists of 'naturally international'
functions. They have been spread on the record in the North-
South dialogue - timidly by the North, polemically by the South
and analytically by a range of non-governmental organizations.
For our present purpose it will be enough to present them as
topic sentences.

First, there is a requirement for the management of problems which are unmanageable except in a global context. The
now familiar examples are climate and weather reporting, forecasting and modification; traffic through, and pollution of,
the atmosphere and the oceans; the protection of the ozone
layer; the management of ocean resources; the human uses of
outer space, including satellite communications, and of vacant
spaces (such as Antarctica) on earth.

Second, there are systems required to make sure that nations and their citizens, in the exercise of their separate
sovereignties, do not transgress the ecological bounds of the
biosphere we must all inhabit together. The needed systems are
not yet in place, but the imperatives are clear enough. The
world community needs:

● A system that negotiates and monitors agreed standards of
air and water quality, and reviews national actions that pollute beyond national frontiers.
● A system that keeps under review the damage and potential
damage from human processes, and blows the whistle on those
that may affect people beyond national frontiers.
● A system that promotes exploration for, and keeps a world
inventory of, nonrenewable resources that may be needed by
people outside the nations where the resources happen to be
found.
● A system that monitors world production of food and fi-
bers; seeks international agreement to limit overcropping,
overgrazing, overcutting and overfishing; and provides for the
exchange of timely information on national harvests and food
requirements.

For all these functions, it will be necessary sooner or
later to create an international system for the use and protection of resource data derived from the constantly improving
sensors operating from space vehicles.

Third, the global fairness revolution and the drive for

universal human rights will bring into being a system for establishing and reviewing international standards for individual entitlement to food, health, education, employment and any
other agreed components of 'basic human needs'; and for relating international economic cooperation, including aid, to progress toward these standards. Along with an internationally
certified 'poverty floor' may come a demand for an 'affluence
ceiling': that is, an international system for the review and
monitoring of national decisions about growth, affluence and
waste in the more developed countries.

Fourth, there is a growing requirement for international
institutions to facilitate the 'planetary bargaining' among
nation-states on issues that are usually called 'international
economics' but which reach deep into the 'domestic' economic,
social and financial policy - and therefore into the politics -
of every nation. The most obvious systems waiting to be born
are those needed:

● To hold, finance, and manage buffer stocks of major world
commodities, in order to assure continuity of supply and stability of prices for producers and consumers in relation to
long-term market forces.
● To assure access by developing countries to markets in
the industrial countries.
● To help manage constructive shifts in industrial geography, and help nations plan investment in their own industries
in the light of investment policies of other nations.
● To push agricultural productivity in the developing nations, and meanwhile to make sure there is enough food for
all through a world food reserve.
● To promote cooperation between oil producers and consumers, to help reduce energy waste in the industrial nations,
to encourage international research and development of alternative energy sources, and to assist developing countries in
devising sound energy strategies as a crucial part of their
development planning.
● To resolve differences among transnational enterprises,
host countries and home countries over such issues as taxation,
employment, competitive practices and contributions to meeting
basic human needs.
● To raise funds for development financing directly by fees
and taxes related to the use of international 'commons', and
to marry the allocation of these funds to the meeting of basic
human needs.
● To provide for effective international consultation on
actions by international monetary authorities which substantially affect the money supply, and create international money in
a manner and at a rate that is compatible with economic growth
at reasonable rates of inflation - the definition of what is
reasonable being itself the product of an international process.

● To regulate conflict, promote research, develop protein,
conserve fisheries, and explore, exploit and share the revenues from the oceans, the continental margin and the deep sea-
bed.
● To limit conflict by international conciliation and medi-
ation, the development of international peacekeeping forces,
and (through arms control) the institutionalization of military uncertainty at the lowest possible cost.

LIFE SIGNS; TOWARD PLANETARY BARGAINS

Some years ago an international working group assembled
by the Aspen Institute for Humanistic Studies studied the political economy of this new kind of world order, and called it
a 'planetary bargain'. The group observed that:

> The complexity of the issues and the congestion of inter-
> est-groups involved (159 nation-states, a hundred major
> transnational corporations, dozens of nonprofit multina-
> tionals, all meeting in 700 intergovernmental conferences
> and more than 3,000 international association meetings a
> year) make nonsense of the notion that with one great po-
> litical act a New International Economic Order might be
> created. The process, if it works, will be more like a
> global bazaar, in which negotiators are continuously en-
> gaged in parallel negotiations about strategically relat-
> ed but tactically separable matters. Yet the environment
> for constructive bargaining has to be created by a shared
> sense that bargains can be struck which advance the inter-
> ests of all, that a political consensus can be formed by
> widespread realization that peoples of every race and na-
> tion are in dangerous passage together in a world of fi-
> nite resources, ultimate weapons, and unmet requirements.
> (3)

We are still very far from such a political consensus;
the distance yet to be traversed is obvious from the stridency
of the rhetoric and the emptiness of the dialogue between
'North' and 'South'. Yet there is evidence of trends which
might in time add up to the political underpinning for institutions as wide and deep as the 'naturally international' functions that are somehow going to have to be performed.
One trend is the growing awareness of a shared human predicament. Science and technology have brought us close to the
ultimate in military weaponry and close to the margins of biospheric damage. The need for a farseeing collective prudence
on both scores is now very widely understood - even if that
inchoate comprehension has not yet filtered into the pragmatic

chancelleries where short-term politics often wins the arguments about long-term destiny.

Science and technology have also made possible - and
therefore necessary soon or late - the meeting of human needs
at a level nearly everybody would agree is a human right. The
requirements side of the human-needs equation is already global. The supply side - meeting the needs - is still mostly regarded as a national responsibility. But the rapid spread of
a basic-needs ideology - centering on the notion that the
meeting of basic needs should be a first charge on world resources - may provide a basis for 'next steps' at the international level.

At the same time, in the existing international agencies,
there are signs of common sense about procedures for cooperation. One life sign is the increasing tendency in international organizations to eschew two-sided adversary proceedings
and avoid voting procedures - moving instead toward action by
consensus. People and even diplomats have noticed that voting
leads to rapid and acrimonious disagreement about general
principles, whereas consensus procedures can lead (often at
tedious length) to quiet agreement about collective action to
be taken on particulars.

Another life sign is the invention of new kinds of international organizations - short of the 'supranational' institutions described by theorists of world government, but an improvement on arrangements that are bounded by the least common
denominator of what can be agreed from day to day in a committee of instructed national representatives. One such 'extranational' organization is the European Commission, whose Ca-
binet-level members are appointed by but cannot be removed by
their own governments, and which (under the Treaty of Rome)
exercises the initiative on some classes of actions on which
national governments have agreed not to make national policy.

There is a place for extranational institutions - with a
wider reach and stronger power than a U.N.-style committee of
governments, yet not a world government from which there is no
earthly appeal - in tackling many of the tasks that will have
to be tackled. Most of the institutions will not need to be
global: the interests of people and nations vary greatly according to size and structure, geography and geology, priorities and purposes. A pluralistic world order will be made up
of regional and functional communities of the concerned. But
it will nearly always be important for the community-of-the-
concerned to keep in touch with a wider circle-of-the-consult-
ed - through a broad political body such as the United Nations
General Assembly, or an *ad hoc* world conference such as Stockholm 1972 and its successors, or a special-purpose standing
assembly such as the one established for Intelsat.

The priceless ingredient of pluralistic governance is a
common feel for shared problems, as a basis for that "shared

sense that bargains can be struck which advance the interests
of all". To produce and project the analysis on which such a
common feel can be rationally and emotionally based is the
primary task for international political leadership. Only thus
will the national 'representatives' and the international
specialists be enabled to face the most puzzling dilemma of
all: that in a pluralistic system, where "planning is improvisation on a general sense of direction", each 'faction' has
to think hard about strategies for dealing with the whole predicament in order to act relevantly on any part of it.

There is nothing in the United Nations Charter that pre-
vents the development of policy planning staffs and extranational institutions, to organize the kind of planetary bargaining that is already overdue. The corrosive sludge of procedure admittedly stands in the way, even though most of it
is not required by the Charter. (The Charter describes voting
arrangements, for example, but does not require them in preference to consensus procedure). But the primary obstacle to
next steps is the still widespread illusion that the mutation
of international institutions must follow the double helix
of the nation-state.

The crisis of national governance provides the occasion
- for theorists of a New International Order, the opportunity
- for a breakthrough in the development of international institutions. The way to start is not to replicate at the global level the formulas that are failing to cope with complexity at the national level. Something new is going to be needed.

NOTES AND REFERENCES

(1) Nothing is more pitiful than to watch national military
planners trying to fashion defence strategies for the next ten
years, based on military hardware and deployment decisions
made ten years ago, often under extremely different circumstances and assumptions.
(2) I have elsewhere suggested a rough and ready test for
non-governmental organizations to apply to their programs: Is
the non-governmental organization working on issues that are
still too vague, too big, too interdisciplinary or too futuris-
tic for governments that are too busy, too crisis ridden and
too politically careful to tackle?
(3) See Aspen Institute for Humanistic Studies, *The Planetary
Bargain. Proposals for a New International Economic Order to
Meet Human Needs*, Report of an International Workshop convened
in Aspen, Colorado, July 7 - August 1, 1975, p. 9.

The Institutional Dimension of a New International Order
Richard A. Falk

THE EVOLUTION OF AN INSTITUTIONAL
PRESENCE

There is now a virtual consensus that the reform of international society requires some significant institutional build up at the global level. This consensus is relatively new, the culmination of some tendencies that can be traced back at least to the formation of the first international institution in the late nineteenth century. At an earlier stage in international society some idealistic interpreters of the global scene thought it unnecessary (and perhaps undesirable) to advocate international institutions as part of their program for global reform.

For instance, Grotius in his great treatise on the law of war, devotes no more than a few lines to the suggestion that some loose tradition of periodic meetings among heads of state would be beneficial. Immanuel Kant in his essay *Perpetual Peace* argues that global reform is dependent upon the prior successful establishment of republican forms of governance at the state level; no additional superstructure to assure peace or justice is needed or desirable. Lenin argues to the same effect, simply substituting the socialist reorganization of national political life for then prevailing bourgeoise or liberal modes.

Of course, it is also true that some older reformist conceptions called for institutional growth at the supranational level. These conceptions were generally of two varieties, occasionally a mixture of both. On the one side, were imperial conceptions of global unification based on universalizing a principal center of state power, usually that of the author. Thus Dante saw the necessity of the global extension of the

Roman Empire in *De Monarchia*. On the other side were utopian
conceptions of a world governing authority that transcended in
all respects the limitations of the state system. Abbé de
Saint Pierre in the early eighteenth century evolved such a
conception, apparently believing (to Rousseau's ironic amuse-
ment and disbelief) that such an edifice could be built just
as soon as the main rulers of the day could be persuaded that
the aim of a fulfilled human society would be thereby promoted.

In our century, the main stimulus for new proposals for
global reform was the experience of two mutually destructive
world wars, with the widespread fear that even worse tragedies
could follow. In the practical realm of diplomacy, at the same
time, both imperial and utopian schemes seemed irrelevant. The
puzzle confronting policymakers of leading sovereign states
was how to respond to these reformist pressures while remaining sensitive to the constraints of a world order system dominated by the values, attitudes, and structures of state sovereignty and nationalism.

Two sorts of 'solutions' were forthcoming, yet neither
has generated great expectations. The first approach was to
establish the chrysalis for world government in the form of a
comprehensive international organization operating on the basis of a very general constitutional document. The League of
Nations and the United Nations are embodiments of this approach. Woodrow Wilson, Franklin Roosevelt, especially American liberal leaders, regarded these infant world organizations
as the seeds for the eventual flourishing of an effective and
equitable global governance system. Of course, the results
have been generally disappointing for anyone holding such ex-
alted expectations. The League, and even more so, the United
Nations, serve mainly as extensions of the state system (not
as alternatives to it) and register shifting tendencies within
that system. At most we can say that such a global forum for
communication and mobilization is accepted on all sides as an
inevitable, if marginal, feature of the present international
order. Attempts to detach the UN from the state system by
granting it more independence vis-à-vis funding, capabilities,
and staff have been half-hearted and, as matters now stand,
lack any serious promise.

The second twentieth century 'solution' is generally
identified as 'functionalism', involving the emergence of special purpose international institutions operating within the
broad framework of the United Nations. There has been a steady
growth of functionalist activity if measured in terms of number of institutions, budget, or size of staff. (1) These institutions are assigned specific roles, often involving technical specialization. Experts set policy. Politics enter to varying degrees and generate varying assessments as to whether
politicalization is beneficial or detrimental. (2) Typical
actors that fall within this category are the ILO, WHO, FAO.

Such actors have not produced any significant transformation
of international order, nor is there much prospect. Their competence and capabilities, as with the general purpose international institutions, are derivative from and dependent upon
statist logic and geopolitical constraints. Modest contributions to problem-solving, standard-setting, and consciousness-
raising have been made by these specialized institutions, but
in no sense can their present or potential role be understood
as more than one of system-stabilization.

The same comments apply, perhaps with even great force,
to general purpose and specialized regional actors, with the
partial and controversial exception of Western Europe. In
Europe, an impressive degree of sovereignty-cutting has been
carried out under the auspices of a regional institutional
framework, and has seemed to have had the additional effect of
reducing the intensity of conflicts and prospects for war within the region. Internal (past warfare, homogeneity) and external factors (Soviet security threat, scale of American economic competition) have encouraged measures of European integration, but statist considerations have prevented European regionalism from proceeding very far in a supranational direction. Indeed, the European experience is still one of statist
adaptation to a peculiar set of strains in geopolitics created
after World War II. Other regionalist build-ups, as in Latin
America, Africa, Middle East, or South Asia have been even
less significant from a system-transforming perspective. For
instance, the OAS is, in part, an alliance framework and, in
part, an arena for hegemonial leadership by the United States.
The Arab League has served some state interests in having a
flexible regionally managed peacekeeping capability and as an
anti-Israeli alliance. The OAU, also, serves mainly to help
make Africa safer for statism, and thereby less vulnerable to
extra-regional penetration.

Perhaps, more significant, are intergovernmental institutional frameworks that seek revision in the international order, in the intra-structural sense of rearranging relative positions of power. OPEC has had that ambition, at times, and
even created a climate within the United Nations that gave temporary leverage to militant demands for a NIEO. And generally,
in a variety of North-South settings, loose institutional arrangements aiming at promoting solidarity (amid diversity)
have exerted an influence on bargaining style, and perhaps,
outcomes over a period of the last 15 years. At most, however,
such institutional developments have corrected some distor-
tions in the state system, as well as enabling this system to
adapt more successfully to shifting currents of power. Perhaps
a slightly more equitable set of relationships between rich
and poor, and between North and South, have emerged, but only
slightly more. Of course, a few states in the South by virtue
of their leverage have been able to demand participation in

principal geopolitical arenas as the price for their willingness to play non-disruptive roles.

The general conclusion, then, is to notice that the international institutional presence in the present world system is
marginal to the state system, and is often a derivation from
it that has little or no independence. Its general role is to
make the system function more smoothly, as well as to make
some cosmetic concessions to those who argue that a more struc-
tured/centralized form of international order is needed at
this historical time to avoid general warfare and to facilitate a level of international cooperation needed for economic
growth and stability.

APPROACHES TO INSTITUTIONAL REFORM

At this time, almost 35 years after World War II, there
is a general agreement that a more elaborate institutional
presence is required in international society just to keep the
old system functioning. This agreement, however, obscures a
more fundamental disagreement, that is, as to the appropriate
scale and form of institutional buildup required for purposes
of system-maintenance, system reform, or system-transformation.
(3) Even the Trilateral Commission emphasizes the importance
of a strengthened institutional capacity to meet the challenges of interdependence within the economic sphere. In essence,
the minimum current focal point for any reformist perspective
on international society is the need to manage a world system
of shifting geopolitical patterns, growing complexity, interdependence, and fragility, especially in the economic sphere.
To some extent management must be accomplished vis-à-vis problems of the global commons. The objective of such institutionalization is to contribute toward the achievement and maintenance of a moderate international order which is perceived by
conservative and liberal policymakers as the necessary alternative to mutually destructive conflict and, possibly chaos. (4)
This perception arises out of a post-imperial frame of reference which acknowledges the need for transnational patterns of
coordination as essential for the succesful functioning of the
capitalist sector of the world economy. The case for institutional reform and extension is partly an historical argument
that the organization of the capitalist sector under American
hegemony is no longer tenable given the weakness of the dollar, the rise of non-American centers of economic power (e.g.
Germany, Saudi Arabia), as well as the problems posed by un-
regulated MNCs operating out of several different home economic bases.

In more concrete terms, this outlook acknowledges the importance of extensions of the existing institutional framework

to deal with the stabilization of commodity prices and the regulation of multinational corporate activities (e.g. 'a GATT
for investment'). It also supports institutional innovations
to oversee oceans policy, to manage fishery domains, to sustain environmental quality, to resolve ocean disputes, and to
minister ocean minerals regimes. (5) Such a reformist outlook
is mindful of political constraints, insensitive to equity
concerns, and seeks no more than adaptation. To an extent some
normative components enter, as even the most conservative glo-
balist perspective concedes that some deliberate effort must
be made to assure Third World participation and support if new
international institutional initiatives are to be successful.

This attempt at a managerial fix for international society deliberately leaves structural issues untouched. Hegemonial
geopolitics are presupposed (implicitly endorsed). The more
fundamental problems posed by fragmentation at the state level
are ignored. As well, the war system is accepted as part of
'the given' that cannot and, perhaps, need not be altered by
the managerial quest. It is apparently taken for granted that
only the resources of traditional statecraft will be available
to curb military conflict and arms races, as well as restrain
the spread of weaponry to all parts of the world. That is, the
Trilateral Commission image of a preferred world is one of
adaptation to achieve moderation, which under present circumstances calls for some redesigning and strengthening of central
guidance machinery, especially in the economic spheres, together with a benevolent gradualism that works to incorporate
rich Third World countries as equal partners in the international economic order and to offer poor countries some token concessions. The basic motif is to strike a bargain or reach a
series of bargains that provide enough positive incentives for
most governments to encourage their constructive participation
in the existing system of world order (i.e. without generating
fundamental disruption or challenge).

Another side of world order thinking, although far less
influential, derives from those who are ready in the wings
with a blue-print for some grand design of world order, usually
world government in some form. Here the preoccupation with war
and especially with the menaces posed by new weaponry of mass
destruction motivates the advocates of this approach. The argument is that unless we transcend a world of states quickly
and decisively we will bring human history to an apocalyptic
end. Such an outlook has been reinforced by the inability of
separate sovereignties to act for the benefit of a general global interest. In effect, advocates of this line argue for the
evolution of full-scale central governmental institutions complemented by general and complete disarmament, by management
and planning capabilities for global resources, and by dispute-
settlement procedures. The Clark/Sohn plan for *World Peace
through World Law* is the most influential and carefully elabo-

rated example of this kind of approach to world order based on
comprehensive institutional centralization.

The difficulties with such institutional centralism are
quite obvious. Most stark, of course, is the absence of recep-
tivity on the part of the main political actors on the world
stage, namely, leaders of national governments. If most governments are not prepared to work seriously toward such a goal,
it seems impossible to mobilize the political will. This clo-
sure is reinforced by the absence of popular enthusiasm for
grand designs. Attachment to sovereign rights and symbols is
too high, anxiety about global centralization is too great,
and the whole enterprise appears too abstract and remote to a-
rouse significant levels of serious support even from among
those who are most worried about and victimized by the failures
and dangers of the existing system of world order. As matters
now stand, the advocacy of world government is dismissed as
foolish and sterile, an idea that has been around for some time
without winning any relevant support in either elite or popular
circles.

On a deeper level, anxiety exists that even if some kind
of world governance structure could be brought into being in
the near future, its execution would likely be so seriously
flawed as to make us nostalgic for a world of states. Some
kind of ordeal of bureaucratic centralism is imagined as the
likely consequence of a premature shift from the states system
to a more integrated global political structure.

In any event, these poles of perception dominate the political imagination, and inhibit other modes of creative and concrete thinking about the place of institutions in global reform. In fact, serious images of 'restructuring' of world order
have concentrated on the interplay of dynamic factors involving
trade, investment, and economic goals, regarding institutional
innovations as either fanciful (given statism), superfluous
(if the political will should emerge, then institutional requirements will be easily satisfied and do not require advance
specification) or inappropriate (emphasis on policy at the margins overcomes concern with modifying underlying structures).

The effect of this general climate of opinion has been to
encourage analysis of prospects for global reform to concen-
trate on the interplay of factors relating to power, interests,
and attitudes without any independent attention to the structures of world order. Global models constructed in accordance
with econometric theory have, in particular, sought to depict
as objectively as possible the interactive workings of the international system under carefully delineated sets of conditions. The institutional dimension has been consistently down-
played in this work, being regarded as trivial or formalistic
given the solidity of the present system of world order. And
with respect to structuring the future system institutions have
been generally regarded, if at all, as a sequel rather than a

cause in relation to forming the requisite political will. In
such a setting, to posit institutional innovation in a serious
way, is either to be engaged in imperial geopolitics or to embark upon an exercise in sterile utopianism. Therefore, institutional innovation has not seemed very pertinent to the most
fashionable recent work of global reform, except in various
ancillary roles as facilitators or obstructors of existing policy. Is this neglect justified? How might it be overcome?

GUIDELINES FOR A POSITIVE APPROACH

Let us set forward two goals: a commitment to *normative
change* (i.e. change associated with explicit values) and a
commitment to *political relevance* (i.e. proposals sensitive to
issues of feasibility). Some other elements condition the analysis: an overriding concern with minimum order, especially in
superpower relations (i.e. avoidance of general war as major
priority); an image of feasibility (e.g. 10-100 years) not
restricted to the exceedingly short time horizons of governmental leaders (i.e. 1-5 years); a conception of feasibility
that is not shaped by the normative receptivities of existing
governmental leaders. These presuppositions of world order a-
nalysis should be explained and justified in considerable detail. Here, it is only possible to mention them so as to suggest a particular orientation toward global reform.

The analysis of the positive place of institutions in a
program or image of global reform proceeds from this orientation. My own appraisal has been heavily influenced by the work
of the World Order Models Project (WOMP) over the past decade.
This work arose out of the conviction that a program of drastic global reform was essential and was inescapably political
in its fundamental character. To be political in a world system that is at once hierarchical and characterized by ideological, geopolitical, cultural, and ethnic pluralism meant that
agents of global transformation would have to proceed outward
from the nation-state, and hence, would have to exhibit the
diversity of national situations around the world. No master
plan, devoid of ideological and cultural content, could skip
such a step without assuring its irrelevance. At the same time,
without some shared normative framework, it would be difficult
to consider the effort at transformation to be an enterprise
with a coherent direction, capable of growing into a global
social movement, and committed to the construction of a new
system of world order that was beneficial and sustainable. An
acceptance of this tension between pluralism of interpretation
and universalism of aspiration is at the center of WOMP's attempts to be relevant without being accomodationist. As an organizational matter it has produced a shared value framework

at a high enough level of abstraction to encompass the principal diversities of the world, without being so amorphous in
its implications as to avoid some definiteness of commitment.
This consensus of values has generated a series of transforma-
tive images and strategies that depict the contours of a preferred world order system and articulate, as well, transitional scenarios of the momentous shift from *here* to *there*. (6)
Institutional changes played an important role in the main
WOMP models of relevant utopias or preferred worlds, yet a
subordinate one to the main shifts in values/orientation. (7)
The approach taken to institutional issues can be better ap-
preciated within the wider context of world order methodology.

Values: an agreed framework of values associated with
Peace (minimization of large-scale violence, including structural violence), Economic Well-Being (satisfaction of basic
human needs, together with a movement toward equality between
and within societies), Social and Political Justice (realization of non-economic human rights for individuals and groups),
Ecological Balance (achievement of environmental quality, conservation of resources, preservation of endangered species),
and Humane Governance (collective organizational and constitutional arrangements on national, regional, and global levels
that promote the integrated realization of the other four values). It is understood that these values are, depending on
context, interrelated, mutually reinforcing, and in conflict,
i.e. the promotion of one (e.g. peace) cannot succeed unless
correlated with the others, and paradoxically, choices must be
made at each state as to whether to foster economic well-being
if it involves environmental harm or depletion of scarce resources. The tension among values and ways of resolving it are
features of transition strategy; the preferred world, while
generating its own agenda of concerns, is defined as a world
order system in which the five values are simultaneously realized. (8)

Preferred World: the goal of transition as defined by value realization and manifest in structures of human governance.
The shape of the preferred world cannot be reliably predetermined, nor can its emergence be anticipated before the year
2025 or so. That is, there is no sense in which history will
stop because a preferred world has been achieved; whatever horizon of aspiration is reached, discloses a new horizon. However, it is here in the effort at prefiguring a preferred
world that the institutional (constitutional) dimension re-
ceives its greatest attention.

Transition: the period from now until the time that a
preferred world emerged is specified as the time of transition.
In a methodological sense, the analytical purpose of focusing
on transition is to insist upon a deliberative attitude toward change in which certain goals are pursued (as related to
the valued ends set forth) by reliance on appropriate tactics

and strategies. In effect, the challenge of the transition
period is a call for the acceptance of human responsibility
for the political organization of the planet. This call for
political commitment is conditioned by the realities of various national settings (repressive or liberal), of distinct
issue-areas (human rights or disarmament), of the stage of
development and culture, of the scale and situation of a particular national society. The transition question can be expressed in political terms: what activity, given the actor
(person, institution, government, party, religion) is most
conducive to the realization of the valued ends proposed as
dominant in the preferred world? At one end of the scale, a
transition activity might be the promotion of solar energy,
vegetarianism, and voluntary simplicity, the profoundly political statement made by the choices that individuals make a-
bout how to lead their own lives. At the other end might be a
more conventional political commitment to a liberation struggle or to the advocacy of a stand-by peacekeeping force or
global taxation plan at the United Nations. The issue of institutions arises as follows: how can a given direction or program of institutional reform serve as a means in the transition period to realize world order values (i.e. more peace,
economic well-being, etc., as measured by indicators, e.g.
battlefield deaths, per capita daily caloric intake, etc.)?
Part of a response may involve the construction of transnational nongovernment institutional arrangements (e.g. a privately
promoted peoples' tribunal to assess state crime in the human
rights sphere).

COMMENTS ON INSTITUTIONAL DESIGN

1. With respect to *world order values*, there are no institutional implications, *per se*, from the values adopted. Of
course, other values or world order goals could be formulated
so as to have institutional implications, e.g. the desirability
of maximum regional or global integration as an end rather than
as a means.
   The opposite normative bias is contained in the substance
of 'humane governance' as a valued end. Ideas of minimum bureaucratic presence consistent with achieving the other four
values are a value, as in discerning a humane scale for governing units. The emphasis, then, is on decentralizing existing
concentrations of institutional authority, on separating authority from power, and on softening the first and second systems
of sovereign states and market forces rather than on hardening
the third system of global institutions. Such an image of human
governance also presupposes some success in activating the
third system (i.e. the popular sector). (9)

Images of humane governance, including its array of institutional embodiments, are discussed below in connection with
the idea of a preferred world (see figures 1-4). Insofar as
world order thinking is informed by a coherent ideology of
transformation, it must have some sense of the optional role
and character of international institutions, their distinct
character, their interrelationship with one another (i.e. the
reorganization of the second system) and their interrelationship with the first and third system.

2. With respect to designing a *preferred world*: let us assume here that the concept of preferred world is conditioned
by an agreed set of world order values and a conception of
transition. Thus, not all conceivable reorganizations of the
political life of the planet are relevant (e.g. world empire
or hard world state). Nevertheless, there are a range of models
of preferred world systems that potentially qualify (e.g. soft
world state, small state world, regionalist solution, functionalist solution). For each, an institutional framework seems
implied, and can be schematically summarized, but it is difficult, if not arbitrary, to draw invidious comparisons at this
stage as to which of the four general types of restructured international order would be most desirable and feasible. Perhaps, as developments in the future unfold, more detailed assessments of strengths and weaknesses can be made, although
their utility will depend on the degree to which appraisal is
not torn from the context of actual global political developments.

Also the types of restructuring portrayed in the four figures are intended only to be illustrative of some world order
organizing logics that could mitigate, if not eliminate, the
disadvantages associated with world order organized in deferen-
ce to the primacy of statist logic. In actual circumstances,
however, these organizing logics can be combined in a wide variety of ways to produce a coherent system of world order capable of realizing the values adopted here as criteria for
world order performance.

3. With respect to the *transition process*, as already indicated, the emphasis is upon guiding choice in relation to a
given course of commitments to global reform. The question of
institutional design is, of course, complex in a variety of
transition settings. A given issue of institutional reform or
creation (e.g. for a new law of the oceans) should be assessed
as beneficial or not, in whole or part, depending on whether
it appears to enhance the prospects of structural transformation under approved value auspices or embodies approved values
in the present working of the world political system.

World order is a composite of ordering logics having a
variety of normative effects. Especially in a time of transition these logics and effects tend to produce contradictory international patterns. As the 'old' structures are challenged

Figure 1: Soft World State

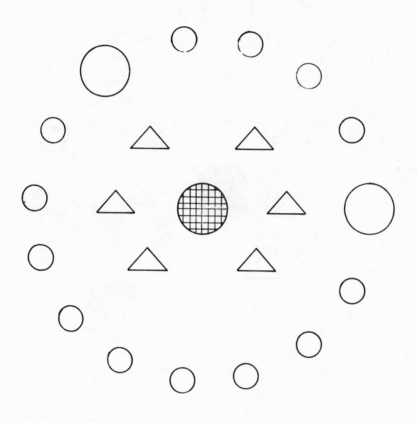

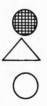 Central Government System

Functional Institutional Actors

Subordinate Governmental Actors

Figure 2: Small State World

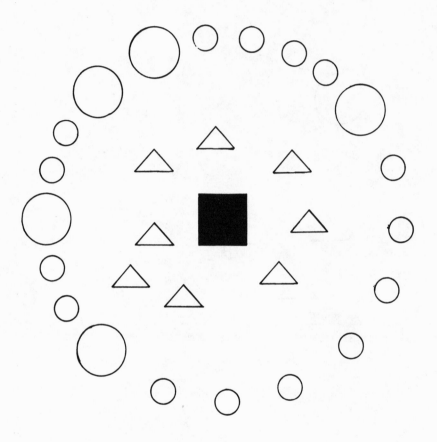

  State Actors

Functional Institutional Actors

Coordinating Capability

Figure 3: Regionalist World

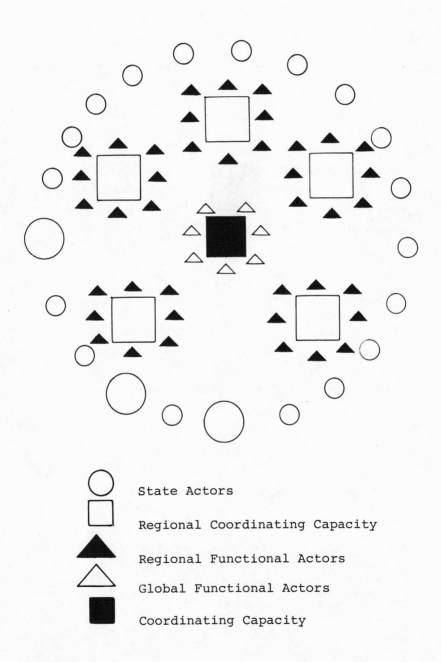

○ State Actors

▢ Regional Coordinating Capacity

▲ Regional Functional Actors

△ Global Functional Actors

■ Coordinating Capacity

Figure 4: Functionalist World

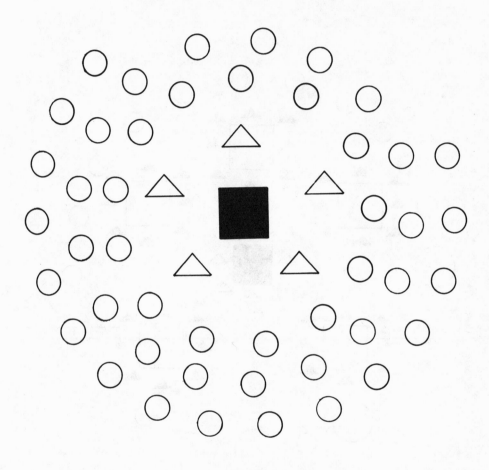

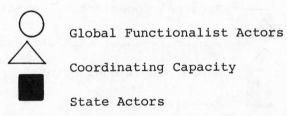

Global Functionalist Actors

Coordinating Capacity

State Actors

and/or superceded by the 'new' structures, it becomes confus-
ing and contradictory to interpret what is happening, much less
to be confident about what will be beneficial.

A NOTE IN CONCLUSION

The question of the place of institutions in the work of
global reform is necessarily elusive. As well, it is beset by
the flaws of the past: utopianism and sly proposals to foster
national, regional, or special interests. At the same time, the
institutional dimension is essential, as it provides the most
visible and stable indication of how life is to be organized in
an alternate international political system. We need new ways
to introduce the institutional dimension into the work of global reform so that it does not fall prey to either the fallacy
of *premature specificity* (i.e. positing a structure detached
from the emergent political context) or to the maneuverings of
covert imperialism (i.e. positing a structure in which one *part*
of the world order system maximizes its gains at the expense of
the well-being of the *whole*).

NOTES AND REFERENCES

(1)   For data and interpretation of these trends see Johan
Galtung, 'Non-territorial Actors and the Problem of Peace', in
Saul H. Mendlovitz, (ed.), *On the Creation of a Just World Order*, Free Press, New York, 1975, pp. 151-188.
(2)   An important study of the relationship between politics
and functionalism is E.B. Haas, *Beyond the Nation-State*, Stanford University Press, Stanford, California, 1964.
(3)   For an illustration and discussion of these distinctions
see Richard Falk, 'Contending Approaches to World Order',
Journal of International Affairs, 31, Fall/Winter 1977, pp.
171-198, viz. pp. 184-189.
(4)   See the argument to this effect in Miriam Camps, *The Management of Interdependence*, Council on Foreign Relations, New
York, 1974; and Stanley Hoffmann, *Primacy or World Order*,
McGraw-Hill, New York, 1978.
(5)   See, for example, Trilaterial Commission Task Force Reports, viz. Nos. 9, 11 and 14, 1976-77.
(6)   Rajni Kothari, *Footsteps into the Future:Diagnosis of the
Present World and a Design for an Alternative*, Free Press, New
York, 1974; Ali Mazrui, *A World Federation of Cultures:An African Perspective*, Free Press, New York, 1976; Gustavo Lagos and
Horacio Godoy, *Revolutions of Being:A Latin American View of
the Future*, Free Press, New York, 1977; Richard Falk, *A Study*

of Future Worlds, Free Press, New York, 1975; Johan Galtung, *The True Worlds:A Transnational Perspective*, Free Press, New York, 1980.

(7)   The institutional dimension of each perspective in note 6 is summarized in essay length in Mendlovitz, note 1; my own discussion of the institutional dimension in a preferred world system is in Falk, note 6, Chapter IV, pp. 224-276.

(8)   Discussed in Falk, note 6, Chapter 1, pp. 11-33.

(9)   I have worked out a conception of the dynamics of international order based on this image of three linked and interlinked systems of actors. See Falk, *Third System Initiatives in a Militarized World Order*, Poona, July 1978.

The United Nations as a World Development Authority

Johan Kaufman

INTRODUCTION

.This paper sets out to assess the capacity of the United
Nations and its family of agencies to evolve over time into a
genuine world development authority. (1) It is assumed that
this capacity is determined by three main sets of conditions
which can be summarized as follows:

(i) The willingness of governments to transfer essential economic functions to a world authority;
(ii) Changes in the structure of the United Nations system of
organizations, and in particular in its methods of decision-
making, to enable it to accept tasks transferred by governments;
(iii) The evolution of world economic and technological conditions towards real interdependence, thus creating the preconditions for the U.N. system to assume tasks related to the
management of the social economic affairs of the international
community.

I shall assume, in the light of recent economic trends
and developments, that the third of these conditions is fulfilled. This paper will thus deal with the remaining two conditions.

READINESS OF GOVERNMENTS TO
TRANSFER AUTHORITY

The experience of the last 30 years has shown that govern-

103

ments are prepared to transfer certain prerogatives to a supranational authority once they are convinced of the advantages which can be derived from doing so. While certain obviously international activities, for example, those related to
aviation, weather control, shipping or the world-wide control
of contagious diseases, are readily entrusted to international
organizations, others remain obstinately reserved for national
governments. A typical example is the management of monetary
affairs: experience since 1972 indicates that in this field
governments are not prepared to submit to international control but rather seek to retain autonomy of decision-making.
The idea of a real role for the International Monetary Fund
is only very slowly gaining ground.

It is clear that certain requirements must be met before
a government is willing to hand over national prerogatives to
an international organization. It is essential that:

(i) The issue dealt with must be sufficiently international
to give a world-wide or regional approach a reasonable chance
of success;
(ii) The results of international action must yield net benefits in terms of what each government (or more precisely 'a
majority of governments, including the principal governments
involved in an issue') wishes to achieve;
(iii) There must be a certain degree of consensus among the
governments on the objectives to be achieved and the methods
to be used to attain the objectives. Unfortunately, governments often have conflicting views with respect to both objectives and methods. As a result, they are reluctant to hand over
tasks. The question of international commodity policy and the
related one of the establishment of a so-called common fund
are examples in this respect;
(iv) There must be confidence among governments as well as between governments and the international secretariat which will
administer a certain international program.

Each of the above conditions is often unfulfilled. The
development of a global decision-making capability thus requires the formulation and implementation of transitional strategies designed to rectify this situation. It is to such transitional measures that we will now turn.

                    The Internationalization of Issues

Problems can be made transparent by effective studies.
Unfortunately, in many cases there are too many studies on any
particular subject going on simultaneously. The traditional
method of making a problem transparent is to establish an international group of experts which is requested to prepare a

report on it. Only if the composition of the group of experts
is really fully balanced, reflecting a wide range of views, and
the report is attractively written, has 'realistic' proposals,
and is published in various countries in the right way, is
there some measure of hope that the right action will follow.
(2) An example of a report which generally meets these requirements is the one prepared by the 'Group of Eminent Persons' on
transnational corporations. (3) However, the follow-up to this
report shows that underlying problems unavoidably surface a-
gain, and that even the best possible report by experts does
not automatically guarantee international action. Yet, it can
be said that the act of 'making problems transparent' is an
absolute condition for further action.

Cost-Effectiveness and Cost-Benefit Monitoring

One of the important deeper reasons why governments are
reluctant to hand over tasks to a supranational authority is
that they are not convinced that the money and other resources
to be invested in an international endeavour will yield net
benefits which are really worthwile. The main factors involved
can be represented as follows:

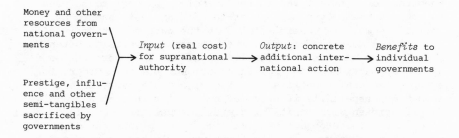

Money and other resources from national governments

Prestige, influence and other semi-tangibles sacrificed by governments

Input (real cost) for supranational authority → *Output*: concrete additional international action → *Benefits* to individual governments

This suggests that the transfer of responsibilities from
national governments to supranational authorities should be
subjected to much more rigorous cost-benefit and cost-effectiveness analyses than has so far generally been the case. The efforts being made under the auspices of the U.N. Committee on
Programme and Co-ordination are a distinct step in the right
direction: uniform methods of program and budget presentation,
and subsequent analysis, are a *conditio sine qua non* for adequate cost-benefit and cost-effectiveness measurement. The two
concepts should, of course, be adapted to the characteristics
of intergovernmental cooperation: cost-benefit analysis would
take place where international action results in quantitatively
(i.e. either in monetary terms or in terms of some relevant
non-money standard) measurable terms.

Cost-effectiveness analysis would take place in all other cases, where the benefits are more or less intangible. This would apply, for example, to the numerous studies and reports requested in every intergovernmental organization. The effort should then be directed at analyzing the follow-up given to a report, the distribution and reading it has received, the comments made on it during discussions in intergovernmental organs, etc. A points-system should be elaborated so that each of these factors could be afforded an appropriate quantitative weight.

As a *transitional measure*, cost benefit and cost-effectiveness measuring methods should be established as soon as feasible, on a uniform basis, in all the organizations of the U.N. system.

Consensus on Objectives and Methods

In many cases, the most important question is whether a compromise can be found between those who base themselves on the 'free market system' and those who advocate 'interventionism'. The issue of the common fund for the stabilization of the prices of certain commodities is a case in point.

As a *transitional measure*, a greater effort should be made to obtain at least a minimum degree of consensus on the most important objectives, and on the principal methods to be used to achieve them. Systematic cost-benefit analysis should be applied as much as possible, also in the case of 'objectives'.

In the question of objectives, semantic confusion often prevails and hampers conceptualization: because there was no agreed definition of the New International Economic Order, for example, several countries objected vigorously every time the term NIEO, especially if preceded by 'the' rather than by 'a', and if written with capital letters, was used in some draft resolution. These objections, as a minimum, meant loss of time in reaching agreement and, as a maximum, blocked or rendered ineffective any decision-making. As this is written, this problem has largely disappeared due to the fact that the United States has accepted the term, although only after it had been interpreted in a special way: "The international economic order is a system of relationships among all nations. The process of change, therefore, must be through an evolving consensus that takes into account the economic systems, the interests and the ideas of all countries. Thus we are talking about a process, or a broad framework for dialogue and progress, as much as an 'order'".

Suggested transitional measure: the U.N. might look at the pros and contras of establishing an Ad Hoc Committee on Concepts and Definitions, composed of scholars and practitioners, and enlarged for particular purposes with sector-oriented experts, to work towards agreed definitions. U.N. draft resolutions provid-

ing definitions might be referred to this Committee, although
care would need to be exercized to ensure that this did not
become an excuse for delaying action. Although definition-ma-
king would not overcome fundamental problems, it could prevent
some difficulties and much time-consuming and sterile discussion.

The Confidence Factor

The confidence factor is one which has been almost totally neglected by both practitioners and scientific observers of
international cooperation. Yet, in the first and last instance,
it may well be the deciding factor in determining progress towards international cooperation and the acceptability of supranational organs, including a World Development Authority.

There is certainly a general lack of confidence in international secretariats. Even if confidence in them could be res-
tored, however, there remains the overwhelming factor of the
distrust which states have for each other. A better understanding of the behavior of states and of the fundamental lack of
confidence in each other would seem dependent on us gaining
real insights into the psychology of nations and of their leaders.

As far as nations are concerned, efforts in the direction
of psychological analysis are meagre indeed. (4) As far as individuals, in particular political leaders, are concerned, a
wider literature is developing, some of it in the evolving realm of psycho-history. (5)

Some basic questions arise:

● Is it possible to isolate in the behavior of States what
is called preconscious or unconscious processes, i.e. mental
experiences of which they are not aware but which can be de-
tected?

● How do various types of frustration lead to specific types
of behavior of States?

● Can we detect psychological stages in the development of
States, comparable to those in the development of children? (6)

● Can the distinction between personal and environmental
frustration be applied to States?

● Can we apply the three types of patterns of conflict,
known from the theory of psychology, to States: the double approach conflict, in which a choice must be made between two
attractive goals; the double-avoidant conflict, in which a
choice must be made between to evils; and the approach-avoidant
conflict, in which the decision must be made whether or not to
move toward a pleasurable goal, the attainment of which involves
painful consequences.

It would be worthwile to pursue the question of whether
States, like individuals, can be analyzed in terms of abnormal
psychological behavior. Can we detect in States, for example,
various known schizophrenic reactions? Can we say that certain
States seem to have a 'persecution complex', others a 'big
power complex'. The answers to these questions can perhaps not
be based on theoretical analysis, but must derive from specific case studies.

As a *transitional measure* I would recommend that such
studies be undertaken on an interdisciplinary basis.

The question of confidence of governments in international secretariats has also received little attention. It is apparently assumed that international secretariats are not subject to political influences and are thus able to behave in an
absolutely correct way. In practice, the secretariats are constantly pushed and pulled by various pressures coming from
governments or others. However well intended, the actions of
an international secretariat are likely to receive the support
of some governments whilst antagonizing others.

As a *transitional measure* there could be a pact among
governments to refrain from trying to influence the secretariats in a non-open way. In particular, governments should refrain from trying to push 'their' candidates for secretariat
positions. Recruitment should take place on a fully internationalized basis. This could be achieved if the names of candidates were proposed by independent offices rather than by
governments. International secretariats could then refuse the
nominations for posts made by anyone other than these independent bodies.

Of course, such procedures will not in themselves produce
the required confidence in international secretariats. For this
it will be necessary that the secretariats gain a high reputation, in every sense. (7)

THE STRUCTURE OF THE UNITED NATIONS

Fundamental changes in the structure of the U.N. system
are necessary in order to enable it to execute more difficult
tasks. It must unfortunately be noted that the recent restructuring exercise has had limited effects. (8) The U.N. system
is still divided along 'vertical' lines: there are separate
agencies for agriculture, industry, health, trade, etc.

The existence of these separate agencies as fully autonomous units will interfere with the effective functioning of
any World Development Authority, as and when established. Does
this mean that specialized agencies have to be subservient to
a World Development Authority in every respect? The answer
would seem to be both yes and no. On essential policy questions,

a World Development Authority should be able to issue directives. On technical questions and questions of secondary importance, the specialized agencies could retain a great deal
of autonomy.

It is, however, also necessary that the present set-up of
the specialized agencies be critically reviewed. Attempts to
establish a World Development Authority would inevitably give
rise to inter-agency rivalries. Agencies are also likely to
band together in an effort to prevent its creation. It would
be helpful, therefore, if the existing system of specialized
agencies could be fundamentally modified. This, obviously, can
only be a long-term goal. The recent U.N. restructuring exercise has shown that the existence of each agency is sacrosanct;
not even the 25 Experts who prepared a valuable report dared
suggest drastic changes in the present set-up.

Towards Clusters of Specialized Agencies

The reorganization of the specialized agencies could logically aim at creating clusters of agencies around broad substantive areas. Such clusters of agencies, either merged, or
closely restructured with a single advisory or legislative intergovernmental council for each group of agencies, could be
formed along the following (proximate) lines:

(1) A group dealing with *basic production sectors*: industry,
agriculture, resources. This cluster would consist of the present FAO, ILO, IAEA, UNIDO and the parts of the U.N. Secretariat which deal with resources;
(ii) A group dealing with *trade and current monetary problems*:
GATT, UNCTAD, IMF. Strong reasons probably militate against a
full merger of these three agencies. GATT is a contractual a-
greement, IMF has its own very special statutory form. The
joint intergovernmental council could therefore only be advisory;
(iii) A group dealing with *basic infrastructural sectors*:
health, education, intellectual property, telecommunications.
The present WHO, UNESCO, WIPO, ITU and UPU would establish especially close links for this purpose. ITU and UPU could be
fully merged, since both deal with communication.
(iv) A group dealing with *operational development assistance*:
the World Bank and its affiliates (IDA, IFC), UNDP, IFAD
(International Fund for Agricultural Development), UNICEF, U.N.
Fund for Drug Abuse Control, and various other funds now existing separately. The Bank should continue to exist separately,
for reasons similar to the IMF.

A reclustering along these lines would also tend to give
an entirely different focus to the *Administrative Committee on*

Coordination, which is made up of the heads of the specialized
agencies, and chaired by the Secretary-General of the U.N.
Presumably, the effective functioning of a World Development
Authority would be preceded by a lengthy period during which
the specialized agencies would be restructured and the clusters
formed. During this period, the Administrative Committee on
Coordination would have the very important task of assuring a
smooth transition to a system which, through its very structure
would be much more cohesive and intrinsically coordinated than
the one it replaces.

Other Improvements

Many of the recommendations in a *New United Nations Structure for Global Economic Co-operation* remain valuable and deserve to be carefully reexamined. It is to some of these recommendations that we should now briefly turn.

Concerning the U.N. Secretariat, a substantive unit should
be created as early as possible to perform the functions foreseen in para 61 (a) and (b) of Resolution 32/197. This para
states:

> (61) In support of the relevant intergovernmental bodies,
> the United Nations Secretariat should concentrate on the
> following functions:
>
> (a) Interdisciplinary research and analysis, drawing as
> necessary upon all relevant parts of the United Nations
> system. On the basis of the relevant legislative authori-
> ty, this function includes:
>
> (i) Preparing, on a regular basis, global economic and
> social surveys and projections to assist the General As-
> sembly and the Economic and Social Council in the dis-
> charge of their responsibilities as set out in sections I
> and II;
> (ii) Undertaking in-depth intersectoral analyses and syn-
> theses of development issues, in close collaboration with
> those elements of the United Nations system engaged in
> similar work and taking into account relevant work in the
> various sectoral components of the United Nations system,
> and preparing concise and action-oriented recommendations
> on those issues in accordance with the requirements of
> the General Assembly and the Economic and Social Council,
> for consideration by those organs;
> (iii) Identifying and bringing to the attention of Govern-
> ments emerging economic and social issues of international
> concern;

This function would accordingly cover, *inter alia*, the provision of substantive support services for the work of the Committee for Development Planning;

(b) .Cross sectoral analysis of programmes and plans in the economic and social sectors of the United Nations system with a view to mobilizing and integrating, at the planning and programming stages, the inputs and expertise of the organizations of the United Nations system for the following tasks:

(i) Concerting in an effective manner the implementation of policy guidelines, directives and priorities emanating from the General Assembly and the Economic and Social Council;
(ii) Developing the co-operative and, whereever possible, joint planning of programme activities decided upon at the intergovernmental level, with a view to system-wide medium-term planning at the earliest possible time;

This function would accordingly cover, *inter alia*, the provision of substantive support services for the relevant work of the Committee for Programme and Co-ordination and the Administrative Committee on Co-ordination.

On the intergovernmental side, governments should take as quickly as possible action designed to come to terms with the present proliferation of intergovernmental meetings. This proliferation has resulted in a reduction in the qualitative level of attendance.

The UNDP Governing Council should serve as the governing body for all U.N. funds. Another important step in the right direction would be to merge ECOSOC, the Committee of the Whole (established under General Assembly Resolution 32/174), the UNCTAD Board, the World Food Council and the UNIDO Board. This would result in improved levels of coordination within the system.

THE IMPROVEMENT OF NEGOTIATING METHODS

An improved U.N. system structure will require improved negotiating methods. The following aspects deserve special attention:

(i)   speech-making;
(ii) negotiations between groups;
(iii) the acceptability of change in conjunction with the time factor;

(iv) the use of escape clauses;
(v)   agreement on long-term policies and commitments.

(i)   *Speech-making*. Speech-making and negotiation occur on one
and the same meeting, thereby reducing the time available for
the process of negotiation.
      Suggested transitional measure. An effort should be made
to put speech-making in separate meetings which do not necessarily precede negotiating sessions. Some of the more successful decisions of the U.N. Security Council were possible precisely because 'explanation of vote' took place and statements
were read after a consensus decision, which was negotiated in
private sessions. In delicate negotiations, for example those
on the Common Fund, a similar practice might help.
(ii) *Group negotiation*. The process of negotiating between
groups, for example between Group B (developed market economies) and the Group of 77 in UNCTAD, leads to automatic rigi-
dities, in some cases to a confrontation between maximum demand and minimum offers. The position of each group, as experience shows, tends to cluster around the extremes and not
around the average, especially if important countries in each
group take extreme positions.
      Suggested transitional measure. There should be an insti-
tutionalized practice that group positions are flexible, and
small contact groups should be created which are empowered to
negotiate compromise resolutions at the start of any negotiating meeting. This would avoid the dangerous technique of
'five minutes before twelve' decision-making, and it may prevent frictions due to artificially arrived at group positions
in situations where groups are in fact divided.
(iii)*Change and the time factor*. Nations do not like abrupt
change. They usually maintain that their parliaments and/or
their business community or other sectors and/or their public
opinion will not accept change which appears sudden and rapid
and, in particular, in times of unemployment or recession.
This constraint involves the question of timing. The decisions
of the Sixth and Seventh Special Sessions are without a time
frame; developing nations desire the fastest possible change,
the developed countries seem to play for more time. Elections
and changes of government contribute towards absorbing more
time.
      Suggested transitional measure. There should be agreed
time-frames, intermediate between slowness and abrupt change,
perhaps conforming to the old concept 'with all deliberate
speed'. Governments and private organizations should endeavor
to prepare public opinion for change, and of course take effective domestic measures to restructure their economies, including financial support for companies and the retraining of
workers for employment in competitive industries.
(iv) *Escape clauses*. Governments are disinclined to accept spe-

cific quantitative or policy commitments without escape clauses. The General Agreement on Tariffs and Trade, still in its
way one of the more successful examples of international decision-making, continues to function, *inter alia*, because of
its escape clause machinery.
    Suggested transitional measure. An effort could be made,
perhaps within the framework of a new International Development Strategy, to create machinery to relate targets agreed in
principle to 'examination procedures' to which governments can
voluntarily subscribe. An effort should be made to formulate
a fairly precisely defined 'escape clause' in relation to each
target, and to apply agreed 'examination procedures' to the
use of escape clause machinery. Care should be taken that the
use of escape clause machinery is subjected to international
scrutiny (as is done in GATT and in certain OECD agreements)
so that a minimum of equitable burden-sharing is maintained.
(v)   *Long-term policies.* Governments have distinct short-term
views, often linked to parliamentary or presidential elections.
They are, therefore, reluctant to accept long-term policy
changes, unless it is in their interest to do so, as was the
case with the Treaty of Rome which created the EEC. A World
Development Authority by its nature requires long-term commitment.
    Suggested transitional measure. There should be an inter-
national effort whereby countries concert in seeking to convince their parliaments of the need for long-term commitments.
OECD countries could work out joint long-term commitment procedures and then seek to convince Eastern European countries
(perhaps through the Economic Commission for Europe) to accept them. A global long-term 'commitment' policy should be
negotiated in a U.N. body and include OPEC and other nations.

CONCLUDING OBSERVATIONS

    It should again be emphasized that most of the structural
deficiencies in the United Nations system are the result of
actions taken by governments. As the Report of the Group of
Experts on the structure of the U.N. system has observed:

> Every serious reform proposal (as opposed to marginal
> proposals that amount to mere 'tinkering') is bound to
> cut across someone's vested interest in the *status quo*.
> A meaningful reform of the system, to take account of new
> requirements and developments, may involve the foregoing
> of some short-term interests and entrenched habits in fa-
> vour of long-term interests in a workable international
> economic order.

The ability of mankind to master the awesome challenges
confronting it depends largely on the political will of
Member States. International institutions can be an important factor in mobilizing that political will. If the
United Nations system is to play a central part in meeting the challenges of our time, it must reflect a number
of realities in the present world situation - the trend
towards relaxation of tensions and universality of participation in the international community, the growing interdependence between Member States, the increasing interrelationship between sectoral issues, the active discon-
tent of a substantial segment of mankind with the present
status of international economic relations and the fact
that not only is the world divided between developed and
developing countries but that the composition of each of
these groups reflects an increasingly variegated pattern
of countries with different levels of wealth, development
and technological capability and diverse social systems.
(9)

Finally, it should be obvious that public relations methods will need to be used to bring about a change in the behavior of States. Within the framework of transitional strategies it would no doubt be worthwhile to give serious examination to the possibilities of using on a much wider scale than
is presently the case television and other mass media to demonstrate the advantages of the global management of resources to those who oppose it. Obviously, it would be foolish to
believe that things will 'happen by themselves'. In particular,
it must be clearly shown that a World Development Authority embodied in a strengthened United Nations system is not synonymous with 'world central planning'.

NOTES AND REFERENCES

(1)   Parts of this paper were previously published in 'Deci-
sionmaking for the New International Economic Order' contained
in Antony J. Dolman and Jan van Ettinger (editors), *Partners
in Tomorrow:Strategies for a New International Order*, E.P.
Dutton, New York, 1978, pp. 174-181. Certain proposals are
also incorporated in Johan Kaufmann, United Nations Decision
Making, Sijthoff & Noordhoff, Leiden 1980.
(2)   It should be noted that what is 'idealistic' to some is
'realistic' to others and that what is 'idealistic' at point
X in time, often becomes 'realistic' at point X + Y.
(3)   United Nations, *The Impact of Multinational Corporations
on Development and International Relations*, (U.N. Publication
E.74.II.X.5), New York, 1974.

(4)   With a few notable exceptions. See, for example, Harold
D. Laswell, *Psychopathology and Politics*, new. ed., University
of Chicago Press, Chicago and London, 1977; Irving L. Janis,
*Victims of Groupthink:A Psychological Study of Foreign Policy
Decisions and Fiascos*, Houghton Mifflin, Boston, 1972; and
H. Kelman (ed.), *International Behavior:A Social-Psychological
Analysis*, Holt Rinehart and Winston, New York, 1965.
(5)   For example, Erik H. Erikson, *Childhood and Society*, 2nd
ed., W.W. Norton & Company, New York, 1963; Saul Friedländer,
Histoire et Psychanalyse, Ed. du Seuil, Paris, 1975; Alexander
L. George and Juliette L. George, *Woodrow Wilson and Colonel
House*, John Day, New York, 1964; and Ernest Jones, *Psycho-Myth,
Psycho-History*, 2 vols., Stonehill Publishing, New York, 1974.
(6)   Compare, for example, with Erik H. Erikson, op.cit.
(7)   This is not to suggest that there are no secretariats
with such a reputation.
(8)   Resolution 32/197 of the General Assembly, adopted 20
December 1977. See United Nations, *A New United Nations Structure for Global Economic Cooperation. Report of the Group of
Experts on the Structure of the United Nations System*, (document E/AC/62/9), New York, May 1975.
(9)   Ibid, paras 10 and 12.

II

Concepts and Strategies: Issues and Implications

For we are all, like swimmers in the sea,
poised on the top of a huge wave of fate,
which hangs uncertain to which side to fall.

Matthew Arnold
Sohrab and Rustum, 1853

Power and Global Planning and Resource Management
Johan Galtung

ON POWER IN GENERAL

Power is power to move, to move people and things in one
direction rather than others, to move their hearts and minds.
So power is dynamic; it is that which can bring about change
and oppose change - it is the key factor to be understood by
those who want to bring about changes, or to oppose them. It
is to social systems what force is to physical systems - and
of forces there are many kinds: mechanical, electric, magne-
tic, etc. There is force everywhere. When most things nevertheless remain where they are most of the time it is not because there are no forces, but because forces are somehow balanced: there are equal and opposed counter-forces. If something changes this situation it is because there is a force
excess in one direction, or - which is saying the same - a
force deficit in the other direction. (1)

It is usually the *power excess* that interests us in poli-
tiological analyses. A focus on that alone, however, may lead
to a lack of awareness of all the invisible power there is a-
round simply because it is adequately compensated. Thus, why
do cities not exploit the countryside even more than they do,
getting even more foodstuffs for even worse terms of trade with
city-made goods and services? The countryside is in principle
easy to exploit: farmers are fragmented by geographical distance (as opposed to workers who are together not only in the
workshops in general and the factories in particular, but in
the living quarters, the 'working class districts'), and they
are easily made dependent on what cities have to offer: the
services and manufactured goods sold on the markets. Moreover,
they are tied to the farms by the necessity to care for plants
and animals; even one day absent for politics may be catastro-

phic. So why are they not squeezed even further? Probably partly because people in the cities know that the farmers possess
an ultimate weapon, the total delivery strike - and also be
cause there are ties of solidarity, e.g. national ties, uniting
the two. (2) For that reason people in cities may prefer to
exploit farmers in other countries, far away; farmers unable
to articulate their distress directly. In short, we postulate
two forms of countervailing power: the delivery strike, and
solidarity - the former restraining the cities for fear of what
farmers may do to them, the latter a restraint on the cities by
the cities themselves. One might talk about anticipated external and internal negative sanctions.

Power analysis, then, is analysis of social systems in
terms of power in balance and imbalance. (3) It presupposes the
existence of some typologies of power. Without these, it is
virtually impossible to say anything which is non-trivial about
power and how it can be exercised to promote world order values.

And the simplest typology may be one that takes *sanctions*
as the point of departure and sees social processes as an *action dialogue*, as an *action-reaction*, where action is, at least
to some extent, steered by some anticipation of whether the
reaction may be positive or negative. (4) The dialogue may, as
all dialogues, be internal in the actor or external between
actors, so we have four possibilities:

Table 1: Power as Sanction: The Four Basic Types

	Positive Sanctions	*Negative Sanctions*
Internal (personal)	Good conscience	Bad conscience
External (social)	Reward	Punishment

These are mutual steering processes at the micro and ma-
cro level of social organization. The terms used in the table,
however, may seem too moralistic, too much derived from reli-
gious/theological and legal/juridical languages of discourse.
There might be nothing wrong in this since these are institutions profoundly concerned with power; with steering people
along the road of correct behavior and thought, partly by the
carrots of positive sanctions, mainly by the stick of negative
sanctions: bad conscience in the form of a more or less permanent guilt consciousness, fines and imprisonment, eternal
punishment in the afterlife. Whether these forms of power are,
in fact, effective is another matter: they have been exercised
for a long time and people still seem to engage in both wrong
behavior and have wrong thoughts. But that, of course, proves
very little: one would have to know how people had behaved
had these forms of power not existed. Moreover, it could also

be that there is some countervailing power at work which neu-
tralizes the possible effect of these forms of power. To see
this, however, more concepts are needed.

Let us simplify Table 1 by collapsing the two forms of
internal power. Essentially they are moral power, and operate
inside the actor. But we shall prefer a broader term than
'moral', a term that also brings in philosophical and political *standards* according to which an actor may evaluate his and
her behavior - not only the religious and legal standards. We
can think of no better general term than 'ideological', or, if
one will, *idea power*. For the point is simply this: there is a
body of thought, more or less coherent, according to which some
behavior/thought is right and some is wrong - and it may serve
to steer actors on the assumption that it matters sufficiently
to them whether what they do is right or wrong.

Hence, we end up with three types of power or power channels:

Table 2: The Three Basic Types of Power

IDEOLOGICAL	REMUNERATIVE	PUNITIVE
by defining *standards*	by administering *goods*	by administering *bads*

Any concrete, empirical situation may, of course, be a mixture
of all three, partly as manifest power, partly as latent power
not yet released into action - but the knowledge that it may
be unleashed, called an expectation, positive or negative, may
have considerable effect. There is, incidentally, one particular advantage of Table 2 relative to Table 1: although ideological power works inside the actor when the actor compares
standards with perception of own actions, those standards have
to come from somewhere. The *source of power* is where the standards come from; they are only put to work inside the actor.
For that reason the *power-receiver* is merely carrying out the
comparison, in a sense decentralizing the power exercise of
the power-sender. But, as will be developed later, he can also
become a power-sender, a source of power, namely, by generating
his own standards, not just using those of others.

We now assume that the material out of which power is made
has three components: *standards of right and wrong, goods* and
bads. The problem to be discussed is how this power material
is transmitted, and for this there are, as is usual in social
analysis, two perspectives: an *actor-oriented* and a *structure-
oriented* perspective. It is never a question of choosing between them: they are simply two different modes of operation
of social systems in general and power in particular.

According to the *actor-oriented perspective*, the exercise
of power is deliberate, intended. Power comes in discrete quan-

ta, in the action dialogue which can be written like a drama
with identifiable actors and sequences of action. What is most
easily identified as power at the common sense level of analysis is a quantum of bad inflicted on the other, in other
words an act of punishment. But the same applies to a quantum
of good, a reward. And to an act of ideological communication,
often known as *moralizing*: this was correct action, this was
incorrect - for I know which is which.

According to the *structure-oriented perspective*, the exercise of power is not deliberate, conscious, premeditated.
Power no longer comes in discrete quanta, or at least that is
not a fruitful perspective: it is more like a flow, like a
water faucet left open: it may be a trickle or flood wave depending on the quantity of power there is. The 'action dialogue'
is no longer a good metaphor, for everything is so automatic;
it is a structure at work. External sanctions are institutionalized and internal sanctions are internalized. (6) In less
jargon-ridden language this means the following: goods and
bads come automatically, according to contract - a *quid pro
quo*, according to the old rule *do ut des*. And the standards
are so built into the mental structure of the actors that a
sense of what is correct and what is not also comes automatically; there is no need for any explicit reminder.

This is the normal exercise of power, the famous nine-
tenths of the iceberg - but much less visible than the preceding type. The actor-initiated exercise of power is dramatic,
it is *news* - and in fact does fill the newspapers; the structurally built-in type is *olds*, so much a part of the ordinary
way society operates that it passes unnoticed by many. This is
actually one of the big differences between liberal and marxist
analysis: the latter is much better at using the structure-
oriented perspective, although overemphasizing economic goods
and bads at the expense of so many others; the former is much
better at using the actor-oriented perspective, but to the
point of developing advanced levels of structure blindness.
Both the religious and the legal perspectives are much stronger
along actor-oriented than structure-oriented lines of thought
and action, because of the high level of significance attached
to intention, to premeditation.

We shall refer to the power exercised according to the
first perspective as *resource power*, and to the power exercised
according to the second perspective as *positional power*. In the
first case, the powerful has an excess of, or at least uses an
excess of, *resources*: the goods, the bads, and standards -
among other things to know what constitutes goods and what constitutes bads. In the second case, what the powerful has and
others do not have is a certain *position* in a social structure.

For the analysis of resource power one would obviously
make use of the categories of economic and military analysis,
the major institutions for the production of goods and bads.

Thus, the factors of economic production - capital, labor, raw
materials including energy, research, organization (for processing and distribution - and the factors of military 'production' (i.e. destruction) - capital (the military budgets), labor (the military forces), raw materials including energy (for
the military hardware), research and organization (for processing and distribution) - would be listed. Just as important,
however, in an evaluation of power, would be the extent to
which the actor can set standards for others - in other words,
the extent to which it is a moulder of culture for itself and
others, a *model*.

    For the analysis of positional power one would have to
make use of the categories of structural analysis. Actually,
there are two dimensions to this analysis: first, an analysis
of the total social structure in which individual, group/class
or state actors are embedded; second, an analysis of the positions of the various actors within that structure. (Actually
this corresponds to the analysis of resource power: one thing
would be to analyze what constitutes a resource, another to
identify the world distribution of resources). The analysis of
the structure, then, becomes a question of to what extent there
is vertical division of labor built into it, conditioning of
some actors by others, marginalization, fragmentation and segmentation. (7) In the extreme case, *the pure alpha structure*,
there is a clear center and a clear periphery: the center benefits from the vertical division of labor, it conditions the periphery, the periphery is kept outside, is marginalized; it is
fragmented, meaning that the actors in the periphery are kept
apart from each other; and the periphery is segmented, meaning
that the actors only participate with a part of their selves,
that part which is useful to the center (as natural resources,
as human resources or 'labor' and so on). Obviously, *to be in
the center of a pure alpha structure*, that is to have positional power.

    Let us now summarize. There are three *types* of power, and
two *modes* of exercising power:

Table 3: Types and Modes of Power

	IDEOLOGICAL	REMUNERATIVE	PUNITIVE
RESOURCE POWER			
POSITION POWER			

It should be noted that the type of power is exactly the same
in the two modes; the differences being whether it is transmitted *ad hoc* or automatically. To take an example: the case of
remunerative power, in international systems. It can be exercised as an *ad hoc* grant/loan in response to some type of beha-

vior very much wanted - and technical assistance is one mechanism for this. Or, it is simply a part of trade, a flow of
something wanted, regulated by contractual relations. At the
international level, this is the difference between the occasional award of premium or bonus, and the regular salary that
a wage-earner may have - and nobody would contest that wage-
earners, as countries, are steered through contractual relations, not only through the *ad hoc* decisions. Incidentally, in
terms of understanding day-to-day relations, the examples indicate how much more significant is the structure-oriented analysis, with its focus on position power, and how inadequate is
an analysis which focuses on the occasional outbursts of the
ad hoc exercise of power.

One brutal fact about social systems can now be brought
into the picture: *power begets power*. This principle actually
works in all directions in Table 2. Thus, resource power can
be converted to positional power, and vice versa. With resource
power, channels of communication can be built; moreover, one
may become a center of attraction by virtue of having something
to offer and this may structure the channels of communication.
Conversely, positional power is by definition not only a guarantee that resources will accumulate in the center (this is
ensured by the vertical division of labor), but also that the
periphery will by and large be unable to prevent this from happening (this is ensured by means of the other four structural
factors that can be seen as auxiliary to the major one).

The same applies horizontally in Table 3. Thus, punitive
power can be used for conquest and be converted to remunerative
power - that was the old story of, for instance, Western imperialism; just as the new story is how remunerative or economic
power can be converted to punitive power simply by placing
strong economic machinery at the disposal of the military which
can be used to turn out an ever increasing, and increasingly
sophisticated, array of means of destruction. The conversion of
either into ideological power may be deplored but is nevertheless a frequent phenomenon: might is right, he who is powerful
commands attention, that attention is already the nucleus around
which ideological power can crystallize. (8) Conversely, ideological power may give an edge of superiority that the charisma-
tic but poor actor can utilize, slowly accumulating a reservoir
of resources for good and for bad.(9)

This type of analysis could now lead to a very interesting
dimension: complete vs. incomplete power configurations, or -
expressed differently - equilibrated vs. disequilibrated actors.
The equilibrated actors are consistently high on all power dimensions, on all three types and both modes, or consistently
low. (10) In short, they are perfectly *powerful*, or perfectly
powerless; they have all kinds of resources and are in the center of the structure, or they have very little in terms of resources and are in the periphery. We know both types from the

world today; these are the 'haves' and the 'have-nots', and
with all the mechanisms of conversion between types and modes
of power it is not strange that the *world as a system* becomes
so polarized once some actors have some edge over the others.
(11) Nevertheless, the most interesting factor in the international system may be the disequilibrated actors, those who
are high on some dimension of power and low on some other, for
the simple reason that they are likely to be sources of some
dynamism - the equilibrated topdogs being too complacent, too
happy about the present state of affairs, too concerned with
defending the *status quo* with all kinds of means, and the equilibrated underdogs often being too incapable, powerless, apa-
thetic to be able to bring about any change.

Obviously, there are many types of disequilibrated actors
in any system, using the categories of Table 3. For instance,
playing first on the types of power: an actor may be high on
ideological, remunerative *or* punitive power, low on the others,
(the Vatican, the oil states, the terrorists). The obvious prediction would be that *actors will tend to strive for a full
configuration*, particularly if they are high on two so that
there is only one missing (China, strong on ideology and on
goods, now obviously also going in for the production of bads,
or at least for their acquisition). However, as we shall see
later, such predictions may be too simplistic for there is
also an attrition factor at work: one type of power may coun-
teract the other. Thus, ideological power may be driven out by
too much remunerative power (the clouds of doubt over the Vatican if/when it is seen as too rich); and punitive power may
drive out remunerative power (if the oil states acquire many
more arms, will that not inspire even more the trend to become independent of their major resource?). In short, there
may be power in the incomplete configuration.

And the same applies to the types of disequilibria that
relate to the mode of power. Countries very high on resources
but low on positional power (China), like countries high on
positional power but low on resources (Switzerland) will always represent an element of deviance, of the atypical; and in
their strivings to convert at least some of their advantages
on one mode of power into some upward mobility along the other
dimension(s), some dynamism will be created. More particularly,
the former can be expected to create structures around themselves so that they obtain high positional power; that is, if
they cannot or do not wish to move into high positions in existing structures. (12) And the latter will slowly but safely
accumulate the resources that accrue, almost with certainty to
the actor in a central position in a structure, not the least
because of the informal control (not only *having* more information than others have, but also to some extent deciding what
they *should* have).

Finally, a word about *formal vs. informal systems*. It is

not a very important distinction except if it is made in such
a way that the informal systems in fact are the systems of ultimate power, and for that reason often steering the formal
systems. We shall identify the formal power system with the
non-territorial system of (multilateral) organizations in which
actors (in our case, above all, *countries*) relate to each other
and the informal power system with the *territorial system* of
(bilateral) relations amoung countries. (13) The organizations,
particularly the United Nations, then stand out as a formal
system on top or in front of the system of states relating directly to each other with their ideologies and ways of distri-
buting goods and bads. Let us only add to this that everything
else said above applies to both systems: there are all three
types and both modes of power in both systems, as a moment's
reflection will show. Thus, international organizations certainly also have their structure in which power flows unabated
but also largely unnoticed, between the splashes of *ad hoc*
decisions - which, incidentally, may be made at regular intervals. (14) In short, the structure of the secretariat vs. the
decisions made by the general assemblies!

ON COUNTERVAILING POWER

   Our concern is with change in the present world system.
For that to happen some countervailing power has to come into
the picture. And how is that at all possible: the powerful, especially those with a complete power configuration, look so
powerful, so equipped by virtue of the positions they have -
and the powerless so totally, absolutely powerless. Actually,
the situation is not that bad. If it had been so bad, the underdogs would always remain underdogs and the topdogs always
topdogs. Yet history teaches us that quite a lot of changes do
take place. Consequently, there must be ample opportunity for
changes in the power configuration to take place, otherwise
history would not be as dynamic as it is. What we need to understand this is a theory of how the powerless can become more
powerful, a theory of countervailing power at least as rich as
the one-way theory of power so far presented. Actually, they
both belong, equally, to any fully fledged theory of power.
   The point of departure would be a distinction, not so far
made, between *power-over-others* and *power-over-oneself* as the
two major types of countervailing power. (15) In the field of
remunerative power, or economic power to use a more evocative
term, it is quite clear what this means: the first stands for
counterpenetration; the second for self-reliance, even for
self-sufficiency (autarchy). In the field of punitive power,
or military power, the first stands for the famous balance of
power, the second for - what? What is it that corresponds to

self-reliance in the field of military power, and in the field
of ideological power?

Let us first handle power-over-others as an approach to
countervailing power. What it means is simply that the underdog builds up the same types and modes of power as the topdog
until balance is achieved. As the reader will have noticed
this is never completely possible: in this approach there will
always be an element of imitation, of using the topdog as a
power model; which is tantamount to saying that the topdog
retains his ideological power. The underdog is moulded by the
topdog even if he should manage to pass him both in the ability
to deliver goods and bads, both in resource power and position
power. Of course, the underdog may sincerely wish this to happen, but in that wish is already embedded the internalization
of standards set by the topdog. And then there is, of course,
the problem of whether it is *possible* thus to 'catch up', to
'bridge the gap'; leaving alone whether it is *desirable*. We
shall return to these issues but first we have to explore the
other type of countervailing power: power-over-oneself. The
point of departure is a more subtle aspect of power than has
been touched upon so far although it is implicit in the concept
of a power-*receiver*. Power has to be *received* to work; in the
effective exercise of power there is always an element of underdog cooperation with the topdog. The physical analogy may
be of some value here. A nail is made so that the force of a
hammer can have an impact. The hammer is helpless relative to
many other shapes and sizes - for instance cotton - from which
it does not follow that these other things may destroy the
hammer; they simply render it ineffective. Similarly, the force
of lightning, an electric discharge, is rendered rather powerless against rubber. So, what are the social equivalents of
cotton and rubber. (16)

To explore this we can use the types of power in Table 2
and apply the same reasoning for resource power and for positional power. For ideological power to be effective, there has
to be an element of *submissiveness* in the power-receiver, an
admission that the power-sender is somehow superior. For remunerative power to be effective, there has to be a corresponding
element of *dependency*, an admission that one needs what the
topdog has to offer. And for punitive power to be effective,
there has to be an element of *fear*. And is this not precisely
the 'portrait of the underdog' (17) - submissive, dependent
and fearful - in other words not only a question of the lack
of resources and the peripheral position but also of an attitude, a psychological make-up, that goes with these deficits
and make them bite.

Having said this, it is obvious what the conditions for
a less receptive attitude to power exercises would be: *self-
respect, self-sufficiency and fearlessness*. If one respects
sufficiently one's own standards and ability to define what is

correct and right, what is incorrect and wrong (18); further,
if one is no longer dependent on what the topdog has to offer
and no longer fears his arms - well, then one is no longer a
power-receiver, an underdog, *one is autonomous because one has
power-over-oneself*. And the beautiful thing about that type of
power is that it can be developed by anybody even under the
most adverse circumstances. It may not work under all circumstances, at least not equally effectively, but the process of
moving away from being a power-receiver toward a more autonomous status can always be initiated. (19) Incidentally, this
process is what puberty is about, with all three elements;
and it is identifiable in the history of many countries that
simply refuse to submit, to depend and to fear (Albania relative to Yugoslavia, to the Soviet Union, and ultimately to
China; almost all countries that in some period or another have
been exposed to economic sanctions). (20) To the topdog it
looks like defiance, like some kind of adolescent fad the
country has to get through, and the parallel to puberty is actually meaningful. (21) But to the country itself, or at least
to those who are the carriers of this kind of policy, it may
belong to the *Sternstunden* of that country, to the periods of
transcendence when people feel they are born anew. (22)

So much for the attitudes that are seen as crucial, with
their psycho-manifestations. In the concrete world of behavior
and action, what would be the concomitants of a declaration of
autonomy? *Above all, it would be to pay less attention to the
topdogs*. (23) There are two ways of being authoritarian: one
is to be systematically submissive, the other to be equally
systematically unplacable. Both of them are indicators of the
same: that the topdog has a profound influence on one's own
behavior. To be autonomous is to develop one's own personality
- be that for individuals or for countries - not to be steered
in everything, positively or negatively, by some model. Consequently, it does not mean splendid isolation, that would be an
expression of fear. He who is fearless does not fear contact
with others, interaction, but retains a capacity for self-sufficiency that would make him independent if the wanted to, i.e.
if the topdog tries to make use of any dependency for ulterior
purposes. (24)

The upshot of all this is that self-reliance, so often
discussed narrowly in an economic context alone, merely as a
question of using better one's own economic factors, should be
seen as a power strategy. Its three pillars, self-respect,
self-sufficiency and fearlessness point much beyond economics
toward politics and psychology, and the key to it all is to
gain more power over oneself. In this, the mental declaration
of independence is indispensable, but in saying so we are not
proclaiming that the key to countervailing power is psycholo-
gical/ideological - only that this is an indispensable element.
Prior to that declaration of independence there is probably

also a history of power abuse, of *exploitation of the middle range*, sufficient to stimulate counterreactions, not so strong as to lead to total subjugation, to a state of perennial submissiveness, dependency and fear. The problem is whether the total pattern of power exercise leaves us with that kind of open window, with a pressure sufficient to stimulate but not to subjugate. In short, it is a question of that fruitful range that turns a challenge into a creative response. (25)

At this point another crucial aspect of general power theory has to be brought into the picture: the theory of *power bridgeheads*. It has been alluded to above: it is a question of whether and how the topdog is built into the underdog, capable of exercising all types of power through both modes, so to speak. In psycho-analytical theory, at the individual level, this is the famous *super-Ego*, the internalized presence of the source of standards, of morals (we would say ideology) - sometimes personalized as the mental image of a stern god, a father, an easily saddened mother. In the theory of imperialism, among states, the bridgehead takes very concrete forms: the colonial forces, above all foreign troops, administrators, businessmen of various kinds, missionaries; the neo-colonial forces, usually the same categories with the same values and trades, but with local skin. In a sense, the neo-colonial situation is to the colonial situation what the more mature child is to the smaller one: for the latter the super-Ego is still very concrete, even the concrete presence of parental authority; for the former it is already a part of the person's self, gradually being rooted in the personality, moulded with other forces. (26)

Thus, to attain autonomy from colonialism one has to fight others; and to attain autonomy from neo-colonialism (which is not only found in the Third World, but in the First and Second Worlds as well), *part of the fight has to be against oneself*. The borderlines between self and other are never clear - not even in the colonial case for that reason; the power always being a little bit rooted, institutionalized, internalized (for that reason the borderline between pure, *ad hoc* resource power and positional power is not too clear either in practice; these are analytical categories). Needless to say, this does not make the struggle for autonomy any easier. Incidentally, it also serves to explain why people alienate from their societies often are important in revolutions: they have less to fight against inside themselves.

Translated into the politics of today, what has been said so far is simply the following: countervailing power, relative to the colossal power structure in today's world, *would have dissociation, delinking from that structure as a major component*. In this type of struggle, elites in the underdog countries (the 'centers in the periphery') may fall on either side; most likely they will split, one part joining the center, in the

world power structure,(27) another part joining the newly forged autonomy, trying to work out a viable future. As we all
know this is very far from any abstract kind of reasoning; it
is exactly what has happened in the world a number of times in
this century - sometimes identified with the word 'revolution'
However, that word may block innovative theory and practice
rather than stimulate it, so let us try to continue with the
problem of countervailing power as such, and expose what has
been said so far to some obvious criticism.

Critic: So, some countries undergo this process after the first
seeds have been sown by what I guess you would call
progressive groups within the country. They become
autonomous - they develop self-respect, self-sufficiency and fearlessness. I grant you that this happens to
nations and countries; there are these instances of
euphoria, 'transcendence' you would probably call it.
But is it viable, can it last?

Author: Nothing lasts forever. Yet, it is almost incredible how
long the euphoria accompanying what has happened in Cuba has lasted, in spite of elements of repression. (28)
However, it should be pointed out that this is not
something a country would have to do alone - collective
self-reliance (as opposed to the major falsification of
that concept, collective bargaining with the power
structure) is an effort to become autonomous together.

Critic: I grant you that. However, if the power structure in
the world is that strong, what will prevent it from doing what is in its power to do: unleash all the bads
at its disposal, from economic blockade to more or less
open support of its own bridgeheads to right-out invasion? The local people may declare themselves imbued
with self-respect, enjoy their self-sufficiency and be
fearless - yet, with an economic blockade biting, with
internal and external military in the streets, a dead
man is a dead man whether fearless or not.

Author: Right, and for that reason what has been said so far is
too simplistic. Delinking is not enough; it is also too
crude as a category. As is said, it should only be regarded as one component. At the same time there could
be another component of more conventional countervailing power: counter-ideology, counter-penetration, coun-
ter-force. The basic point with the present power theory is only that this is never sufficient, regardless of
how necessary it may be.

Let us then try to summarize in a more complete and syste-

matic fashion some of the obvious possibilities of the underdog. In doing so we have to make use of Table 3; if these are
the basic forms of power then the basic forms of countervailing power should be responses to them, to all six of them.
With one autonomy and one balance approach for each one that
should give a total of twelve forms of countervailing power:

Table 4: Types and Modes of Countervailing Power

	IDEOLOGICAL (a)	REMUNERATIVE (b)	PUNITIVE (c)
RESOURCE POWER *Autonomy* (1) *approach*	*self-respect* building own ideology	*self-sufficiency* using own fac-tors for own use	*fearlessness* decentralize, less vulner-able
RESOURCE POWER *Balance* (2) *approach*	counter-mission	counter-penetration	counter-deterrence
POSITION POWER *Autonomy* (3) *approach*	building own structures, dissociation	building own corporations, dissociation	building own non-alignment, dissociation
POSITION POWER *Balance* (4) *approach*	joining on equal terms, recoupling	joining on equal terms, recoupling	joining on equal terms, recoupling

In this tabular presentation there is also some hint or
hypothesis as to *strategy,* that term being used not only in the
sense of defining the goals, but also of laying down the rough
time order of some of the major steps on the way. Of course,
that time order can never be linear; there is always a back-and-
forth movement in any political process - but *grosso modo* the
table may nevertheless be indicative.
    Thus, a basic point is to start with the recognition that
the fundamental assets, the basic resources, are with oneself.
Consequently, to gain control over them is where everything
starts. Part of this is a psycho-political process of building
autonomy in one's own mind, part of it a question of gaining
control over the economic cycles - both nature (raw materials,
energy),production facilities and the distribution machineries.
All this should primarily be for own uses as long as there is
a need, particularly as long as basic human needs are left un-
satisfied. But this has to be accompanied with an ideological
build-up, and a truly endogenous one. Here it should be remem-
bered that marxism is a product of the West, perhaps indispensable to understand how Western capitalism works; but it is
not the same as an endogenous ideology. (29) No culture, to
our knowledge, preaches submissiveness to a world power struc-

ture; consequently there are elements on which to build in any culture. But this task, obviously, cannot be done from the outside. And the same applies to fearlessness: in the table there is an indication of a structure that might be conducive to the state of fearlessness - a decentralization of the country to the point that it becomes less vulnerable to an outside attack. (30) Possibly, this may be combined with preparations for guerilla and non-military types of defense.

Imagine now that this is carried out, that there is more control over one's own resources - cultural, economic and military resources. In that case one can start playing the other party's game, penetrating the topdog. Today this is best known in the economic field and in the form of investment and buying of property.

So far little is done by the world periphery in terms of counter-missionary activities, and by that is not so much meant the creation of buddhist, hindu and islam centers - more or less proselytizing - around the world, but a much broader approach . The Third World does not seem to be aware that one of its major assets has to do with its way of life; itself more integrated, more based on togetherness than the extremely segmented and fragmented life styles that have been developed in the West. Playing the Western game in the reverse would mean not only developing faith and pride in one's own way of life - to the extent it is still there - but also defining the West as underdeveloped (which in many regards it is) and start propagating for changes.

Nor has the Third World so far really started opening a Pandora's box that sooner or later will have to be opened: the question of a credible counter-deterrence. Of course, today the capitalist West would like to see parts of the Third World organize itself militarily against military penetration organized by the socialist part of the West, and that socialist part might well like to organize similar alliances against interventionist operations from the capitalist part of the West. What will probably come, if only after painful years of attachment to either camp, would be a credible Third World deterrent against any kind of penetration (31) - but it is quite possible that this cannot take place before a process of autonomy relative to neo-colonialism and the vestiges of colonialism has progressed further. It should not, of course, be ruled out that this deterrent will also have a nuclear component, and any attempt by the *status quo* powers in nuclear affairs to delegitimize Third World nuclear power more than their own will naturally be counterproductive. (32)

With this autonomy basis, preparatory work is done for attacks on the structure of power itself. Whether those attacks will be successful depends very much on whether the autonomy approach work of phase 1 above has been sufficiently well done. If all that is done is to get rich quickly through improved

terms of trade on some commodities and investing or wasting
excess accumulated capital (33), then it is more likely than
not that the world power structure will be able to readjust,
for instance by upping the prices on manufactured goods, on
licenses and royalties, etc., all the time claiming that they
refer to new products, not to last year's product. But if own
resources are believed in, particularly own human beings (not
accepting outsiders' definition of what a 'developed', skilled
educated human 'resource' means), then a necessary condition
for some dissociation or decoupling from the world power structure is present.

Two clarifying remarks need to be made here. Firstly, the
point about decoupling is not so much leaving the world structure of bilateral and multilateral relations as to focus more
on one's own situation, and those in the same situation objectively speaking, paying less attention to those above and
more to others in the same position as oneself. It means acting
and thinking more in horizontal terms, less in vertical terms,
so to speak. From the topdog point of view, however, this is
already delinking since they ask for almost undivided attention,
being highly jealous of others. And in a sense it is - given
that any country's or any actor's potential for interaction is
limited, interaction resources have to be taken from somewhere.
A real emphasis on horizontal solidarity will have to be combined with some decrease in attention to those on the top, at
least relatively speaking. It does mean redirection of trade,
for instance.

The second clarifying remark is this; decoupling does not
have to apply to all fields of interaction. There are fields
that are more critical than others. Again, the parallel to adolescent autonomy building activities can be made use of: it is
more important, at least in western culture, for the young boy
or girl to find their own way in the world of ideology than in
the world of commensalism and convivialism - to be independent
ideologically is completely compatible, in many families, with
continued living together. How partial or complete a decoupling
has to be will depend very much on what kind of 'family': there
are world topdogs who may learn to let go even in essential relations; there are others who will try to keep whatever vertical link there is. (34)

Imagine now that this phase 3 has been carried out with
some success - what would then be the basic point of phase 4,
the balance approach within the position approach?

The point, as the two words 'balance' and 'position' indicate, is to obtain some parity in world structures. The formal
approach to this, in organizations, is well known: much attention paid to the national origin of the officers of the organization, parity obtained through quotas and rotation, occasionally also to the location of headquarters, or at least to conferences and assemblies. One should not belittle this: changes

in the formal structure toward parity may not only mystify the
gross asymmetries in the informal structures by throwing a
veil of equality over them; they *may* also contribute to some
change in these informal structures. However, the basic thesis
here is that a much better approach is to build up one's own
structure first, gaining autonomous experience, and then re-
couple or relink on the basis of a parity that already exists
in the informal structure.

In short, the order in which things are done is important.
The strategy of countervailing power recommended here is this:

ending up with a world where both resources and positions are
more equally distributed than in the present world. However,
there are also many other more or less articulated strategies
in this field, such as

2b

In other words, simply engage in counter-investment. Or,
for that matter:

3c

the strategy of non-alignment. Or an example often found in
more pious, small groups in the First World (and also in the
Third):

1

forgetting how easily such a tiny structure can be overrun by
the roller-coaster of the world power structure.

Let us then again confront a critic with a rather important objection:

Critic: But what is in Table 4 looks so much like what is already being done! I have heard the verbiage of phase
1 for ages, and much of it is in the resolutions and
charters of the New International Economic Order. Moreover, OPEC countries are already engaged in counter-
penetration; and as to building own structures for
ideological transmission, I guess this is what the new
international information order is about; (35) and

there has been non-aligment around for a long time,
since Beograd in 1961 or Bandoeng in 1955 if you will.
There has also been joining, relinking, recoupling -
particularly of the so-called socialist countries.
Even that champion of decoupling, China, now seems to
be relinking with world capitalism at full speed!

Author: Right, I agree with this analysis. But some points are
missing. First, the countervailing strategies of the
underprivileged of this world have so far been very
fragmented: sometimes this, then a little bit of that
- some countries specializing in phase 2 approaches,
others in phase 3 approaches, and so on. What is contained in Table 4 is a more complete set of strategies, with efforts to see how they combine into something quite meaningful if more actors were practising
all of them. Second, the order has not been right. Much
of what passes for countervailing power is actually a
way of playing up to the existing power structure,
e.g. by supplying it with capital in the form of re-
cycled petrodollars. And then, third: why should it be
that different? I actually want to show that what the
underprivileged countries have been doing *does* make
sense or *can* make sense provided it is pursued with a
more total strategy in mind. What has been done is part
of a historical process that has already changed this
world and is going to change it further - the present
paper merely tries to point to some of the pieces that
may still be missing in the puzzle.

Critic: But then another point: do all that, and where would
we be? Definitely in the world where today's underprivileged countries have a fairer share of the total
world product. But that is a rather mixed bag. It contains very big and powerful countries and small and
powerless ones; it contains elites perhaps more privileged than almost anybody in the First World and masses
worse off than anyone else. Even if one redistributes
between the First, Second and Third Worlds one does not
necessarily make for any redistribution within the
Third World!

Author: With this I agree entirely, and that is the reason why
so much of the general theory is in terms of 'actors'
not in terms of countries. Also, Table 4 is prefaced
with some remarks about 'the obvious possibilities of
the underdog' - again leaving it open who the underdog
is. Thus, I take it that all that has been said so far
in a sense applied to at least three levels: *between
the regions* in the world conveniently referred to by

counting 'worlds', *within these regions* as a way in
which the weaker states can stand up against the
stronger ones, and *within these states* as a way in
which the masses can stand up against the elites.
Power works like a set of Chinese boxes: there is
power within power within power; and within the most
powerless there are again the powerful and the powerless. These three levels correspond to regional, national and local levels of self-reliance, respectively.

In fact, all of what has been said so far can be summarized in that term: *self-reliance* - which we would like to interpret as a *process*, not as a state of affairs - at at least
these three levels and with something like the content that is
given in Table 4. In other words, self-reliance as a concept
should comprise both autonomy, decoupling and recoupling strategies.

SOME CONSEQUENCES FOR GLOBAL PLANNING, MANAGEMENT AND INSTITUTIONS

The basic consequence of what has been said in the preceding section can be formulated in one simple thesis: *if change
is wanted, very little can be obtained through negotiation with
the holders of power*. Think of what they possess; the positions
of command in most structures that matter, formal or informal,
overwhelming resources to throw into any bargain that may be
struck as a result of the negotiation. Look at the way the
structures are made, particularly the informal structures in
the territorial system: there is already built into them a
fragmentation that makes it so easy to deal with the powerless
one at a time through the capacities of the foreign ministry
machineries in the capitals of the powerful countries - just
calling in the ambassador, offering his country something special, the understanding being that he will not look too much in
any horizontal direction, informing his equals. And there is
built into the formal system, the international organizations,
a very high level of *segmentation*: the organizations are so
specific, so tuned to a small spectrum of the total world situation, so hedged around by rules as to what constitutes relevant matters. And think of the *marginalization* built into the
formal system: the powerful countries have so many more organizations with secretariats well endowed both in capital, research and organization; the powerless are not members and more
often than not have nothing corresponding in terms of organizations. In short, by using the existing systems or, rather, by
relying on them, the results are already given. The agendas are

built into the structure of the system, the results are an almost foregone conclusion. The cards are too well stacked in
favor of the haves.

It should be pointed out that this does not necessarily
depend on any bad will or intention on the side of the powerful. Of course, they may have their tricks: they may feign a
resistance in the direction they want the agreement to go so
as to give the powerless an impression of victory. But much
more basic than the whole ritual of night long negotiations,
the dramatic breakdown and then breakthrough with the champag-
ne bottles taken out of the coolers (where they have been all
the time), is the automatic working of the structures. Thus,
if there is negotiation about economic relations between non-
industrialized and industrialized countries, the negotiations
almost have to be about terms of trade; how much of the commodities for how many of the manufactures. The very fact of meeting together guarantees that this topic will be brought up one
way or the other because their relationship is structured around
that theme. And in doing so, energy of all kinds is taken away
from the other possibilities: processing at home for own use
(import substitution), and trade along horizontal lines. But
for the former a meeting with oneself, *ad hoc*, is sufficient;
for the latter there is no need to devote too much time to
discussions with the overprivileged. Hence, less time should be
devoted to North-South conferences (like the Paris dialogue)(36)
- rather wait till time is ripe.

To define 'development' in such a way that it is spearheaded by rich countries is structurally similar to defining
'disarmament' in such a way that it is spearheaded by the superpowers. (37) It is a good indicator of the extent to which
these powerful countries have been able to impress their standards on others that there are many people, some of them of considerable prominence, who still - after so much evidence to the
contrary - manage to believe that this is the only 'realistic'
approach. To the contrary, this is the approach that the rich
countries, wanting it or not, will make use of to further increase the wealth gap, and the superpowers to further increase
the force gap - the former by making development dependent on
trade with rich countries, the latter by imposing conditions
on others that they do not live up to themselves. It is realistic in the sense that it is feasible; the powerful want it and
the powerless think they have no alternative and are often
flattered simply because they are within talking distance of
their structural masters, rewarded by some mini-concessions.
Some of them may even feel flattered by being offered the opportunity to serve as an 'engine of growth', helping the rich
countries out of their current crisis by placing a sufficient
number of orders in order to provide jobs for the unemployed
in countries used to produce for the entire world market without other competition than what they can muster among them-

selves. (38)

So, if the 'realistic' approach is unrealistic, what is
then the 'unrealistic' approach that may prove to be realistic? How does the adage, *'pay less attention to the powerful'*
translate into concrete politics in the field of global planning, management and institutions?

To start with the formal system, the system of organizations: *by creating many more autonomous Third World organizations*, at least in all fields of any significance for the distribution of ideology (including news!), goods and bads. This
does not mean leaving any world organization in the same field;
the struggle within that organization should continue - but
it should be strengthened by autonomous organizational experience.

To take the United Nations as an example: an organization
encompassing all types of power, an organization for the dis-
bursement of resource power and the flow of structural power,
an organization where all types of countervailing power can to
some extent be promoted, and counteracted - the latter mainly
through co-optation, absorption. The system of Afro-Asian or
Third World caucuses are good cases of effective use of the
dialectic between fission and fusion: withdrawal to discuss
and form a position, then a thrust forward inside the organization. Bloc voting is another and related expression and in-
dispensible, in spite of the obvious that the motivations behind a certain vote may differ considerably inside the highly
heterogeneous Third World bloc.

But this is not enough, for whereas the nations of the
First World have their views well prepared not only through
their governments but also by their powerful intergovernmental
secretariats (particularly OECD and the EC), the Third World
is not in a similar position. It may perhaps be said that they
have been able to some extent to make use of UNCTAD as a secretariat - as a minor compensation for the way in which GATT,
WIPO and so many other U.N. organizations have served predo-
minantly First World interests. But even this is to play into
the hands of the powerful because of the functional specificity of UNCTAD, its economism and not negligible intellectual
rigidity and conservatism.

What is needed is obviously a *Third World Secretariat*,
maybe brought about by some fusion between the machineries for
the non-aligned countries and for the Group of 77 in order not
to disperse energies too much. The difficulties are of course
exactly the same as those witnessed by the OECD and EC secretariats (the latter has the somewhat pretentious name of 'commission'): nationals of some countries may have a too dominant
position (to make no mention of such organizations as NATO or
OEA, WTO or CMEA, where superpower dominance is built in from
the very beginning). More precisely, in the case of a Third
World Secretariat, it could some time ago have been feared that

the production of development intellectuals was so much higher
in Latin America and India that there would be space for little
else, and particularly not for Africans. (39) But, not the
least due to the U.N., a high number of qualified people with
an adequate geographical dispersion now exists as a reservoir
for staffing a secretariat of that type. Incidentally, that
secretariat would of course add greatly to its power and influence by doing the same as done by the OECD and the EC: having
some First World *stagiaires* and resident researchers; and by
undertaking studies of the problems of the countries of the
First World, not only to understand them better, but also with
a view to providing them, one way or the other, with fresh
views.

Obviously, a secretariat of that type would be located in
a Third World country and it would be concerned with relations
within and among Third World countries (autonomy-building!) as
well as with relations with the First and Second Worlds (balan-
ce- building!). It would prepare background and position papers,
not only for the formal system of organizations, but also as
advice in connection with bilateral relations - as does the
First World (and indeed the Second). There would be a U.N. section with sub-sections for U.N. organizations. All this is obvious. But if one might be permitted one little piece of advice then it would be to have a maximum of exchange between the
secretariat and positions of theory and practice, universities
and research institutes on the one hand, and concrete work on
the other, even practising Chinese patterns of rotation in and
out of villages and industries (but on a more voluntary basis).
In no way does this preclude work in the U.N. and contact
with the First World: as a matter of fact, it would probably
increase it. But it does mean that the Third World would have
a chance, on a continuous basis and large scale, to be much
better prepared. That would very soon pay off, not only for
the Third World in the sense that it would be more able to take
care of its own interests, but also for the whole world because
the Third World would see itself more, not less, in terms of a
world role. Why? Because of the significance of being autonomous relative to being at the bottom of the world table - in
some cases even in the position of Lazarus, down at the floor,
hoping for some crumbs to 'trickle down'.

Thus, after some years the Third World Secretariat would
be surprised to see how many readers they would have among the
disenchanted in the First World, just as Third World business
and power elites in general have been avid customers of the documents churned out by First World machineries - because they
speak to their bridgehead interests.

In general, this pattern could be repeated in many, even
most, of the international organizations of any significance.
It will only serve to enrich our world, in addition to building
autonomy for the underprivileged - just like separate organiza-

tions for women are not only a necessity for their liberation,
but also something from which everybody will ultimately benefit.

But will the First World benefit from this? Even with a
growing world pie - to use that economistic language - the
rate of change of redistribution may be higher than the rate
of growth of the pie so that the First World actually does
lose. The argument would then be that the First World already
has enough, even more than enough, and that it should worry
much more about its internal redistribution and its many symp-
toms of overdevelopment, and less about continued power balance in its favor relative to the Third World.(40) As it is not
very likely that the arrogant power elite of the First World
will see matters this way, they will probably have to learn
it the hard way: by the Third World gradually unleashing all
its potentials for countervailing power. An intelligent First
World elite, however, would have a deeper understanding of
power and would understand how much latent power there is in
the Third World, how much power can and probably will be unleashed - and be more accommodating and encouraging.

Then, the informal power system, the territorial system,
where rules are less explicit in spite of all the codification
in international law, and where power is more extreme, both in
terms of rewards and in terms of punishment, than it can ever
be in an organization (where maximum reward is to become president and maximum punishment is to be excluded - compare that
to a lasting trade surplus and a military invasion!). The basic
rule would be the same: a sign of health would be a growing
preponderance of horizontal, bilateral relations over the vertical ones generated in various forms by five hundred years of
colonialism. This has to be a gradual process, and some care
has to be exercised to chart a course between the Scylla of
accommodating too much to the *status quo*, and the Charybdis
of provoking too much of the ire of the power-holders. (41)
Again, it is felt that the Third World is not necessarily doing
too badly in this regard: those who go fast do provoke that
ire, and either have to gamble on the other super-powerholder
(Yugoslavia, Cuba) or will suffer intervention in one form or
the other (Czechoslovakia, Chile); unless they have the power
resources of a China, that is. And those who go too slow will
suffer from continued exploitation by the world power structure and its bridgeheads. But those who go quickly will pave
the way for others, in the longer run (and will have to pay for
that heroic contribution), and those who go too slowly will pay
by not moving at all but benefit from the moves by others in
the longer run. (42)

In all of this, it may very well be that the conservative
regimes, moving slowly or not at all, are rather grateful to
the progressive regimes for the task they carry out, on behalf
of so many. It may also be that the local bridgehead elites are

keen to reap the last benefits before their regimes crumble
into socialist, populist or whatever the future will bring
regimes. (43)

What is the correct approach: to start with the informal
or with the formal system, using the twelve approaches of
countervailing power? The answer seems to have to be in terms
of both, and the informal system is more important, the formal
system more feasible. *Small steps in the former, big steps
in the latter!* For instance, why not already now establish the
Law of the Sea section of the Third World Secretariat, having
it ready, working out what cannot be worked out except· in a
very watered-down form at the world level? After all, the
Third World borders on a considerable portion of the world
oceans. And then the small steps; an occasional warning against
a superpower warship, a refusal to accept the notion that it
should somehow be treated like a sacred cow.

As mentioned many times, the system offers many opportunities. It is not so monolithic as it may look: there are
cracks, there are points of attack, there are levers - for
those who want to make use of them.

NOTES AND REFERENCES

(1)   Thus, I am deliberately using Newton's three laws as a
heuristic for thinking about power. When things remain the same
it is not because there is no power but because power is balanced; when they change it is because there is imbalance, and
that *actio* provokes a *reactio*. Maybe even some good social interpretation could be given to the concept of 'mass' in mechan-
ics, the level of inertia, meaning that for a given force (F)
the rate of change (a) is inversely proportionate to the mass
(m) - $F = ma$?
(2)   To what extent these ties are operative is another matter.
Many Third World elites seem to be very callous about the plight
of their compatriots in the countryside, and people in the First
World at least equally callous about Third World peasantry - far
away, in geographical and social terms; unable to exercise
political pressure through national institutions, and hardly
even through international organizations.
(3)   This type of analysis is almost totally absent from such
well known 'world models' as *Limits to Growth* (1972), *Mankind
at the Turning Point* (1974) and *Reshaping the International
Order* (1976). It is also generally absent from the essays contained in A.J.Dolman and J.van Ettinger (eds.), *Partners in
Tomorrow; Strategies for a New International Order,* Sunrise
Books, New York, 1978. It is actually also absent from the
Bariloche 'world model' *Catastrophe or New Society* (1976). One

may speculate on why: perhaps the expertise made use of is that of the economist, unaccustomed to think in terms of manifest and latent power systems - although the economic system is both conditioned by, and itself a way of generating, power at work. The other explanation is, of course, some kind of gentleman's agreement: 'we know there are power differentials and that power matters but let us try to get around it by working toward an understanding and a consensus on other matters, perhaps more technical, including images of future world orders. Let us then hope that there is something like the power of conviction, that out of this may grow a commitment that will move the (power) mountains'. There are those who see this as pious thinking and remain sceptical of the intention and also capability of a power structure to dissolve itself at the instigation of such gentle pushes. I am rather inclined to share that view.

(4) For another analysis along such lines, see Johan Galtung, *A Structural Theory of Revolution*, Rotterdam University Press, Rotterdam, 1974; also in *Essays in Peace Research*, Vol. III, Ejlers, Copenhagen, 1978, pp. 268-314, particularly p. 280.

(5). For more on these perspectives, see Johan Galtung, *The True Worlds: A Transnational Perspective*, Free Press, New York, 1980, chapter 2, particularly 2.1.

(6) Institutionalization and internalization processes are major subject matters of sociology and psychology respectively, as are the opposite processes: de-institutionalization and externalization.

(7) For an analysis of this, see Johan Galtung, 'A structural theory of imperialism', *Essays in Peace Research*, Vol. IV, ch. 13, Ejlers, Copenhagen, 1978.

(8) But this also works the other way: the powerful on the way down is despised by his accolytes, and wakes up to discover that his friends have become scarce.

(9) This, of course, is some of the power basis of the smaller Western countries in Northern Europe, and of Canada.

(10) For more details see the work referred to in footnote 4, or 'A structural theory of aggression', ibid., pp. 105-132.

(11) The circular and cumulative causation implicit in this principle is consistently used in Immanuel Wallerstein's brilliant *The Modern World System*, Academic Press, New York, 1974.

(12) One may think of the socialist powers: both the Soviet Union and China have tried to create their own systems; in the case of the former with the same structure as the Aeroflot world map - subtracting some obvious routes to Western capitals.

(13) This is explored in detail in the work referred to in footnote 5 above, in chapters 6, 'The territorial system' and 7, 'The non-territorial system'.

(14) That decisions are made at regular intervals means that decision-making is institutionalized, not that the decisions

(e.g. the distribution of sanctions) are institutionalized.
For more on that, see 'Patterns of diplomacy', *Essays in Peace
Research*, Vol. IV, ch. 3, Ejlers, Copenhagen, 1979. In the same
volume there is also an article 'Non-territorial actors: The
invisible continent' (ch. 12) with much more detail about the
non-territorial system. Also, see 'Non-territorial actors and
the problem of peace', in Saul H.Mendlovitz (ed.), *In the
Search of Peace*, New York, 1974, pp. 151-188.
(15) Apart from the work referred to in footnote 5, this is
also developed in *The European Community, a Super-power in the
Making*, Allen & Unwin, London, 1973 - translation into Danish,
Swedish, Finnish, German, Spanish, Japanese and Greek, chapter
3, 'On power in general'.
(16) Cotton and rubber may remind us of another and more human
parallel in the Japanese concept of zyu-zyutu (jiu-jitsu) -
there the analogy with the bamboo yielding to the wind, not
breaking, is often used.
(17) The title of the famous article by Geneviève Knupfer.
(18) This concept, of course, includes cognitive standards, in
other words, research, science. A critical attitude to Western
science has so far mainly come to the social sciences; for an
example see Ikenna Nzimirio, *The Crisis in the Social Sciences:
The Nigerian Situation*, Third World Forum Occasional Paper No.2,
Mexico, 1977.
(19) History abounds with cases of how people, even when con-
demned to death, awaiting their execution, refuse to submit to
the powerwielder.
(20) For more on the use of economic sanctions as a form of
power, and why it usually does not work (because it stimulates
so much countervailing power), see 'On the effects of international economic sanctions', *Essays in Peace Research*, Vol. V,
Ejlers, Copenhagen, 1979, ch. 4.
(21) The present author will never forget a remark made to him
in 1966, after having given a lecture at an institute of the
Soviet Academy of Sciences in Moscow, asking for views on the
Chinese Cultural Revolution: "You see, China has been that
little yellow child on the road to socialism, and it was our
task to show them that road. That child has now come to puberty,
a very difficult phase indeed - and the best we parents can do
is to withdraw, stand by and wait....".
(22) For a list of *Sternstunden*, please study the world calendar
of national independence days, etc. - bearing in mind that these
may be *Sternstunden* of elites, not of the masses whose plight
often is about the same before and after.
(23) Yonna Friedman has suggested (in a dialogue on future
societies at the GPID meeting in Geneva, 9-13 January 1978)
that one way of doing that would be to read newspapers less,
particularly newspapers that are centered on the power machina-
tions of the topdogs. But then reading them might also give

some useful insight into countervailing power!
(24) This is developed in considerable detail in Johan Galtung,
Peter O'Brien, Roy Preiswerk (editors), *Self-Reliance*, Georgi,
St.Saphorin, 1978.
(25) Toynbee's formula - only that he applied it to the topdogs,
to those in the center of civilization, not to the underdogs,
to the barbarians "knocking on the door ten times" (Braudel)
for instance.
(26) The Freudian Super-Ego/Id/Ego relationship, a rather complex one.
(27) They often do so very literally, ending up in Miami (Flori-
da) and the sanatoria on the Crimean peninsula.
(28) See 'Cuba: anti-imperialism and socialist development',
Essays in Peace Research, Vol. V, ch. 7.
(29) See Johan Galtung, 'Two ways of being western: Some simi-
larities between marxism and liberalism', *Papers*, Chair in Conflict and Peace Research, University of Oslo.
(30) "The government of Cambodia, which now calls itself Kampu-
chea, consists of nine people at the top, no regional organization that is discernible, and a communal structure "in the
style of the 14th century" in villages throughout the land",
Mr. Pike (a Foreign Service Officer, Washington) said. "An in-
vading force would have to take control of every village", he
added, "and such an enterprise of uncertain prospects would be
"stepping deeper into the swamp"". 'McGovern suggests raid to
oust Cambodia rulers', *International Herald Tribune*, 23 August
1978. Maybe the 14th century was not all that bad?
(31) The French-Belgian-U.S. action against the Kolwezi attack
of 1978 has stimulated work toward an African force - a force
capitalist and socialist West will no doubt try to twist to its
own purposes.
(32) The talks between Morarji Desai and Jimmy Carter are clas-
sical expressions of this contradiction.
(33) These are the most visible aspects of the New International
Economic Order so far; although it would be unfair to judge it
all by the spending patterns of the ruling sheikhs in feudal
social formations, evidently enjoying total control of the surplus generated.
(34) Intuitively it looks as if Britain (no longer 'Great') is
more able to adjust than France - but then the latter still
sings la Marseillaise whereas the former seems to prefer the
Beatles song 'Love is All You Need' to 'Rule, Britannia,
Britannia Rule the Waves' - much to the credit of the British.
(35) For an excellent presentation, see Juan Somavía, 'Can we
understand each other? The need for a New International Information Order', in Dolman, van Ettinger (eds.), op.cit., pp.
228-235.
(36) The fruitful conference is the one that is neither fragmented (the Third World can appear together), nor segmented
(there is a chance to deal with the total relationship, not

only with specific issues like 'energy'), nor marginalized
(there is parity in all parts of the conference organization).
UNCTAD comes closest to this in the present flora of international organizations.
(37) Thus, we agree entirely with Silviu Brucan in his excellent *The Dissolution of Power*, Knopf, New York, 1971: "In the
author's own view, the U.N.'s ineffectiveness stems from two
major fallacies: (a) peace and security must be safeguarded
primarily by the big powers; and (b) development, the name of
peace today, is to be promoted chiefly by the rich and advanced
nations". (p. 354).
(38) A typical example is given in 'Can the rich prosper without the progress of the poor?', by John W. Sewell, Overseas
Development Council, for the Society for International Development North-South Round-table, Rome, 18-20 May 1978: "A simple
calculation indicates that if developed countries were to grow
in the next decade at roughly the same rate as in the 1960s --
and if the U.S. share of the developing country imports were
to remain the same as in the last decade -- the developing
countries might be expected to import an additional $ 27 billion
of goods from the United States per year by 1985. Using standard projections, this increase might mean as many as two
million additional jobs in American export industries" (p. 6).
Noticing in passing that the author does not know the proper
use of the term 'American' (he interprets it to mean the United
States), this is almost incredible: maintenance of the *status
quo*, with the rationale that the poor countries should help in
providing jobs for the rich countries, and even maintain "the
U.S. share of the developing country imports".
(39) I am indebted to Peter O'Brien for pointing this out to me.
(40) As an example see a report from the Alternative Ways of
Life sub-project meeting of the Goals, Processes and Indicators
of Development Project, U.N. University (Cartigny, April 1978)
by Johan Galtung and Monica Wemegah, 'Overdevelopment and Alternative Ways of Life in Rich Countries'.
(41) And they are concerned with the same: to proceed softly so
as not to stimulate too much the powerful batteries of countervailing power.
(42) *Gracias, Fidel!* was the headline in an important Latin
American paper after the concessions made by the U.S. in the
famous Punta del Este OEA meeting in 1961. How well they used
those concessions is another, and important, matter.
(43) And here one should not underestimate the demoralizing
effect of countervailing power: it may look as if everything
is the same - goods and bads flow more or less as before - but
the power-holders/wielders/senders no longer believe in the
legitimacy of what they do. They still issue standards in the
form of moral and cognitive ideologies, they proclaim what is
right, but they no longer say/think/feel that their standards
for saying what is right are themselves necessarily right.

The Multinational Corporation and the New International Order
Stel Kefalas

INTRODUCTION

The process of establishing a New International Order
started with the 1975 Seventh Special Session's Ad Hoc Committee under the Chairmanship of Jan Pronk, the Dutch Minister
for Development Cooperation. The sixteen-day meeting of that
session reaffirmed the strong feeling of its members with respect to the following: (i) that nations can no longer ignore
the daily increasing consequences of world interdependence;
(ii) that a process has begun aiming at overcoming some of the
side disparaties existing within and between nations and dis-
tributing more equitably the world's wealth; and (iii) that
confrontation and conflict between 'developed' and 'developing'
countries is slowly given way to cooperation. The specific a-
reas of concern in the new economic order are documented in a
20-page Assembly report. In perusing this document, one gets
the impression that the world has indeed reached a crucial
turning point which calls not only for putting nations on a
more equal economic footing but also for giving them a more
equitable participation opportunity in decision-making.

The proposal for reforming the international system which
was finally endorsed by the Seventh Special Session of the
General Assembly contains specific programs regarding the following seven areas: (i) international trade; (ii) transfer of
resources for development and reforming the international monetary system; (iii) science and technology; (iv) industrialization; (v) food and agriculture; (vi) cooperation among developing countries; and (vii) restructuring the United Nations
system. (1) As can be seen from this list, the demand for reshaping the international order indeed goes beyond mere economics - although economics is at the heart of the entire propo-

sal. In short, the quest aims at "bringing about a more equitable distribution of income and wealth, social justice, efficiency of production, income security, employment creation, safeguarding the environment, and improving facilities for education, health, nutrition, housing and social welfare(which) must go hand and hand with rapid economic growth and the reduction of existing regional, sectoral, and social disparities". (2)

Is is apparent from the last paragraph that the Multinational Corporation (MNC) is at the center of the entire world reshaping scheme. Yet precious little effort has been devoted to a comparison of the compatability of the goals of an MNC with those aspirations of the new international order designers. This paper presents a brief sketch for a new MNC which will facilitate the transformation of the world into a new world.

THE ISSUES

The MNC's potential for bringing about more equitable material wealth distribution around the globe has been recognized for some time now. However, a more thorough examination of the nature and magnitude of this potential has only recently been initiated. Indeed, less than five years have passed since the U.N. Economic and Social Council, recognizing the truly holistic nature of the phenomenon, established the Group of Eminent Persons, a multinational, multidisciplinary, and multi-interest group of experts mandated with the project entitled 'The Study of the Impact of Multinational Corporations on Development and on International Relations'. (3)

The phenomenal expansion of economic activity in the First World which accompanied the first three quarters of this century has provided sufficient latitude for calculated exaggerations with respect to the positive role of the MNC as well as ample opportunity for some thorny problems to be swept under the rugs of corporate and governmental executive boardrooms. The skillfulness of these executives in shifting from pre-war 'gun-boat politics' to post-war 'Wall Street and Madison Avenue Politics', has been the subject of numerous fiction and non-fiction writers. Against this rosy background of plush red-carpeted executive suites equipped with a panoply of the latest computerized information systems, the vision of a Third World mother assembling television sets for $1 a day with which she is expected to feed her six children is a scandalous anomaly.

Nature inherently rejects anomalies. As most scientists know, few disharmonies have persisted or survived for more than a fraction of a moment in the evolutionary time clock. The corrective attempts set in motion at the beginning of this decade to effectively deal with the environmental crisis, the monetary

crisis, the energy and resources crises, the food crisis and
the world economic order crisis have now developed a degree of
momentum. It is becoming increasingly evident that the economic prosperity of the West is reaching a limit. (4)

It is the objective of this inquiry to provide a reconcep-
tualization of the role of the MNC in the process of transition from undifferentiated to organic growth. At the center of
this framework is the corporate executive of the MNC, the multinational manager. The selection of the manager as the 'client',
so to speak, is the result of the author's belief that the true
agents of change in an organization are the people who devote
most of their lives to planning, organizing, executing, and
controlling the goals and operations of their organizations.
The best-conceived intellectual and governmental schemes may be
severely hampered and even nullified if the men and women who
run the main logistic systems of this organizations-dominated
globe perceive them as threats to their drive for self-actuali-
zation. Therefore, by appealing directly to these managers much-
needed changes can more readily and more successfully be effect-
ed than by attempting to by-pass them and ultimately, to coerce
them.

THE EVOLUTION OF THE MULTINATIONAL
CORPORATION: AN OVERVIEW

The evolution of international business began with the
exchange of goods among nations (i.e. with international trade).
Its second stage developed with the partial exchange of physical corporate assets of one company for the capital assets of
another (i.e. portfolio investment). It evolved into the third
stage with the acquisition and takeover of an entire company
and the establishment of productive facilities owned and managed by a firm with economic interests in more than one country
(i.e. direct foreign investment). It finally reached its apex,
its *homo sapiens*, so to speak, with the multinational corporation which is involved in international trade, portfolio and
direct foreign investment.

The literature on the subject of multinational corporations is reaching gigantic proportions. In general, it incorporates four main areas of investigation: (i) the definition of
a multinational corporation; (ii) the various aspects of the
decision to invest abroad; (iii) the growth of the multinational corporation; and (iv) the impact of the multinational corporation's activities upon the firm itself, upon the home and
host country, and upon world economic and political welfare,
stability and peace.

There exists little general consensus in the literature
with respect to any of the above issues. However, progress is

underway The definitional problem is close to being solved.(5)
The various aspects of the decision to invest abroad, despite
their enormous complexity, have been lent considerable clarity.
(6) The phenomenal growth of the MNC has become a major area of
investigation for the UN, OECD and other institutions.(7) And
finally, the most far-reaching problem, the impact of the mul-
tinantional corporation's operations on itself and on its home
and host countries, has been allotted the lion's share of the
research. (8)

   Multinational corporations can perhaps best be defined as
business enterprises which are engaged in all activities of
international business, namely in international trade, portfo-
lio and direct foreign investment. As such, they share certain
common characteristics: they are large, usually $1 billion in
annual sales; they have numerous affiliates in many countries;
they do most of their business inside the First World; (9) and
they represent a threat which is perceived as both potential
and real to purely national companies, to the labor of the host
countries, (10) to the labor of home countries, (11) and to the
international economic order.. (12) Finally, they rank very high
in public distrust in both investing and recipient countries.
(13)

   The present author is inclined to believe that the MNC has
exhibited a remarkable ability to mobilize resources over much
of the globe and to create wealth. In doing so, it has developed into a species that has begun to show signs of 'tumerous
overgrowth', which could indeed bring about its extinction. If
the MNC manager persists in his commitment to feeding the overgrowth process, this undertaking will lead to the MNC's deterioration and demise. It is a cardinal requisite of sound management that managers devise conceptual frameworks and operating
procedures which will enable the corporation to adapt to changing environmental conditions. It is imperative that the MNC
manager realize that the policies and procedures which have enabled the MNC to survive and thrive thus far provide absolutely no guarantee that they will do so in the near future.

                    THREE VIEWPOINTS ON THE MNC AND ITS
                      ROLE IN THE NEW WORLD ORDER

   Few issues, if any, have been more controversial than the
role of the multinational corporation in domestic and international affairs. As with most controversies, the arguments gra-
vitate along the two ends of a continuum as indicated in Figure
1. At the extreme left hand side of that continuum one finds
the so-called optimists. These are scholars and practitioners
who conceive of the MNC as the best thing to have come along
since the industrial revolution. They envision the MNC as play-

Figure 1: Three Viewpoints Regarding the MNC's Role and its Future

	Optimists — Past →	Pessimists — Present →	Meliorists — Future →
Nature	The MNC is the most creative international institution representing man's highest accomplishment in the art and science of organizing material and human resources.	The MNC is the most destructive mechanism ever invented by humans. Its current structure and function represent man's worst accomplishment.	The MNC has a rather high potential for becoming a very useful vehicle for improvements in the human condition all over the world.
Role	The MNC must and will play a more active and more visible role in domestic and international human affairs. There is basically nothing incompatible between the nation-state's plan and the MNC's objectives and specific goals.	Since the MNC's existence in an area undermines the power of the nation-state to maintain a political and economic stability within its sovereign territory, the MNC's role must diminish.	By its very existence the MNC will continue to play a very important role in human development. This is an organization-dominated and dependent world which will continue to be more so.
The MNC and The World Order	The Third World's demand for a 'new' economic order seems to be justified but must be accomplished by 'putting their own house in order' and not by handouts from the MNCs. They must create an environment conducive to more freedom for the MNC, not less. Those Third World nations that have made progress toward industrialization have done so through the offices of the MNCs.	The Third World's demand for a new economic order is not only legitimate and justified but it is a manifestation of a final coming to the end of the economic imperialism which has through years of exploitation of the poor by the rich created a yawning gap in economic development between the North and the South. The new order will give the South its just share.	The Third World's demand for a new economic order reflects certain changes in man's conception of the earth's carrying capacities and man's purpose on this provisional life. Specifically, man is becoming more and more 'limits-conscious' and at the same time man is adapting a 'long range' perspective. As a result, people attempt to prolong the use of their finite resources.
Future Proposals	Leave the MNC alone to evolve into a more effective and efficient wealth creating mechanism. Do not kill the Golden Goose. Both the host and the home country will depend on the MNC to lay the golden eggs of a peaceful, prosperous and viable world. The invisible hand is still alive and well and has been doing an excellent job. There are more people today living better than the kings of the yester-year.	The MNCs must be controlled. Their objectives and goals are basically incompatible with the aims of the nation-state (particularly the Third World). The invisible hand does not exist. There are multinational managers creating a world which is unbearable for those who work for them and have to live with them. Nothing short of an international, supra-governmental agency will suffice.	The MNC must change drastically, in terms of its goals and objectives and its structure. Although some degree of institutionalization of this change appears necessary it is by no means sufficient. Both the MNC and the nation-state are complex and are confronted with diverse problems. There must be changes in the MNC's policies and procedures.

ing an ever more active role in both domestic and international affairs and see no conflicts or incongruencies between the
state's objectives and the MNC goals. In addition they consider the newly publicized demands of the Third World for a New
International Economic Order as highly unrealistic, unfair and
extremely naive. As the *Wall Street Journal* put it in an editorial entitled 'A Word to the Third World': "Don't expect the
US to serve you up prosperity and don't think you can get it
through extortion". Along the same lines, the *Journal* further
warned: "And if the Third World countries want to be rich like
us, they might try doing a few things our way". (14)

   This rather polemical attitude of the particular organ
of modern capitalism is not the exception at all. Rather, one
could venture to say that it appears to be the prevailing opinion of the contemporary executive. It should be no surprise
to learn that the recommendation by this side of the continuum will read as is done: namely there is nothing wrong with
the way things are... what's good for the MNC is good for you.
No more controls, no more policing, and please, not another
United Nations; enough is enough.

   At the other extreme end of the continuum one finds those
scholars and some ex-practitioners who would argue that apart
from dealing with man's most elegant and useful creation of
the 20th century, as Mr. Moynihan baptized the MNC, we are
faced with one of the most dangerous beasts since the Hydra.
Not only does there appear to be nothing congruous between the
MNC and the nation-state but as a rule the MNC is keeping the
nation-state concept and the nation-state itself at 'bay', as
one of the most best-known scholars from an equally well-known
business school has put it.

   These pessimists consider the demands of the Third World
as very just, and as a justice long overdue. Based upon this
philosophy regarding the role of the MNC and the new world realities and knowing that most, if not all agents of private
profit-motivated enterprises will not do anything until and
unless they 'have to', they recommend the creation of super-
and supra-national agencies which will control the MNC. This
supra-national agency will domicile in a less developed country and will be under the general aegis and jurisdiction of
the United Nations.

   As is always the case, when an issue has been polarized
into two extreme interpretations, the most acceptable interpretation will be somewhere in the middle. This point will
usually be more or less around the center and will represent
a synthesis in the Hegelian sense or a compromise in common
language parlance. This 'middle of the road' kind of perception of the interface between a nation-state and a MNC is a
composite of the least controversial point of argument from
both camps. In that fashion this third viewpoint may be interpreted as representing the maximum amount of agreement over

the issue.

In Figure 1, this third viewpoint is given the name 'me-
liorists', and is chosen to include those people who subscribe
to meliorism, i.e. the doctrine, intermediate between optimism
and pessimism, which affirms that the world can be made better
by human effort. However, as can be seen from the figure the
meliorist viewpoint is not positioned between the two extremes
of the pessimists and the optimists for it does not represent
a synthesis or compromise. In other words, the main theses of
this viewpoint do not constitute the best of both worlds in
an effort to avoid a collapse of an on-going negotiation or to
forestall an oncoming battle. This viewpoint represents recognition and acceptance of the evolutionary changes which have
taken place over the last quarter of a century regarding the
relationships between man and man, and man and nature.

Another interpretation of the relationship among these
viewpoints which can be made by looking at Figure 1 is that
these three viewpoints represent the three stages in the process of man's organizationability, i.e. man's ability to combine human and material resources for the purpose of satisfying man's needs and desires. At the beginning of this human
endeavor there was a more or less perfect and indisputable
congruency between the aims of the corporation and the needs
of human society. This stage, which has been referred to elsewhere as the Age of Congruency, is characteristically described by the adage 'what is good for the company is good for society', to paraphrase the First Secretary of the Treasury of
the USA. During that stage it was obvious to almost everyone
concerned that the butcher, the baker and the candlestick maker
were superior to the common housewife. Soon it became equally
obvious that the butcher, the baker and the candlestick maker
were far inferior to the General Foods and Baking Company, and
General Electric Light giants.

By the middle of the current century, some people, driven
either by their unselfish intellectual curiosity or by selfish
reasons, began to suspect that this human cooperative effort,
the corporation, had developed a mind of its own and that it
seemed to be a bit more ambitious than originally envisioned
by society. Some of the more industrious scholars and investi-
gators even proved that the new corporation, aside from being
useful to society, was getting to the point of becoming exceedingly dangerous. Soon these voices overcame the pandemonium of
the machines and horns of the industrial establishments and
made their way to the capitols where legislators began to edu-
cate themselves in the art and science of management. With the
help of interest groups this education process was indeed very
rapid. In no time society experienced the dawn of the 'Age of
Regulation'. These regulations reflected the scepticism and
even the pessimism regarding the corporations' true intentions
and actual practices. The adage "what's good for the corpora-

tion is good for society", which dominated most textbooks in economics and management, seemed to be replaced with a new lengthened one reading "what's good for the corporation is good for society as long as the Federal Agency or ministry does not prove otherwise".

It is now becoming increasingly, and one could add, painfully clear that neither of the two aforementioned viewpoints reflect contemporary reality as it unfolds and determines to some extent the most likely near future. The optimist's viewpoint which centers on and depends on the basic premise of the perfect and indisputable congruency between societal and corporate needs, intentions desires and practices is definitely outmoded and could not be substantiated by any empirical evidence, no matter how sympathetically one is looking at it and packaging it. The pessimist's philosophy which rests on the premise of complete incongruency between societal and corporate intentions and which assumes malignancy in corporate intentions which can be cured through a heavy dose of regulatory medicine is equally naive. One really wishes that reality were that simple but it is not. This is indeed the Age of Uncertainty - uncertainty which is created by the numerous discontinuities in the present world.

The meliorist believes that the MNC is indeed a potentially useful instrument and must play a definite role in the orchestration of the new world order. The meliorist's point of departure is that an unattended Golden Goose will lay too few eggs in too few or too many places. Some of these might turn out to be 'not golden' to say the least. By the same token, a closely attended Golden Goose might not lay any eggs at all. What is recommended is a new MNC. A MNC whose objective, goals and practices will take into consideration the new world realities. Although this concern for the new world realities by the manager of the MNC might require a certain degree of external institutionalization, (i.e. the creation of supranational organizations or institutions which will induce, influence or coerce the manager) that alone does not constitute a sufficient condition, albeit a necessary one, for the kind of MNC transformation the meliorist envisages. For that transformation to take place the external institutionalization must be supplemented with an internal i.e. corporate change in the company's *Weltanschauung*, policies, strategies, objectives and operations principles. Only when the manager of an MNC has been convinced that the new long-range planning and day-to-day operations must be in tune with the changes in the external business environment (i.e. the political, scientific, economic, social and ecological conditions) can the MNC become a useful vehicle in a new world order.

Although the majority of the meliorist's camp is composed of Third World scholars, there are a number of First World intellectuals and, most important, practicing high executives of

MNCs becoming more and more visible. Space does not allow us
to go into great detail on this change in the mood of the
First World toward a meliorist attitude regarding the role of
the MNC in a new world order. We therefore confine ourselves
to a few examples. In addition to the academic recommendations
for a minimum of external institutionalization along the lines
of: (a) an international treaty suggested by scholars of the
stature of Charles Kindelberger, Eugene Rostow and Paul Gold-
berg; (b) an international charter as proposed by professors
Kindelberger and former Under-Secretary of State George Ball;
and (c) procedures, codes and international institutions, proposed by Professor Joseph Nye, one finds here and there hints
offered by active high-ranking executives of some of the largest MNCs in the world.

In 1976, the prestigious *Christian Science Monitor* published a series of thirteen articles condensed from a report
entitled *Corporate Citizenship in the Global Community*, published by the International Management and Development Institute (IMDI). In these articles under the title 'The Global
Corporation: Views from the Top', one finds the opinions of
such corporate figures as Henry Ford II, Chairman of Ford Motor Company, Reginald H. Jones, Chairman and COE of General
Electric Corporations, F. Perry Wilson, of Union Carbide Corporation, E.M. deWindt, from Eaton Corporation, Walter B.
Wriston, from Citibank, Donald M. Kendall from Pepsi Cola
along with the heads of the UN, the International Chamber of
Commerce, the US Secretary of the Treasury William Simon, and
other influential corporate and governmental leaders. Although
the main messages offered to the public by these corporate and
public giants are still along the conventional lines of the
'free enterprise flag wavers' one finds rather overt and clear
hints at the graveness of the situation the MNC currently faces
and the seriousness of the future survival of the contemporary
MNC.

Most of the hints to be found in contemporary corporate
speech giving and public relations releases seem to relate
either explicitly or implicitly to certain discontinuities reflecting certain major changes in the underlying social and
cultural reality which call for a "reordering and reexaming of
corporate priorities, policies and operating practices", (16)
to paraphrase Union Carbide's Chief Executive Mr. F. Perry
Wilson. It was Peter Drucker who over then years ago pointed
to these discontinuities as a "build up of tension between a
new underlying reality and the surface of established institution and customary behavior that still conform to yesterday's
underlying realities. (These) discontinuities tend to develop
gradually and quietly and are rarely perceived until they have
resulted in the volcanic eruption or the earthquake". (17)

In this paper we will zero in on four major discontinuities which seem to threaten the MNC manager's conventional mo-

del of the relationship between the MNC and the world around
it. Subsequently we will offer a meliorist's proposal for the
drawing of a new blueprint for the future MNC. This modest
proposal calls for a reexamination and a rewriting of the MNC's
corporate philosophy on the one hand and a redefinition and
reformulation of ten important operating practices or principles.

THE NEW WORLD REALITIES:
SAME GAMES, NEW RULES

A rudimentary review of the literature on what has come
to be known as 'world problematique' reveals that the contemporary world picture is being completed by the emergence of certain new diverging and converging phenomena, which may be considered as major discontinuities some of which are the following:

(i)   Globalism - Nationalism
(ii) Abundance - Scarcity
(iii) Development - Survival
(iv) Growth - No-Growth

It should be noted at the outset that the concepts on the
lefthand side of the continua (i.e. Globalism, Abundance, Development and Growth) have traditionally been regarded as typical characteristics of the so-called Developed or First World,
while those at the other end of the continua (i.e. Nationalism,
Scarcity, Development and No-Growth) have generally been recognized as the attributes of the Underdeveloped or Third World.
Today, however, it appears that although the indication of a
180 degree turnaround is still in its embryonic stage, at
least a fairly discernible movement in that direction has been
set in motion. This section presents a brief overview of this
moment.

Globalism   -   Nationalism

The remarkable developments in transportation and communication which followed the end of World War II have enabled its
pioneers and main beneficiaries to look at the world as their
'oyster'. By the same token, these same forces caused the
Third World to become more aware of the pearl in this oyster
and to demand its fair share. Thus, during the last thirty
years or so some hundred small and divided 'sovereign' nations
have been fighting the united economic world action of the

First World. More frequently than not, these smaller, fragmented nation-states found themselves in a dilemma where, in order
to provide for some degree of economic welfare for their citi-
zenry, they were faced with 'Faustian bargains' in which their
political and social integrity was at stake. Thus, the issue
of territorial and political sovereignty ultimately had to bow
to the need for economic development and sufficiency.

It gradually became obvious to the intellectual forces of
the Third World that the strategy of individualistic nationalism was an ill-suited instrument for dealing with the extensive economic and, to some extent, political coordination of
the First World. Thus, the 'sixties witnessed the emulation of
First World strategies of regional economic and potentially
political integration by Third World nations. (18)

The drastic changes in the rules of the game of world e-
conomic order have caused confusion in the First World. Reactions have ranged from mild warnings by high political representatives, to attempts to create counter-organizations such
as the Organization of Petroleum Importing Countries (OPIC)
aimed at 'busting the oil cartel', to such unthinkable strategies as the use of military force against the new villains who
want to 'destroy the West'. (19) While some First World observers consider these reactions not only justified, but
healthy, others, primarily from the Third World, interpret
them as the beginning of a new era of nationalism, capitalis-
tic style.

Abundance - Scarcity

The First World's opulence with respect to natural resources and man-made products in contrast to the scarcity that
has plagued the Third World has been vividly documented over
the last two decades. It therefore hardly seems necessary to
reiterate the voluminous mass of statistics and their inferences with respect to the affluence of the 'North' and the
misery of the 'South'. What does seem appropriate, however, is
a brief overview of the swing of the pendulum from abundance
to scarcity inside the First World and from scarcity to abundance in parts of the Third World.

Although the concepts of abundance and scarcity allude
to physical dimensions of resources it is obvious that what is
of importance is their potential for utilization. It is this
potential, which is essentially economic, technological and
social in its dimensions, that, up to a point, determines resource use, and therefore its utility. Thus, the Third World,
despite its physical abundance of resources is still burdened
with scarcities. On the other hand, Japan and most of Western
Europe represent examples of abundance in spite of their lack

of resources.

It now appears that due to certain economic, technological, social and ecological developments in both the First and Third Worlds, the physical existence of resources has become the invariant against which economic, technological and social availability must be measured. By using this new, pragmatic measure, one can see that the scale seems to be tilting in favor of the Third World. Although most US Government officials and other forecasters foresee no real possibility that the Third World will be as succesful in experimenting with the implementation of their power as the few favored oil countries, (20) others view this as a treacherous attitude. (21)

While the increasing organization of the Third World countries into materials cartels may not be as successful as OPEC which deals with a very unique resource extensively used and having low substitutability, and while Bergsten's prophecy of "cannibalistic competition" among the rich for the resources of the poor may indeed not materialize, the inescapable fact is that traditional and historical concepts of abundance and scarcity are just that - history.

                    Development   -   Survival

It has long been suspected, argued, and documented that the First World with its consumption-oriented societies has 'overshot' its development process. At the same time, the chronic inability of some 80% of the world's population to provide the bare minimum requirements for physical survival has been colorfully and dreadfully brought into the homes of most First World inhabitants via satellite by television reports on the massive starvations which followed the devasting droughts in Asia and Africa. Suddenly the ecstatic, exaggerated Third World governmental reports on the phenomenal growth rates of their countries were darkened by the blackness of the corpses resulting from what some blinded observers still call a 'natural' disaster.

Paul and Anne Ehrlich in *The End of Affluence* redefined the terms 'developed' and 'underdeveloped' in a way which sheds considerable light on the dark figures of the quantitative statistics of growth rates and per capita income. Their main criterion for this definition is 'per capita resource demand' rather than the per capita income and growth rate employed in conventional approaches. By using this new yardstick, the Third World is still underdeveloped while the First World become 'overdeveloped', to the extent that population levels and per capita resource demands are so high that it will be impossible to maintain their present living standards without making exorbitant demand on global resources and ecosystems. (22)

Growth   -   No-Growth

Perhaps no other phenomenon has caught the 'North' by
such surprise as the downturn trend in economic activity in
recent years. After some twenty years of remarkable performance, the weighted average growth rate of the twenty-four industrialized countries reached zero in 1974 after a record of
6.2% in 1973 and ended up around -2% by the end of 1975. (23)
Whether this trend resulted from decreasing population growth,
shortages of raw materials and energy, market saturation, or
just the normal "aftermath of a go-go decade"(24), the subject has been analyzed by a number of Europeans and Americans,
who, "for some reason or another, found fault with the prevailing economic and political orthodoxies which, in their view
relied too heavily on the concept of continued growth". (25)
    In the Third World the issue of growth vs. non-growth has
been resolved. In addition to considering growth desirable and
necessary, it is looked upon as a necessary and sufficient condition for economic development and survival. The prospects
for growth in the Third World depend, however, on the impact
of trends in the First World (a combination of declining production, consumption and high inflation and unemployment) upon
the development plans of the diverse regions of the Third
World. This World, which used to be considered a homogeneous
region has recently been divised into three distinct areas:
(1) the 'Least Developed' Countries(LLDCs): those with no resources, investments and no exports; (ii) the Middle-Income
Developing Countries: those with some exports and considerable
foreign investment; and (iii) the Oil-Exporting 'Developing'
Countries: those with a massive inflow of foreign exchange due
to increased revenues from oil. (26)
    In summary, a brief survey of the new world realities
points to a number of discontinuities: (i) *World outlook*: some
First World countries are reversing their world outlook from
globalism toward regionalism and even nationalism while most
of the Third World is moving away from nationalism toward regionalism aimed at a united front which encompasses some 80%
of the world's population. At the same time, however, there is
an encouraging trend toward First and Third World cooperation
as well as between the First and Second World; (27) (ii) *Existence of resources and material wealth*: the physical existence
of resources is becoming a more decisive criterion for determining their availability. According to this criterion most of
the First World will be resource-poor; (iii) *Economic development*: there is strong suspicion and considerable documented
evidence that the First World has reached its limits to growth
whereas most of the Third World needs and would substantially
benefit from economic growth.

TOWARD A TRANSFORMATION

The transformation of the MNC requires the abandonment of
the model of managerial philosophy and practice so successfully used over the last three quarters of the century. This model, which is referred to here as the Surrogate, has outlived
its usefulness and must therfore be replaced by a new model
which better reflects the realities which a MNC manager faces.

The Surrogate: An Obsolete Model
of MNC Management

The majority of managers who run today's MNCs were educated by institutions which looked at the world through 19th century spectacles. As a result of this education the manager
formed a conceptual framework of his organization and its societal role which conceived of it as a closed system capable
of generating changes in its environment while maintaining complete immunity from any demands emanating from the changes it
generated.
The contemporary MNC manager's framework could be much
more easily characterized as a surrogate than as a true model
of reality. Its logic rests on four pillars - all of which are
beginning to develop severe cracks. The first pillar is that
of the Myth of Other Stolidity or Padsnappery. This myth asserts that the MNC manager knows best what the most appropriate
strategy of wealth creation is and that the 'others' will never
catch on to the sophisticated managerial methods and techniques.
The second pillar of conventional MNC wisdom represents the manager's view of the world: the Myth of Divisibility, Isolation
and One-Way Dependence which lures the manager into conceiving
the world as a conglomeration of divisible parts whose existence depends on the MNC's helping hand. Machiavellianism or
the Myth of Other Manipulation, the third pillar, has very recently developed the most severe cracks as a result of the US
Congress' investigations of MNCs. Finally, the last pillar,
Allomentry or the Myth of Continuous and Undifferentiated
Giantism, is literally crumbling as demonstrated by the latest
incidents of forced disinvestment, nationalizations, expropri-
ations, and outright confiscations by midget nations of property owned by the giants.
In summary, the MNC manager who perceives the world from
the distorted viewpoint of the Surrogate considers the activities, philosophies and values of others as misguided, conceiv-
es of others as being extremely slow in learning, and views
the world as divided by political ideologies and legal systems
which are in need of MNC manipulation. Under these conditions
he falsely believes that MNCs can grow indefinitely along a

path of undifferentiated growth characterized by replications
of some 'ideal' form of organization.

The Premises

Before going into the basic steps of the MNC transformation process, the following statements seem essential:

(i) The MNCs are real, i.e. they are affecting people's daily
lives and future plans. For this reason it will be advisable
when thinking of and talking about them to do so in real terms
rather than in terms of the surrogates of money and power. One
is able to form a better understanding of the role of the MNC
in one's own life if one thinks of the quantities of resources
consumed by the MNCs in their wealth-creation processes, the
number of people who derive a livelihood by participation in
the MNCs' activities, and the amount of output they generate,
both useful and wasteful, and so on.
(ii) The presence of a MNC in a country is frequently a necessary condition for the country's economic development, but it
is by no means sufficient. By the same token, the absence of a
MNC from a country, which can come about as a result of expro-
priation of existing facilities or as a result of making difficult new entries, will not necessarily lead to a country's
economic and social development through native business concerns. An excellent case in point is France. During the De
Gaulle era and the zenith of Servan-Schreiber's *American Challenge*, MNCs - and primarily US-based MNCs - left France because
of the "unfavorable and hostile climate". Today France is attempting to generate a return of US investments through adver-
tisements in *Business Week*. In one such advertisement the
chairmen of DATAR began his invitation with "Dear American
Friends". The same method has been used by Sweden's young mo-
narch King Carl XVI. (28)
(iii)The post-WW II era has been characterized by a tremendous
drive for economic activity all over the globe and a relatively stable political climate. The MNCs have played an important
role in this economic activity. As a result, their agents, the
people at the top and the bottom of the organizational hierarchy, have gained a blend of knowledge and experience of the
intricate process of combining human and physical resources
and transforming them into marketable products and services
which is unprecedented by any measurement. It is, therefore,
to the benefit of humanity to evaluate this vast storehouse of
knowledge and keep what can be used and what can be improved
upon.
(iv) If the goal of 'a new economic order' is to be accomplished, a rather complex and sophisticated process of need-assess-
ment and need-fulfillment via a more equitable distribution of

material wealth must be set in motion. History teaches that
at some point in this process, at the implementation stage unfortunately, international business concerns are brought aboard.
It should, therefore, be self-evident that dismantlement or
break-up of the MNCs is neither feasible nor desirable. It is
due to this stark reality that the strategy of transformation
through the enhancement of the MNC manager's understanding of
his complex role and his responsibility to societies well beyond the 'bottom line consideration' appears the only viable and
realistic alternative.

(v)   Finally, the MNC transformation contemplated here can only
be realized *mutatis mutandis* and *pari passu* with a larger transformation of the world's societies. In addition, the desire for
this transformation must be incorporated into the philosophies,
policies and standard operating procedures of the corporate establishment. There can be no transformation of any sort if the
MNC manager always perceives his or her role as being constantly caught between the Scylla of societal demand and the Charybdis of corporate orders.

In summary, the vision which underlies the strategy for
transformation of a MNC is a rather optimistic one. On the one
hand, the world is viewed as pursuing the goals of (a) world
security; (b) increasing world agricultural productivity; (c)
stabilizing the world's population; (d) sustainable economic
growth; (e) equitable conditions for development; and (f) world
monetary stability; and on the other, it sees the MNC as possessing a great potential for facilitating the accomplishment
of these goals. For the latter to materialize, two conditions
must be satisfied: (a) the MNC must be recognized as a full-
fledged partner in the new world order design along with intel-
lectually, nationally and internationally organized bodies
(this true and equitable participation should minimize the
probability of resistance to change and the accompanying back-
lash that has characterized past attempts to regulate business
enterprises at national and international levels); and (b) the
MNC corporate commonwealth must engage in a process of 'self-
assessment' for the purpose of bringing its philosophies, policies and operating procedures in line with the new realities of
an interdependent world of diverse but unified societies.

Philosophical Principles

Managers manage their corporate affairs through models. The
process of abstracting from reality pertinent events and organizing them into a coherent and manageable whole (modeling) is
governed by the modeler's view of the world. By choosing from
among many alternative models and by experimenting with a few
of them (simulation) the manager formulates the company's main
policies which then become, as they are diffused throughout the

organization, specific objectives, goals and standards or targets for specific individuals. It is then obvious that the
corporate philosophy has a much larger impact upon the individual corporate member's behavior than is commonly believed.
The new managerial philosophy consists of the following four
principles:

(i)   *Adaptation and Learning*

     All organic systems, in an effort to reach and maintain
a goal, engage in behavior which is referred to as 'trial and
error'. The chief characteristic of that behavior is that the
number of trials is with time reduced by a process of the communication of feedback information containing a measure of the
deviation between the goal and actual performance. Through
this information the system eventually minimizes the number of
trials required. This process is called learning and adaptation.
     Contrary to prevalent popular belief, Arabs, Africans and
Asians can just as easily learn to be machine operators, computer programmers and operators as can Americans, Europeans
and the Japanese. Professor Vernon dispelled this misguided
example of extreme stolidity with respect to the Third World
as follows: "The cultivation and sale of coffee may have seemed a formidable undertaking to the Yucatecan farmer of 1900;
the management of a sugar plantation may have appeared beyond
the reach of the Cuban poor of 1950. But these pursuits eventually lost their occult quality". (29) The day is not too far
off when these 'hopeless cases' may surpass the managerial ingenuity of the managers of the First World.
     It is imperative that the MNC manager realize that in any
given group of his 'subordinates' in other countries, some
'Sorcerer's Apprentice' may rise up. In contemplating the design and strategies of his organization, the MNC manager should
keep in mind that the collective intelligence of the organization must detect learning potentials and attempt to implement
them rather than to supress them. Any attempt at suppression
will conflict with the basic nature of the organic system.

(ii) *Holism*

     Organic systems are wholes with irreducible properties.
The divided world of the 'fifties and 'sixties represented a
natural phase in human economic and socio-cultural evolution
that seems to be reaching an end. The number of trials and er-
rors have begun to diminish with each new UN conference and
other world conferences. The 'wholes' created by the formation
of the Group of 77, OPEC, and other regional cartels, are exhi-
biting a tremendous capability for learning and a desire to
preserve their wholeness. The *division* of the past is today an

instrument which has lost its effectiveness.

The manager is again advised to look at his organization and especially at himself as a Janus-faced entity who, looking inward, sees himself as a selfcontained unique whole, looking outward as a dependent part. Just as his company cannot be divided into arbitrary parts without destroying its effectiveness, likewise, the world of today must be viewed in the same manner. The holistic properties of the MNC's environment can be expected to strengthen rather than to weaken in the near future. Managerial philosophy, if it is to remain relevant in the future, must accept this trend as a natural property of systemic behavior rather than as an anomaly.

(iii) *Cooperation*

As was indicated earlier, the traditional antagonism among the many nations of the Third World has been replaced with a strong desire for cooperative behavior. What is more significant, however, is the cooperative mood shared by some of the First World nations and the entire Third World. Of particular importance is the cooperative agreement between the EEC countries and the Third World known as the Lomé Convention. This convention links together some 250 million Europeans with close to 270 million people from the Third World and gives 46 ACP countries (37 African, 6 Caribbean and 3 Pacific nations) duty-free non-reciprocal access to Common Market nations for all manufacturing products and most of their farm exports. In addition, the Convention has established a fund of $450 million, spread over five years, to compensate the exporters of 14 important commodities if prices of their exports fall 2.5 percent below the average price based on the previous three years. This plan for export stabilization, dubbed 'Stabex', along with free access to the nine-member EEC countries is the greatest indication of cooperation between the developed and the underdeveloped worlds, for it has provided a degree of security for the supplies of the former and benefits for the latter. (30)

This represents a first step toward world cooperation that no manager, and especially no multinational manager, can afford to ignore. Since he or she will be asked to implement these schemes, it is important that the organizational structure and strategies he or she devises be cooperative in nature.

(iv) *Organic Growth*

The manager will be greatly tempted to endeavor to repeat the allometric growth pattern with which he is so familiar from his past experience of the last two decades. This temptation will be intensified even more by the similar eagerness of the leaders of the Third World, anxious to recover and to make up for lost opportunities. However, this temptation must be resist-

ed by all means. The sirens of the Third World Titan, seduc-
tively calling for exponential growth, must be resisted by the
Odysseus of the MNC, for he must realize that the success of
his endeavors will be endangered, and ultimately terminated,
should he allow himself to succumb to them. There are several
pragmatic reasons why this would happen. For one thing, there
is increased awareness in the world that our resources are
finite, and this awareness is accompanied by the desire to
prolong their existence. For another, the continued exponential growth of economic activity hinges upon substantial growth
in the developed world which will absorb any excess production.
With the downward trend in the First World, the odds that an
African refrigerator will find a place under the saturated sun
of the West are very small.

Nevertheless, there is some room for increasing economic
activity in the Third World, but, as it will be seen immediately, this economic activity will be anything but exponential.
Thus, the manager is strongly advised to cultivate an intellectual commitment toward abandoning the exponential growth
machine and creating, instead, an organic and thoughtful growth
process which will adapt the systemic requirements and dictates
of the finite ecosystem earth.

                          Operational Principles

The above philosophical principles provide an outline of
the new MNC manger's thinking horizon. They constitute, in
other words, the four major pillars of a new managerial ethos.
In addition to that, however, the manager needs some practical
guidelines which will enable him to carry out his long-range
planning and day-to-day operations. The last section of this
inquiry is devoted to outlining the operational principles
which the author considers most important.

(i) *Investment Principle*

The need for corporate growth stands out as being the most
important criterion in deciding to 'go international'. Once
this need has been established then the decision as to whether
and where to invest usually depends on the rate of return on
investment. Thus, regions or nations of the world which promise
a high rate of return on investment receive the lion's share of
direct foreign investment while those regions which do not offer this prospect are by-passed. Of course, the entire process
is considerably more complicated than this, but most executives
will admit that "when the chips come done, that's what counts".
(31)

If the philosophy of the systemic model is adapted, then
the allocation of economic resources and managerial talent will

be initiated and stimulated by the need of a particular niche
of the ecosystem rather than by the needs and wants of the MNC.
According to Mesarovic and Pestel, in their "fourth, or early
action scenario" in which an increased amount of aid to the
Third World by the developed world in the period from 1975 to
2000 must be given so that no aid will be needed thereafter,
"the maximal annual cost reaches 'only' $250 billion, while
the cumulative cost totals somewhat less than $2500 billion".
(32) Given the current preference for private investment in
lieu of public aid, the MNC manager will be expected to invent
'low rate of return' projects which will contribute toward the
economic development of the recipient region. Obviously, the
customary rates of return (10-20%) will be incompatible with
the objective of the aid.

Since much of the extracting industry has been taken over
by national government, MNCs will have to expand into manufacturing, and, more importantly, into agricultural business. The
acquisition of manufacturing and agricultural products requires
large amounts of foreign exchange, a commodity in short supply
in most countries of the Third World. It is, therefore, a need
which must be satisfied although the economic benefits to the
MNC will be less than those derived from the extraction and
export of natural resources.

(ii) *Technological and Production Principle*

The quest for high rates of return on investment, coupled
with certain unique conditions of 'growth societies', such as
a large affluent market, tight supply of labor, etc., has
greatly influenced managerial decisions regarding the kind and
extent of technology utilization and production processes.
Operating under the once sound premises of the Surrogate, managers devised production technologies geared toward producing
large quantities via a continuous process of substitution of
machine power for 'muscle power'. This is a process which began, as already indicated, with the First Industrial Revolution, which was elevated to automated assembly lines in the
post-World War II era, and which is currently reaching its
zenith with cybernation where both mechanical and electronic
equipment is combined to produce highly sophisticated products
with a minimum of human participation.

The MNC of the future will have to abandon both large-
scale production for the large and prosperous market and the
high capital, and technology-intensive production processes
which minimize the need for human participation. There appears
to be an essential principle that governs economic development
which states that for a country to develop, its citizens must
first become employees before they can become customers. West
Germany's and Japan's economic miracles were based on this
simple logic. MNCs that aspire to play a meaningful role in the

world's creation of wealth must abide by this principle and
must provide an opportunity for humans to self-actualize
through participation in production processes.

More specifically, the so-called technology diffusion inside the Third World will have to be of a different kind than
that which has made the First World rich. The most important
and the most abundant resource of the Third World is its people.
It makes perfect economic sense to utilize this abundant and
renewable 'resource'. There is a technology which is designed
to do just that. It goes by the name 'Intermediate Technology',
a technology defined as "a nonviolent technology, based on
small units, that lends itself for use by people who are not
very sophisticated or very rich and powerful". (33) This technology represents something between the indigenous technology
of a typical developing country and the sophisticated, high-
capital-intensive and high-energy-input-dependent technology
of the modern world. It is a technology for production by the
masses and not for mass production.

(iii) *Environmental Acceptability Principle*

Until recently there was an inherent bias against any sort
of ecological consideration in investment decisions, whether
domestic or international. In most business and industrial engineering schools the manager has traditionally been educated
to make decisions by carefully investigating the (i) economic
and (ii) technological feasibility of the proposed project. Any
warnings about the finiteness of the earth as a reservoir of
resources and as a sink for the deposit of the economically
non-reprocessable residues of production were dismissed as nonsense lacking a basic understanding of the price mechanism and
the potentials of the 20th century-*deus ex machina* megamachine.
(34)

The multinational manager has thus far had little to worry about with respect to environmental considerations, especially if his corporation had branches in the Third World. However,
the temporary lack of any environmental controls in these 'pollution havens' of the Third World should not be considered to
be a permanent condition despite all assurances by political
leaders and Chamber of Commerce representatives. (35) It is
absolutely essential that the MNC manager realize this fact of
life and build ecologically acceptable plants from the very
beginning. To fall into the trap set by the con artist consultant that 'the poor need jobs more than they need clean air',
will be like failing into a lobster trap; it is easy to get in
but impossible to get out. (36)

(iv) *Conservation Principle*

Conservation - the careful preservation and protection of

something - is not a completely unknown concept to any manager.
From his basic formal education in engineering and business
schools he learned that a well-managed corporation is one that
utilizes organizational resources in such a way as to conform
to the cardinal rule of economics of least-cost combination.
Thus the effort is aimed at achieving the maximum yield with
the least expenditure. This rule is applied to all basic factors of production such as land, capital, labor and administrative talent.

What seems to be a foreign concept, however, is the idea
of measuring the contributions of these basic factors of production to the overall goal of the enterprise in units other
than money. As a result, organizational resources are considered as being scarce or abundant only with respect to a given
price. The concept of the physical lack of or availability of
resources is for all practical purposes irrelevant. If the
price is right the 'system' will produce the corresponding
quantity demanded.

It is becoming increasingly clear that the physical availability or lack of resources acquires the nature of an invariant in the calculus of demand and supply. However, this idea of
using non-monetary equivalents in planning and managing organizational resources is as foreign to the manager as the idea
of employing the price mechanism is to the ecosystem. Recent
attempts to provide a non-monetary yard-stick have not been
overly ridiculed; see H.T. Odum's sober attempt to provide an
energy accounting system.

If a non-monetary evaluation system for organizational
resources is adopted, then the conventional attitude of 'doing-
more-with-less' becomes questionable. There seems to be strong
hints that a transition towards 'doing-less-with-less' is un-
avoidable.

(v) *The Physical or Geographic Horizon Principle*

With the First World's increasing decline in economic activity, with its increased dependence on the Third World for
raw materials and resources, and with its moral commitment to
help the Third World develop, the conventional planning horizon of the MNC manager which was more or less limited to the
First and recently to the Second World must now be expanded to
include the vast number of territories and peoples of the Third
World. (37) If the excess capacity of the industrial establishment that 'growthmania' has created is to be utilized, the decision to 'go LDC' is no longer an alternative, but rather, a
necessity.

(vi) *The Size of the Adventure Principle*

It has long been suspected and it has recently been docu-

mented that after a certain point the size of the firm begins
to become a disadvantage. (38) Since most MNCs have reached
gigantic dimensions, Schumacher's 'small is beautiful' seems
not only aesthetically sound, but it also makes excellent economic sense. In 'going LDC', existing MNCs must plan and manage their operations in the Third World as 'mini-multis'. This
kind of size strategy is indeed most appropriate, given the
substantial fear that the gigantic size of the MNC will dominate or, for that matter, render the nation-state obsolete.

(vii) *Ownership Principle*

More and more MNCs are abandoning the once-preferred
strategy of 100% ownership. (39) In relinquishing part of its
assets, the MNC must attempt to avoid the most common pitfall
of joint ventures which is the control of the locally-owned
portion in the hands of few rich nationals. Such unorthodox
plans as employee ownership must become more and more common.
The wealth of the firm must be shared by those who need it
most: the marginal worker and clerk, not the already rich
landowner and affluent native.

(viii) *Type of Arrangement Principle*

More and more of the actual production and marketing of
the MNC should be performed by native forces. The role of the
MNC must be more or less that of technology supplier, management consultant, and capital supplier. Such unusual strategies
as project coordinator, turnkey projects, consultation of the
PanAm-Iran type, training projects of the ARAMCO type, and
other innovative schemes would enable the MNC to avoid massive
de-investing of its most expensive and precious investment:
human capital. By the same token, this scheme would save the
Third World s substantial amount of money which would have had
to be invested in re-discovering ideas which can be adapted
with a minimum of expenditure.

(ix) *Location and Personnel Principle*

The conventional industrialization of the Third World by
MNCs has led to massive and inhumane urbanization in these
countries. The MNC's decision to invest in the city is interpreted as a new ray of hope for the rural population, their
longed for El Dorado. But once these hopefuls move into the
city, a terrible process of misery ensues. The MNCs of the future must follow Schumacher's advice and attempt to create an
"agro-industrial structure in the rural and smalltown areas".
(40) The process of the integration of nationals into the managerial ranks of the MNC heirarchy has been extremely slow. Kenneth Simmonds, in a study of 1,851 top managers of leading US

multinationals, found that only 1.6 percent of these high-le-
vel executives were non-Americans. IBM is usually cited as the
most notable exception to this rule. Obviously this discrimination against the 'thinkers' of the Third World is no longer
feasible nor desirable. Upward mobility within an organizational hierarchy should be as much a motivating factor for nationals as it is for 'expatriates'. The recent development in
Canada's requirements that the top executive of a subsidiary
of an MNC be a Canadian national is bound to be universally
emulated in time. It will not be long before 'nationals' will
be sitting on the boards of directors of MNCs.

(x) *Ethical Principle*

     If there has ever been a troublesome concept in most
MNC executives' minds that must be 'ethics'. While their legal
staff and consultants conceive of ethics as a legal concept,
namely, compliance with the law, recently congressional inves-
tigators and business and social critics all over the world,
motivated by the massive uncoverings and voluntary disclosures
of corporate bribes and political contributions of corporate
funds, have shown considerable doubt about this narrow conception.
     Ethics - as the branch of philosophy dealing with values
relating to human conduct, with respect of rightness and wrong-
ness of certain actions and to the goodness and badness of the
motives and ends of such actions - goes beyond the questions
of legality and legitimacy of managerial decision-making. The
MNC manager who aspires to contribute toward the goals of the
new world order should know that ethics consists of "a set of
rules of conduct recognized in respect to a particular class
of human actions or a particular group". The group with which
a manager is affiliated is not only his own stockholders, su-
periors and subordinates, but, moreover, it consists of all of
these plus the entire social and political environment.

                  CONCLUSION: A SYMPATHETIC LOOK INTO
                        THE CORPORATE WORLD

     Is there any evidence that a transformation of the type
described in this paper could be conceived of as anything short
of a utopia? Are there instances where MNC executives have
shown, indicated or even hinted at changes in corporate philosophies, policies, objectives or managerial practices which may
be construed as the beginning of a new era of transformation?
There is no one single answer to these questions. Hard core
evidence of a shift of corporate orientation away from the surrogate and toward the systemic model is very meagre. There ex-

ists, however, considerable evidence in the form of public
statements made by high-ranking executives of some of the largest MNCs hinting at a true 'change of heart' in corporate
boardrooms. Although most concerned scholars would interpret
these statements as purely 'cosmetic colorings' we believe that
the stature and sincerity of the people who made these statement cannot be taken too lightly.

It is important to notice that it is only necessary that
a corporate manager undergoes a change in the main philosophy
of doing business, i.e., adapts the four main philosophical
principles outlined earlier. The redefinition and reformulation
of the ten operational principles would follow more or less
automatically, with a certain time lag, of course. In other
words, once the philosophical principles of cooperation and
organic growth have become part of the corporate philosophy of
an MNC then it would not be too long before the principles of
low rate of return, conservation, environmental quality, and
so on would become standard operating procedures of a corporation.

At the most general level there exists considerable evidence of transformation along the philosophical and operating
principles outlined above. One sees, for example today, a common code of conduct for all MNCs operating within the 24 OECD
members. Although this code has been viewed by the Third World
as an attempt to tell the host countries to grant more and not
less freedom to the MNC a more serious look into the code will
indeed reveal some encouraging rays of hope. To this one could
perhaps add the thousands of self-publicized codes of conduct
which followed the US Congressional Hearings on Multinationals
in 1975. Most recently almost all MNCs which operate in South
Africa have signed and indeed observe the Sullivan Code which
aims at completely eliminating racial discrimination and human
exploitation in that part of the world. (41)

At the more specific individual (company and executive)
level, calls for a new MNC to be kept in tune with a changing
world reality are so numerous that it would require an entire
book to just list them. Here is an example of a statement by
one of the world's largest and most internationalized MNCs.
Reginald H. Jones, Chairman and Chief Executive Officer of General Electrics sees the following changes in the MNC on its
way to a new evolution: (i) the corporation will become more
international in its personnel, management structure, physical
deployment of assets, financing and general strategy; (ii) the
corporation will develop managers who are much more politically sophisticated than in the past; (iii) world corporations
will increasingly respond to social expectations as well as to
the iron laws of economics; (iv) the corporations will allocate
their resources to those needs that the nations feel most ur-
gently; and (v) as the world uses up the most easily available
resources of fuel and raw materials, it is necessary to develop

more expensive secondary sources. In general, Mr. Jones sees
the MNC as a useful vehicle. He concludes his remarks as follows: "The world corporations have a useful role to play in
helping the peoples and the governments of the world to achieve
their aspirations. For this reason, I believe they will thrive
in the emerging world economy". (42)

The close resemblance of Mr. Jones' visions of the future
of the MNC to the main pillars for the transformation described
in this paper need not be emphasized. Elsewhere we have provided some examples of a few corporate responses to and indeed anticipation of most of the changes described under the ten operating principles. (43) In conclusion, here is how the chief of
Citycorp and Citibank, Mr. Walter B. Wriston describes the future MNC managers and the MNC's role in the new world order:

> The development of the world corporation into a truly mul-
> tinational organization has produced a group of managers
> of many nationalities whose perception of the needs and
> wants of the human race knows no boundaries. They really
> believe in one world.
> They understand with great clarity that the payrolls and
> jobs furnished by the world corporation exceed profits
> by a factor of 20 to 1. They know that there can be no
> truly profitable markets where poverty is the rule of life.
> They are a group which recognizes no distinction because
> of color or sex, since they understand with the clarity
> born of experience that talent is the commodity in short-
> est supply in the world.
> They are managers who are against the partitioning of the
> world, not only on a political or theoretical basis, but
> on the pragmatic ground that the planet has become too
> small, that our fate has become too interwoven to engage
> in the old nationalistic games which have so long diluted
> the talent, misused the resources, and dissipated the ener-
> gy of mankind.
> The world corporation has become a new weight in an old
> balance. It must play a constructive role in moving the
> world toward the freer exchange of both ideas and the
> means of production so that the people of our planet may
> one day enjoy the fruits of a truly global society. (44)

NOTES AND REFERENCES

(1) *Survey of International Development*, Society for International Development, Vol. XII, No. 5, September-October, 1975.
(2) Ibid, July-August, 1975.
(3) United Nations, *The Impact of Multinational Corporations
on Development and International Relations,* (U.N. Publication

E.74.II.X.5), New York, 24 March, 1974.
(4)   As Dennis Gabor, world-renowned scientist, inventor and
Nobel Laureate put it several years ago:" It now appears that
a crisis is upon us, long before most people expected it. First
in Britain, then a little later in the United States, production
growth slowed down and even came to a temporary stop, while
prices went up steadily, in spite of growing unemployment. The
present crisis will certainly pass away, production will rise
again through new technological improvement, though their introduction will slow down by the restriction on capital investment
which was necessary to prevent runaway inflation. But the causes will remain with us, and I believe that they will be felt a-
gain in new crises. It is my belief that the present crisis is
already a crisis of *saturation*, foreseen by J.M. Keynes forty
years ago, but fervently disbelieved by most economists in the
long period of year-to-year growth. In the U.K. and the U.S.A.
it manifests itself clearly in the unwillingness of the workers
to work more in order to consume more". Dennis Gabor, *The Mature Society*, Secker and Warburg, London, 1972, p.3.
(5)   Considerable intellectual energy has been expended by academicians, businessmen and national and international governmental agencies to provide a sound and workable definition of
the multinational corporation. Raymond Vernon ('Economic sovereignty at bay', *Foreign Affairs*, Vol. 7, No. 1, October 1968,
p. 114), Professor and Coordinator of the Harvard Business
School Multinational Enterprise Study, employs the term 'multinational enterprise' instead of 'multinational corporation' and
defines it as "a cluster of corporations of diverse nationality
joined together by ties of common ownership and responsive to
common management strategy". Farmer and Richmond (*International
Business: An Operational Theory*, R.D. Irwin, Homewood, Ill.,
1966, p. 13), who prefer the term 'international business', define it as "business operations of any sort by one firm, which
take place within it or between two or more independent countries". Neil Jacoby ('The multinational corporation', *The Center Magazine*, Vol. 3, No. 5, 3 May 1979, p. 38) suggests the
following definition: "A multinational corporation owns and ma-
nages business in two or more countries. It is an agency of
direct, as opposed to *portfolio*, investment in foreign countries, holding and managing the underlying physical assets
rather than securities based upon those assets". Seymour Rubin
('The international firm and the national firm and the national
jurisdiction' in C. Kindleberger, (ed.), *The International Corporation*, MIT Press, Cambridge, Mass., 1970, p. 181), who uses
the term 'international firm', defines it as "business organization that has its roots in one country and operations of various sorts in another". Finally, Charles Kindleberger (*American Business Abroad*, Yale University Press, New Haven, Conn.,
1969) distinguishes between *national* firms that carry on foreign
operations, *multinational* firms that seek to integrate quite

extensively into each national community in which activities
are carried on, and *international* corporations that truly function as an integrated, world economic unit. Businessmen, likewise, lack accord in their definitions of multinational corporations. A.W. Clausen ('The international corporation: An executive's view', *The Annals*, vol. 403, September 1972, p. 14),
President of Bank America Corporation, for example, who prefers
the term: 'transnational firm', states: "Although be concerned
with most, if not all, of the following areas: management,
ownership, financing, resourcing, manufacturing and marketing".
Sir David Barran ('The multinationals: Sheep in sheep's clothing', *Journal of General Management*, Vol. 1, No. 3, 1974, p.13),
of the Shell Centre, London, who adapted the term 'international enterprise' views it as incorporating everything from the
very large-scale type of integrated enterprises to the single-
product manufacturer based in one country who finds himself increasingly driven by the exigencies of his business into successive stages of involvement overseas. The most complete definition, in the author's opinion, has been given by Jacques
G. Maisonrouge, President of IBM World Trade Corporation (in
Bradley and Bursk, 'Multinationalism and the 29th day', *Harvard
Business Review*, Vol. 50, No. 1, January-February, 1972, p.39).
He asserts that "there are five basic criteria for a MNC:
1.   It must do business in many countries;
2.   It must have foreign subsidiaries with the same R&D, manufacturing, sales, services, and so on, that a true industrial
entity has;
3.   There should be nationals running these local companies;
they understand the local scene better than anybody else, and
this helps promote good citizenship;
4.   There must be a multinational headquarter , staffed with
people coming from different countries, so one nationality
does not dominate the organization too much;
5.   There should be multinational stock ownership - the stock
must be owned by people in different companies".
        National and international official agencies have recently
attempted to offer a compromise definition encompassing the
conceptions of both academicians and businessmen. The U.S. Department of Commerce, for example, seems to find Maisonrouge's
definition satisfactory (U.S. Department of Commerce, *The Multinational Corporation,* U.S. Government Printing Office, Washington, D.C. March 1972, p. 7). The U.N. Economic and Social Council on the other hand, suggests a more quantitative definition
(U.N. Department of Economic and Social Affairs, *Multinational
Corporations in World Development*, (U.N. Publication E.73.II.A.
11, 1973, p. 6). The Council recently arrived at the following
definition of a MNC: "In the broadest sense, any corporation
with one or more foreign branches, or affiliates engaged in any
of the activities mentioned (assets, sales, production, employment, or profits of foreign branches and affiliates) may quali-

fy as multinational. More strictly, a particular type of activity (e.g. production), a minimum number of foreign affiliates
(e.g. six), or of sales or assets may be added as conditions
for qualifying for the definition".
(6)   Recent writers on the subject of the multinational corporation or of international business in general have organized
the theories developed thus far concerning 'the decision to
invest abroad' into coherent frameworks. Stefan H. Robock and
Kenneth Simmonds (*International Business and Multinational Enterprises*, R.D. Irwin, Homewood, Ill., 1973) have offered the
following framework: (a) *traditional theories* (international
trade theory and capital investment theories); and (b) *new approaches* (the oligopolistic model, the product cycle model,
international transmission of resources and the evolutionary
model). The best framework seems to be offered by N.S. Fatemi
and G.W. Williams (*Multinational Corporations*, A.S. Barnes and
Company, South Brunswick and New York, 1975). The authors group
the available theories into two categories: the first category
is termed 'the economic position' which explains the growth of
multinational corporations and direct foreign investment as
the result of the economic perception of protected markets
(e.g. the Common Market) and technological advances in transportation and communication. Four theories are included in this
general category: (i) the theory of international oligopoly
(Kindleberger and Hymer); (ii) the product cycle theory (Vernon); (iii) the organic theory of investment (National Industrial Conference Board); and (iv) the currency boundary theory
(Gilpin). The second category is termed 'the public policy position' which argues that the large movement of capital (especially U.S.) is the result of governmental action or inaction.
Needless to say, most research in the developed world attributes the decision to invest to the nature of the firm as a
natural phenomenon. Less developed countries, on the other hand,
interpret it as exploitative and economic imperialism.
(7)   Despite the abundances of quantitative data compiled by
the U.S. Department of Commerce, the International Chamber of
Commerce, the OECD, the U.N. and other institutions, one is
advised to be very cautious in interpreting these statistics
and in drawing any major inferences. Certain statements can be
made, however, with considerable safety. There is widespread
agreement among researchers, for example, that the typical MNC
is a large corporation. For example, the U.N. suggests that
"a central characteristic of the MNC is the predominance of
large-size firms. Typically, the amount of annual sales runs
into hundreds of millions of dollars. Each of the four largest
MNCs have surpassed the one billion dollar level". (U.N., op.
cit., p. 6). *Newsweek*, by using 1971 sales figures ranked twenty MNCs ending with RCA with $3.7 billion.('Global corporations:
Too big to handle?', *Newsweek*, 20 November, 1972, p.96). *World*,
the publication of Peat, Marwick, Mitchel & Co., in organizing

figures compiled by the New York Stock Exchange, *Fortune* and
the Agency of International Development, concluded that, "if
the sales volume of the largest corporations were equated with
the volume of the output of goods and services of the largest
nations, a listing of the non-communist world's one hundred
biggest money powers would contain fifty-three international
corporations and only forty-seven countries. The multinational
corporations account for approximately 1/6 of the world's gross
product". ('Challenges for the multinational corporation',
World, Vol. 2, Spring, 1974, p. 55). In such a listing General
Motors Corporation, for example, would be the sixteenth largest country! In terms of absolute dollars, the total stock of
foreign investment is set by the U.N. (U.N., op.cit.,p.7), at
$165 billion for 1970. *Business Week* estimates that foreign
investment by the five major countries will reach the figure of
$190 billion in 1975 (*Business Week*, 14 July, 1975, p. 65).
(8) See, for example, the U.N. Department of Economic and Social Affairs' study on *Multinational Corporations and World
Development*, U.N. New York, 1973; and the U.S. Department of
Commerce, and Bureau of International Commerce; *The Multinational Corporation:Studies on U.S. Foreign Investment*, Volume
1, U.S. Government Printing Office, Washington, D.C. March,
1972.
(9) Since its inception, the multinational corporation has
been the product of the developed, or 'First World'. By the
end of 1966 seven industrialized countries shared 91.6% of the
world's book value of direct foreign investment. The U.S. owned 60.8%, followed by the United Kingdom, Canada, Germany,
Japan and Sweden. (U.S. Department of Commerce, op.cit., p.9).
Although the American hegemony in foreign investment is declining due to the expansion of European and Japanese multinational corporations, there is no substantial evidence that
any significant emergence of Third World multinational corporations is on the horizon. The 1972 *Business Week* 'Survey of International Corporate Performance' lists no Third World multinational corporations among the 200 giant firms of non-U.S.
origin and includes only three firms from Israel, two Mexican
firms and four South African Companies (*Business Week*, 7 July,
1973, pp. 56-65).
        In terms of geographical and industrial sector distribu-
tion, data suggests than an interesting pattern exists. By the
end of 1966, the majority of foreign investment went to the
developed countries with only 33% to the developing countries
(U.S. Department of Commerce, op.cit.,p.8). 47.3% of the investment which went to the developed countries went into manufacturing with a smaller percentage for petroleum and mining,
i.e. extracting investment. The scene in the developing countries is almost the reverse: 49.0% went into the extracting
industries and only 26.9% for manufacturing (U.N., op.cit.,
p. 10a).

(10) See, for example, Richard J. Barnet and Ronald E.Muller,
Global Reach, Simon and Schuster, New York, 1974; Louis Tur-
ner, *Multinational Companies and the Third World*, Hill and
Wang, New York, 1973; Raymond Vernon, *Sovereignty at Bay: The
Multinational Spread of U.S. Enterprises*, Basic Books, New
York, 1971; H. Stephenson, *The Coming Clash:The Impact of the
International Corporation on the Nation State*, Weidenfeld &
Nicolson, London, 1972; Karl Levitt, *Silent Surrender:The Ame-
rican Economic Empire in Canada*, Liverright, New York, 1970;
George W. Ball, (ed.) *Global Companies:The Political Economy
of World Business*, The American Assembly, Prentice-Hall,
Englewood Cliffs, New Jersey, 1975; Raymond Vernon, *Storm over
the Multinationals: The Real Issues*, Harvard University Press,
Cambridge, Mass., 1977; and 'Multinational at bay', Special
Report, *Saturday Review*, 24 January, 1976.
(11) See, among other, David H. Blake, 'The unions and the
challenge of the multinational corporation', *The Annals of the
American Academy of Political and Social Science*, Vol. 403,
September, 1972, pp. 34-45; and U.S. Senate, 93rd Congress,
1st Session, *Implications of Multinational Firms for World
Trade and Investment and for U.S. Trade and Labor*, U.S. Government Printing Office, Washington, D.C. 1973.
(12) Lawrence B. Krause, 'The international economic system
and the multinational corporation', *The Annals*, Vol. 403,
September, 1972, pp. 93-103.
(13) For a brief summary of an opinion research poll conducted
in 1974 on the public's attitudes towards MNCs, see Robert
W. Dietsch 'The one world of multinationals', *The New Republic*,
14 December, 1974, pp. 8-9.
(14) *Wall Street Journal*, Editorial, 17 July, 1975, p. 18.
(15) A.G. Kefalas, 'The state goals groups and the private enterprise', *Proceedings*, Society for General Systems Research,
1977.
(16) Perry F. Wilson, 'Attack on multinationals - Free enterprises on trial', *Christian Science Monitor*, 13 March, 1976,
p.7.
(17) Peter F. Drucker, *The Age of Discontinuity: Guidelines on
our Changing Society*, Harper Colophon Books, Harper & Row,
New York, 1978, p. x.
(18) This move toward regionalism and away from nationalism is
manifested in such developments as the Latin-American Free
Trade Association, (LAFTA), the Central American Common Market,
patterned after the European Economic Community (EEC) and the
European Free Trade Association (EFTA). In addition, the al-
leged or real cartelization of the oil-exploiting and marketing corporations as well as other giant multinationals was met
by the creation of the Organization of Petroleum Exporting
Countries (OPEC) and the Andean Pact, or the Decision 24 Agreement. Currently, the so-called Group of 77 is demanding "full
and effective participation in the world economy and in the

deliberations and decisions that affect it". Quoted from:
"Group of 77 urges revision of international development strategy to reflect changed aspirations, economic and social conditions", *Survey of International Development*, The Society for
International Development, Vol. XXI, No. 4, July/August, 1975,
p. 1.
(19) See, for example, *Dialogue on World Oil: Highlights of a
Conference on World Oil Problems*, held in Washington, D.C., 3-4
October, 1974, American Enterprise Institute, Washington, D.C.,
1974; Miles Ignotus (Pseudonym), 'Seizing arab oil', *Harpers*,
March 1975, pp. 45-62; and C.Fred Bergsten, 'The response to
the Third World', *Foreign Policy*, No. 19, Summer, 1975, pp.
3-34.
(20) The U.S. National Commission on Materials Policy concluded
its report in June 1974: "As to the possibility that countries
might form effective cartels to deny supplies to major importers
or to raise prices, with the exception of petroleum, the Commission has not isolated any commodities for which the economic
and political basis for such action exists". Quoted in Nicholas
Wade, 'Raw Materials: U.S. grows more vulnerable to Third World',
Science, January, 1974, p. 183.
(21) For example, C.Fred Bergsten, a former assistant to the
U.S. Secretary of State on the National Security Council and
now with the Brookings Institution, has argued that the "United
States' neglect of the Third World is dangerously myopic, in
view of the nation's growing dependence on the raw materials
controlled by Third World countries". Quoted in Nicholas Wade,
op.cit., p. 185. See also, 'Adjusting to scarcity', *The Annals
of the American Academy of Political and Social Science*, July,
1975; 'Materials: Working with shortages', *Technology Review*,
June, 1975; 'Scenario for survival: Coping with shortages',
Business Week, (Special Issue: 'Reappraising the Seventies'),
14 September, 1975, pp. 56-70.
(22) Paul R.Ehrlich and Anne H.Ehrlich, *The End of Affluence*,
Ballantine Books, New York, 1974, p. 21.
Although one might be accused of exaggeration if one were to
interpret the recent isolated instances of water shortages, excessive pollution, traffic congestion, and oil and gas shortages in the First World as the beginning of a new struggle for
survival, Western style, one can certainly not dismiss the
change as irrelevant - at least not as easily as one would have,
say five years ago.
(23) Lawrence A.Mayer, 'The world economy': Climbing back from
negative growth', *Fortune*, August, 1975, p. 150.
(24) Peter F.Drucker, 'Aftermath of a go-go decade', *Wall
Street Journal*, 25 March, 1975, p. 18.
(25) Stephen R.Graubard, 'Preface to the issue 'The No-Growth
Society'', *Daedalus*, Journal of the American Academy of Arts
and Science, Fall, 1973, p.v.

(26) 'The changed economic position of developing countries',
Survey of International Development, January-February, 1975,
p. 3.
(27) See, for example, 'Major new agreement signed between
European Community and 46 'developing countries'', *Survey of
International Development*, March-April, 1975, p. 1.
(28) *Business Week*, Special Advertising Section: France 1976,
10 May, 1976; and *Business Week*, Special Advertising Section:
Sweden, 3 May, 1976.
(29) Quoted in N.Macrae, 'The future of international business:
A survey', *The Economist*, 22 January, 1972, p. xxii.
(30) For a more detailed description of the Lomé Convention,
see *Survey of International Development*, March-April, 1975, op.
cit., pp. 1-2; R.C.Longworth, 'Europe and the 'new working
class'', *Saturday Review*, 6 September, 1975, pp. 12-13; 'The
Lomé Agreement: EC's 9 join 46 of 'ACP' Group in North-South
link', *The Bulletin*, Press and Information Office of the Government of the Federal Republic of Germany, Vol. 23, No. 6, 18
February, 1975, pp. 33-35.
(31) Although it is considered by most experts in the field to
be a truism that 'a prosperous customer is the best customer'
this truism functions as a powerful operational principle in
the case of the contemporary MNC manager. As was pointed out
earlier, about only one third of total direct foreign investment went into the world's regions which account for 90% of the
world's total population. Of that amount a little less than
half went into extraction of natural resources. The remaining
three-quarters of the total investment went to the high growth
areas of Europe and North America. See also footnote 11.
(32) M.Mesarovic and E.Pestel, *Mankind at the Turning Point*,
Signet Books, New York, 1974, p. 63.
(33) E.F.Schumacher, *Small is Beautiful*, Blond and Briggs,
London, 1973, Part II, Chapter 5 and Part III, Chapter 2.
(34) When in 1970 the U.S. passed the National Environmental
Policy Act and created a federal agency (the Environmental
Protection Agency) to deal with environmental problems, it
caught most managers by surprise for they never expected that
the slow conservative mechanism of the U.S. Congress would act
as swiftly as it did. The U.S. scheme soon became the master
plan for other nations. In Western Europe, country after country began to emulate the U.S. experiment and finally the EEC
provided a uniform inter-country environmental policy. This
recognition of the existence of limits in the ecosystem's capacity to carry human and industrial waste led to the simultaneous
conclusion that the ecosystem's capacity to provide for resources
at the rates currently used was also finite. Again, the U.S.
solution, the creation of a Federal Energy and Resources Agency,
is being imitated in most industrialized countries. Although
the initial reaction of corporate executives was to 'fight this

bureaucratic nonsense' it gradually became obvious that the
profitability was suffering much less than originally claimed.
(35) R.J.Barnet and R.E.Müller, *Global Reach*, Simon and Schuster, New York, 1974. The authors cite such an incident occurring
in Mexico City: "In Mexico City's English-language newspaper
the State of Mexico advertises for polluters: 'RELAX, WE'VE
ALREADY PREPARED THE GROUND FOR YOU. If you are thinking of
fleeing from the capital because the new laws for the prevention and control of environmental pollution affect your plant,
you can count on us', p. 345.
(36) J.H.Welles, 'Multinationals need new environmental strategies', *Columbia Journal of World Business*, Summer, 1973, pp. 11-
18. Welles warns that "..... even though a multinational corporation can legally build and operate a high-polluting plant
in a pollution haven today with little or no abatement measures,
there are political risks. Exploiting the right to pollute developing countries is raising charges of "neo-colonialism" and
"economic imperialism". If a multinational inflicts substantial
damage to the host country's environment, it may present a large
and inviting target for ambitious politicians..... locating
plants in pollution havens may backfire at home. Disgruntled
union officials, viewing such a move as exporting their members' jobs, may pressure politicians to impose tariff barriers
on the product produced in pollution havens, thereby threatening important markets of the polluting plants. Indeed, a little
publicized provision of the Federal Water Pollution Control Act
Amendments of 1972 (Section 6) directs the Secretary of Commerce
to study the feasibility of taking such action. Similarly,
citizen environmental groups may call for consumer boycotts of
products produced by plants in pollution havens..... It may
therefore be advantageous to a multinational to expand capacity
in traditional locations despite roughening environmental controls, or to install some degree of abatement measures when
constructing plants in locations where control is not now required. This is in line with a general principle that has successfully guided one of the oldest multinationals, the Singer
Company, for 118 years. According to its chairman, Donald K.
Fircher: "It may sound a bit platitudinous, but you must satis-
fy any government that the totality of your business is to be
of benefit to the country. Sometimes, you must sacrifice short-
term gains to convince them, but if you don't, you're just not
going to last". p. 15.
(37) As recently as October 1974, Peter Drucker, 'Multinational:
Myths and realities', *Foreign Affairs*, October, 1974, pp. 121-
134, pointed to the first myth with these words: ".... the
developing countries are important to the multinational companies and major source of sales, revenues, profits and growth
for them, if not the mainstay of 'corporate capitalism'."
(p. 121). Based upon confidential data in Mr. Drucker's pos-

session on about 45 manufacturers, distributors and financial
institutions among the world's leading multinationals, he argues
that ".... not even India or Mexico - the two 'developing' countries with the largest markets - ranks for any of the multinational companies in my sample ahead even of a single major
sales district in the home country, be it the Hamburg-North
Germany district, the English Midlands or Kansas City", (p. 122).
Mr. Drucker went on to say that "On the worldwide monthly or
quarterly sales and profit chart, which most large companies
use as their most common top-management tool, practically no
developing country even appears in my sample of 45 major multinationals except as part of a 'region', e.g. 'Latin America',
or under 'Others'." (p. 122).
(38) For an innovative approach conceived by the government of
the Federal Republic of Germany aimed at fostering the development of small companies which may be appplicable as well for
multinational corporations, see 'Research ministry fosters
private agency to help smaller firms market innovations', *The
Bulletin*, Press and Information Office of the Government of the
Federal Republic of Germany, 15 April, 1975, p. 93.
(39) Indeed, there is a marked acceptance of this condition. As
J.Paul Lyet, Chief Executive Officer of Sperry Rand Corporation,
recently put it: "Thirty-five percent of something is a lot
better than 100 percent of nothing", *Business Week*, 13 July,
1974, p. 74.
(40) E.F.Schumacher, *Small is Beautiful*, op.cit., p. 174-176.
Schumacher further elaborates that: "The real task may be formulated in four propositions: First, the workplaces have to be
created in the areas where the people are living now, and not
primarily in metropolitan areas into which they tend to migrate.
Second, that these workplaces must be, on the average, cheap
enough so that they can be created in large numbers without this
calling for an unattainable level of capital formation and imports. Third, that the production methods must be relatively
simple, so that the demands for high skills are minimized, not
only in the production process itself, but also in matters of
organization, raw materials supply, financing, marketing, and
so forth. Fourth, that production should be mainly from local
material and mainly for local use".
(41) 'America's South Africa dilemma: Should U.S. firms pull
out or should they stay and work for change?', *Time*, 18 September, 1978, pp. 66-68; also Roger M.Williams, 'American
business should stay in South Africa', *Saturday Review*, 9 September, 1978, pp. 14-21.
(42) Reginald H.Jones, 'The global corporation: Views from the
top', *Christian Science Monitor*, 18 February, 1976, p. 11.
(43) Ervin Laszlo et.al., *Goals for Mankind: A Report to the
Club of Rome*, E.P.Dutton, New York, 1977, Chapter 10 deals with
'Goals for multinational corporations'.
(44) Walter B.Wriston, 'The global corporation: Views from the
top', *Christian Science Monitor*, 21 April, 1976, p. 11.

Expanding the Common Heritage
Elisabeth Mann Borgese

THE COMMON HERITAGE OF MANKIND

The Law of the Sea Conference, having to deal with a
large number of key issues - food and fiber, metals and minerals, communications, science policy, environment, technology,
multinational corporations, to name only a few - is a test
case for the building of a new international order.

We are not concerned here with the problem of *timing*. The
new ocean regime may become a reality in the 1980s, or during
the first quarter of the next century. It is even conceivable
that the Law of the Sea Conference will be only very partially
successful and fail to realize the concepts it was mandated to
enact. These concepts, however, are here to stay. Conceivably,
they may be realized in other areas of international cooperation and return, from here, to the oceans. World order is one
integral system. Where, in this system, the break-through will
occur, no one can tell. But the Law of the Sea Conference has
nursed and matured the new concepts: and the outlines of new
forms are clearly discernible.

The basic principle, the motor force of the 'marine revolution', is the concept of the *Common Heritage of Mankind*. It
cannot be stressed enough, that the adoption of this principle
by the XXV General Assembly as a norm of international law
marked the beginning of a revolution in international relations. It has the potential to transform the relationship between poor and rich countries. It must and will become the basis of the New International Economic Order of which the Law
of the Sea Convention must be an essential part.

It is rather surprising, therefore, that the Law of the
Sea Conference itself has done so little about elaborating the
concept of the Common Heritage and giving it a clear definition

in legal and economic terms. For the outsider or newcomer to
the law of the sea, it is difficult to conceptualize the precise meaning of this new concept which remains somewhat rheto-
rical and etherial. Yet the components of a definition are all
in the present version of the Draft Convention, that is, the
Informal Composite Negotiating Text, and one might use the
components, drawn from four different Articles (136, 137, 140,
and 145) to formulate a definition in two basic articles:

First Article

The Area and its resources are a Common Heritage of Mankind.

Second Article

For the purpose of this Convention 'Common Heritage of
Mankind' means that:

1.   No state shall claim or exercise sovereignty or sovereign
rights over any part of the Area or its resources, nor shall
any State or person, natural or juridical, appropriate any
part thereof. No such claim or exercise of sovereignty or sovereign rights, nor such appropriation shall be recognized.
2.   The Area and its resources shall be managed for the benefit of mankind as a whole, irrespective of the geographical
location of the States, whether coastal or land-locked, and
taking into particular consideration the interests and needs
of the developing countries as specifically provided for in
this Part of the Convention.
3.   The Area shall be open to use exclusively for peaceful
purposes by all States, whether coastal or land-locked, without discrimination and without prejudice to the other provisions of this Part of the present Convention.
4.   Necessary measures shall be taken in order to ensure effective protection for the marine environment from harmful effects which may arise from activities in the Area, in accordance with Part XII of the present Convention.

These paragraphs express the four legal and economic attributes of the Common Heritage concept as they have developed
in discussions and writings since the concept was first proposed by Arvid Pardo in 1967. These attributes, more succinctly are:

●   non-appropriability;
●   shared management and benefit sharing by mankind as a
whole;
●   use for peaceful purposes only;
●   conservation for future generations.

The Concept of the Common Heritage of Mankind, as embodied in the Declaration of Principles, applies to the *mineral resources of the seabed beyond national jurisdiction*. In 1967, and still in 1970, these could be construed to include not only manganese but also offshore oil worth billions of dollars. The concept has since been eroded by exorbitant claims by coastal States to sovereign rights over mineral resources in the outer continental margin, down to the abyssal plane, with ill-defined 'elastic' boundaries, inviting further national expansion should technological and economic interests so suggest.

EXPANDING THE COMMON HERITAGE

This, however, is one side of the story, and there is another side. The *territorial shrinkage* of the Common Heritage might be compensated by the far more important *functional expansion* of the concept, given other political, economic, and ecological imperatives which equally act on the evolution of the law of the sea and on the Conference.

Common Heritage and Living Resources

The first step in this expansion is from the non-living resources of the international seabed area to the living resources in international as well as in national ocean space.

A signpost in this direction is a statement by the Delegation of the Holy See made in the Spring of 1978. (1) "The Contribution which the Holy See can make to the Conference does not consist of technical proposals", the statement reads, "but rather principles which may guarantee just and equitable solutions for the whole international community and, in the first line, the principle which is universally accepted, at least on the theoretical level, namely that the sea is 'the common heritage of mankind'." It should be noted that the statement says "the sea", not "the seabed beyond the limits of national jurisdiction".

"Moreover", the statement continues, "this view constitutes a part of a larger principle of 'The universal purpose of created things'. It is already applied by States on their territory, not as a restriction of their sovereignty, but as an exploitation or use of their natural resources which shall take into consideration the needs of the whole humanity and, above all, of States which are most deprived of them".

In particular the statement points out that while "the principle of delineation of maritime areas adjacent to the coast into economic zones entrusted to the coastal State is

acceptable", on the contrary, "the strictly speaking appropriation of the living resources of these areas is not admissible
because they do not constitute 'res nullius' but they represent goods which belong to the community of nations and, in
addition, because the argument of contiguity which is invoked
as a justification for such appropriation does not represent
a sufficient basis for it".

The statement was well received by many - especially
African - developing countries as well as by socialist States.
It represents a moral force and may constitute a conceptual
break-through. It lays the foundation for further elaboration
of the concept that ocean space and all its resources are the
Common Heritage of Mankind - not only by the Holy Sea but by
others as well. Notice has been given: the expansion of the
concept is on the table.

Its application to the Economic Zone would assure access
of landlocked and geographically disadvantaged States to regional joint management systems, and thus would solve one of
the thorniest, still outstanding, problems of the Conference.
Applied to the international area, it would assure an international management system for the exploitation of a vast new
resource, a multiple, in volume, of the total world fish catch:
the krill of the Southern Ocean. It would ensure that this resource would be exploited for the benefit of protein-deficient
developing nations which, individually, lack the technology
and the capital necessary for its exploitation and processing.
Under the present system, the krill would be exploited, and
most likely overexploited, for the sole benefit of three or
four rich, developed countries.

The krill of the Southern Ocean is the Common Heritage of
Mankind.

Common Heritage and Outer Space

The Treaty on Principles Governing the Activities of
States in the Exploration and Use of Outer Space (1967) defines
Outer Space as "the Common Province of Mankind", and the astronauts as the "envoys of mankind" to Outer Space. No treaty
had ever used such language. But the concepts remained in the
realm of the poetic. With the limits of outer space still unde-
fined, and the economic potential of space technology as nebu-
lous as the more remote stars, there appeared to be no urgent
need to endow the poetic expression with a precise legal or
economic content.

The 'common province' of mankind is, nevertheless, one of
the legitimate ancestors of the Common Heritage of Mankind.
While technological evolution has advanced, revealing ever more
clearly the economic potential of outer-space technology and
its impact on development as well as on sovereignty and on in-

ternational organization - making the Treaty of 1967 obsolete
- the Common Heritage concept, nurtured by the oceans, is now
returning to its ancestral home in Outer Space.

This is illustrated, for example, by a remarkable statement by the Delegate of the Netherlands, Professor Willem Riphagen, during the recent meeting of the Committee on the Peaceful Use of Outer Space. (2) The Netherlands Delegation, Mr.
Riphagen said, was of the opinion that the natural resources
of the moon and other celestial bodies were the Common Heritage of Mankind. That principle implied - he spelled out -
that no State would have sovereignty, permanent or otherwise,
over such resources *in situ*, and that the appropriation of
such resources should not be subject to the rule of 'first
come, first served'. From a more positive standpoint, he explained, that principle implied some form of international management in their exploitation... The international management
of the resources of the moon and other celestial bodies might
take various forms, but the objective had already been agreed
upon.

Meanwhile, history has not stood still. On 3 July 1979,
after seven years of deliberations, the U.N. Committee on the
Peaceful Uses of Outer Space approved a draft international
agreement which declared the natural resources of the moon and
other celestial bodies the Common Heritage of Mankind. The
draft agreement bars contamination of the moon's environment
or any claim to national ownership of any part of the moon. It
is expected to be approved by the XXXIV Session of the U.N.
General Assembly at the end of 1979.

Whether the exploitation of the resources of the moon and
other celestial bodies will ever become economical is of course
an open question. It may therefore be relatively painless for
States to declare them the Common Heritage of Mankind. It is
worth nothing, however, that some States - especially among
those most advanced in space technology - violently oppose the
concept.

The Common Heritage concept, furthermore, is to be applied
not only to the extra-terrestrial resources, but to the *products of space activity* in general. As Mr. Riphagen pointed out
in the same statement, international practice has evolved in
the direction of "application of the concept of the common heritage of mankind to the products of space activities". This
means that the information gathered by satellites, for example,
on earth resources, on pollution, on weather, or on military
activities, is Common Heritage.

Common Heritage and Land Resources

The Common Heritage status of the information on earth
resources affects the status of these resources themselves.

'Sensed' resources, providing the basis for international resource planning, will tend to become Common Heritage themselves. At the intergovernmental level, the expansion of the Common Heritage concept may well take this detour.

At the nongovernmental level, the conceptual route is
more direct.

To realize their goal of a production system satisfying
basic human needs, the authors of the *Bariloche Report* postulate a number of structural changes at the national and international level. (3) The basic features of the postulated new
order are those of a participatory self-management system
(most closely approximated in Yugoslavia today) based on *social ownership* - the national equivalent of the Common Heritage concept. Their description, however, comes close enough
to convey the concept.

> *Ownership and the use of property and means of production*
> play a key role in every society. What is the role of
> property in the world described in the (Bariloche) model?
> It is clear that, in our context, the concept of property
> loses much of its meaning. The private ownership of land
> and the means of production do not exist, but, on the
> other hand, neither does the State own them as is cur-
> rently the case in many centrally planned economies.
> The present-day concept of private ownership of the means
> of production should be replaced by the more universal
> concepts of the *use* and *management* of the means of pro-
> duction... (4)

This sampling of new thinking, from such diverse sources
as the Law of the Sea, the Law of Outer Space, Catholic thinking, and Third-World aspirations, may be sufficient to indicate that the principle of the Common Heritage of Mankind is
here to stay, and to expand.

The concept of the Common Heritage of Mankind does not
conflict with the principle of national sovereignty over natural resources, affirmed in numerous U.N. declarations and resolutions. There is no going back on this principle. Rather,
the Common Heritage principle *transcends* the principle of national sovereignty over natural resources, by *transforming the
concept of sovereignty*, considering it functional rather than
territorial. (5) It also adds a new dimension: that of *participation*. Under the Bariloche as under the Catholic concept
under the Law of the Sea as well as under Space Law, resources
in areas under national jurisdiction may be *used* and *managed*
under national law, provided (i) the nation *participates in
international resource planning*, i.e. in the making of decisions that affect its citizens; and (ii) the State consents
to *binding international dispute settlement* in case of a di-

vergence between perceived national and wider affected interests.

INTERNATIONAL RESOURCE MANAGEMENT SYSTEM

Management, for the benefit of society as a whole, with
special regard to the needs of the poor ('basic needs' strategy), is an intrinsic part of the Common Heritage concept. The
search for new forms of international resource management is
on: it constitutes an essential part of all socially and politically oriented world order studies, whether intergovernmental or nongovernmental.

International resource management is not to be construed
as the operation of a centralized Super-State Super Body, but
as a decentralized, participatory system, based on the principle of *subsidiarity*: that is, resource management decisions
are to be made at the *lowest possible level*, comprising only
those affected by such decisions, whether at the subnational,
national, regional or global level and including the public
sector as well as the private sector, where it exists.

Until now, extensive technical and political work has
been done with regard to only one international resource management system, and that is the *International Seabed Authority*.
Though dealing with an economically somewhat marginal sector
(the mining of the polymetallic nodules from the deep sea-
floor), this Authority thus will have a unique importance as
a *model* for other international resource management systems
which must necessarily be created to implement the Common Heritage principle as the basis for a New International Economic
Order.

The establishment of an international resource management
system is without precedent in the history of international
organization. It would be a break-through. It is not surprising, therefore, that the technical and political difficulties
are enormous, and that the international community, acting
through the U.N. Conference on the Law of the Sea, has not yet
succeeded in solving the problems. The 'glass', however, is as
much half full as it is half empty, and one should consider
it a triumph - a break-through in itself - that the international community has gone as far as it has:

● in accepting, *by consensus*, the need of such a management
system; and
● in having done such considerable and voluminous technical
and political work in preparation for its realization.

The remaining fundamental issue is that of the structure
of the production system.

On this point, unfortunately, the Conference has lured
itself into a dead-end road, by constructing a system in which
the international management sector has to *compete* with the
private sector. We have dealt in a number of papers with the
pitfalls of this approach. Suffice it to restate here that,
given the economic and technological realities of today, it is
impossible for the international management sector to get off
the ground if the very limited capital and technological resources of the private sector are allowed to operate under
what for all practical purposes amounts to a licensing system,
and if their production, while exhausting their capacity, sa-
tisfies the needs of their countries. There is, in that case,
not only no financing and no technology available to the international managing system, but, worse than that, there is no
economic *raison d'être*, no economic incentive, to get it started. If the so-called 'parallel system' really gets incorporated
in the final Treaty, the unfortunate consequence would be that
the Authority, while increasing its demands on the private
sector and the industrial States, will, on the one hand, not
be able to benefit the developing countries and, on the other,
make life too difficult for the industrial States and their
companies (a situation precisely profiling itself already during the present negotiations at the Conference). The consequence of this, in turn, will be that States, taking advantage
of the inadequate definition of the boundaries of the Economic
Zone and the continental margin, will extend their claims to
national jurisdiction, conveniently to include sufficient mining sites so that mining operations can be carried out under
U.S., French, and Mexican jurisdiction rather than under the
jurisdiction of the International Seabed Authority.

An alternative option has, however, been placed before the
Conference. It is an alternative largely devised by developing
countries during the preparatory period for the Conference, and
which was then reintroduced by Nigeria in 1976 and elaborated
by Austria in 1977. (6) This alternative option is based upon
the notion of structured cooperation between the private sector and the international management system. It is an approach
which follows the pattern, well accepted by industry - a recent
private meeting of the Consortia in Geneva looked at this alternative with a quite open mind - of *equity joint ventures*:
any State or State-sponsored or -designated company would have
access to the Area, under the condition that it form *a new
Enterprise*, to which the Authority contributes at least half
the capital investment (including the value of the nodules
which are the Common Heritage of Mankind) and appoints at least
half the members of the Board of Governors (from developing and
small industrialized countries), while the remaining capital is
provided by the States or companies, who appoint also the remaining members of the Board of Governors, in proportion to
their investment. Product, and profit, are divided in propor-

tion to investment.

This approach would solve some of the thorniest problems
still before the Conference: the problem of technology transfer, and that of financing the international resource management system. No other approach would provide such broad participation of developing countries in the management of the resources, and such broad financial participation by the Authority.

Whether the Law of the Sea Conference will or will not
fall back on this solution, which is favored by very many
countries, is an open question. Whether adopted or not, however, the proposal is there: it exists. And it may serve as a
model for international systems in other areas: for the management of living resources, in particular, the harvesting of
Antarctic krill; for the management of satellites (already
foreshadowed by the INMARSAT Convention); and for the management of energy.

At the same time, an *enterprise system* such as outlined
here, could make a second major contribution to the building
of a New International Economic Order. It could provide a model
for bringing transnational corporations into a structured relationship with the international community. While incorporating applicable parts of the UNCTAD Code of Conduct, this would
be a considerable step forward: incorporating also features of
the proposed European Companies and responding to the need for
a democratization of decision-making, and representation, on
the Board, of other than purely financial interests (the Autho-
rity-appointed members from developing and small industrialized
countries could include representatives of labor and of consumers).

Considered from this angle, the applicability of this model could be very wide: as wide as the range of transnational
corporations - the wider, the better for the NIEO.

REVENUE SHARING

Another aspect of the Common Heritage concept is revenue
sharing. If the concept is to be extended to other resources,
so must revenue sharing. (7) In a recent paper attention was
drawn to a series of recent proposals for an international tax
based on use. (8) One should add here that, during the Seventh
Session of the Law of the Sea Conference, the Delegation of
Nepal introduced its proposal for revenue sharing and the es-
tablishement of a *Common Heritage Fund*, in the form of a letter
addressed to the President of the Conference. According to this
proposal, the Fund's income would consist of (i) the revenues
earmarked by the International Seabed Authority for the Fund;
(ii) the revenues due from the Exclusive Economic Zones of

States; and (iii) the revenues from the continental margin
beyond the 200 mile limit of the Exclusive Economic Zone. The
biggest item would obviously be the second, that is, 'a share
of the net revenues from the mineral exploitation of the sea-
bed and subsoil of the exclusive economic zone' as further specified in the proposal. This means, above all, an international
tax on offshore oil, which would run into billions of dollars
which should be collected from companies not included in the
'enterprise system'.

     Not only would such a tax assure the automaticity of
transfers that development strategy has been striving for during the last two decades: it would also create a more workable
financial balance within the international resource management
system itself: i.e., the capital-intensive, costly, and, at the
beginning probably deficit-prone operations of the International Seabed Authority could be financed, largely, by a small part
of the huge profits of the oil industry. There would indeed be
nothing extraordinary in such a method, already widely applied
at the national or corporate level: companies engaged in both
oil production and in metal mining commonly finance the deficits arising from metal mining operations and the losses resulting from metal market fluctuations from the huge profits
they make on oil production.

     What was to be pointed out here in particular, however,
is that an international taxation scheme would be a direct
consequence, an intrinsic part, of the expansion of the concept of Common Heritage.

                    INSTITUTIONAL RESTRUCTURING AND
                    THE INTEGRATION OF THE OCEANS

     In 1971, the Delegation of Malta introduced in the U.N.
Committee on the Peaceful Uses of the Seabed, an *Ocean Space
Draft Treaty* based on the concept that the oceans as a whole
and all their resources are the Common Heritage of Mankind.
It provided for a system of management for all marine resources and all major uses of the oceans. Had the international
community chosen this apparently more complex path many solutions which are now being sought would in fact have become
easier. The Maltese model would have *internalized* many functions and could thus have led to the creation of a more self-
sufficient, more nearly closed, system, which would not have
demanded too many immediate outside changes.

     It became clear immediately, however, that the Maltese
proposal was way ahead of its time. The international community
chose a more limited approach, providing a system of management for one of the marine resources only, viz., the minerals
of the deep seabed. In trying to establish this system, however, the international community, first through the Seabed

Committee, then through the Conference, became ever more acu-
tely aware of the interaction of all uses and the need to deal
with the oceans as a whole. This, however, was now far more
complicated, since many functions had been *externalized*, en-
tailing changes *outside* the new system, and thus the necessity
of restructuring much of the United Nations system.

While providing, to some extent, a code of conduct for
the other major uses of the oceans - the management of living
resources, navigation, scientific research, environmental protection, the transfer of technology - the emerging Draft Convention reveals an awareness that this is not enough and makes
repeated reference to, and demands on 'the competent international institutions'. In some cases, these 'competent institutions' already exist: COFI (FAO) for the living resources;
IOC (UNESCO) for scientific research; IMCO for navigation;
UNEP for the protection of the environment. In other cases -
transfer of technology, regional fisheries management - they
will have to be created. In any case it is clear that the
existing organization will have to be restructured to be able
to assume the newly required functions; and that restructured
and newly established institutions must be coordinated or integrated at the policy-making level, providing for a forum
where problems arising from the uses of the oceans can be discussed by States in their interaction and including not only
their *technical* but also their *political* dimensions. A possible model for the kind of *integrative machinery* needed has
been presented elsewhere. (9)

During the Seventh Session, the Delegation of Portugal
tabled a rather complex resolution, co-sponsored by 17 other
Delegations from developed, developing and socialist States,
to give the necessary official impetus to this process which,
more or less informally, is already in course.

"Considering that the implementation of the Convention on
the Law of the Sea calls for an active and increased role of
the appropriate international organization with competence in
ocean affairs..." the Resolution states, "Recognizing that
further strengthening of these organizations and increased cooperation among them are required, so as to allow Member
States to benefit fully from the expanded opportunities for
economic and social progress offered by the new ocean regime.."
the Resolution calls on member States, on the Secretary General,
the Specialized Agencies and other organizations of the United
Nations, to take the necessary steps to achieve the needed
restructuring and integration.

In this, the structure of the new International Seabed
Authority, being the first to be established to meet the new
requirements, is very likely to influence the restructuring
of the other organizations. For these others, if they are to
discharge their new responsibilities in ocean space, must also
become operational; that is, they must directly manage resourc-

es, engage in scientific research, etc. Besides their traditional, policy-making and executive organs, they will to comprise an *operational arm*, analogous to the Enterprise system
of the Seabed Authority. They also will have to establish organs for *dispute settlement* at a certain level, in response
to provisions already included in the Draft Convention.

TOWARDS A FUNCTIONAL FEDERATION OF INTERNATIONAL ORGANIZATIONS

This restructuring and integrating of the marine-oriented
part of the U.N. system inserts itself into the broad trend to
'restructure the U.N. system', which it is bound to influence
and direct.

The proposed system, or 'functional federation of international basic organizations' is in fact a 'module' system, to
which other 'modules' can be added as needed.

One 'module' could be provided by the Outer-Space sector.

A number of U.N. agencies, organizations, and commissions
as well as other intergovernmental, regional and nongovernmental organizations are presently engaged in outer-space activities. The U.N. Committee on the Peaceful Uses of Outer
Space has the mandate to coordinate these activities, which
are regulated by a number of legal instruments, the most important of which is the *Treaty on Principles Governing the
Activities of States in the Exploration and Use of Outer
Space, including the Moon and Other Celestial Bodies*. The
Treaty, which provides a code of conduct, does not provide for
any kind of machinery for decision-making, nor - as already
pointed out - does it take any account of the *economic* and
development potential of outer-space technology. As this potential becomes more obvious and given the fact that the Common Heritage principle has been applied to outer space and
outer-space activities and resources, it becomes necessary to
create machinery through which all nations can share in policy-making as well as in the management of programs and technologies.

One could imagine a periodic Outer-Space Conference or
Assembly (every three, two, or one year/s), which might either
consist of all member States or, if the model of a functional
federation of international organizations were to be followed,
of representatives of all the international organizations active in outer space. (Which, in turn, are composed of States).
The Committee on the Peaceful Uses of Outer Space might serve
as an Executive Council, or the Conference itself might elect
an Executive Council which would supersede the Committe on
Peaceful Uses of Outer Space and would be chosen on a strictly
regional basis, ensuring equitable representation of all parts

of the world. (10) Obviously there would have to be some kind
of common Secretariat which might well be provided by the U.N.
Secretariat. Such an *International Outer-Space Authority* would
have to have an operational arm, although it may be difficult,
at this stage, to say whether it would be more functional to
create it *ex novo*, following the pattern of the Seabed Authority, or whether the operational arm should be even more decentralized, utilizing existing operational organizations such as
INTELSAT, INTERSPUTNIK, INMARSAT, ESO, which, in this case,
would have to be brought under the policy of the Authority.

Supposing there were six or seven such 'modules' or
'world economic communities' (in the meaning given to the
word 'communities' by 'the European Economic Communities')
dealing with oceans, outer space, energy, food, mineral resources, science and technology, international trade - the whole
system could be drawn together in a restructured ECOSOC, which
might be composed of Delegations from these various module Conferences or Assemblies.

This might be looking a bit too far - and too logically -
into the future. History will fumble along its own way: far
less logical, far less straightforward.

The expansion of the concept of the Common Heritage of
Mankind, however, is in course. If it is indeed to be the basis
of a New International Economic Order, its legal and economic
content has certain corollaries. To explore, however tentative-
ly, what these might be with regard to (i) international resource management; (ii) transnational corporations; (iii) international taxation; and (iv) the structure of international
organizations, has been the purpose of this paper.

NOTES AND REFERENCES

(1)   The statement is entitled *Considerations on Certain To-*
pics Examined by the Second Committee of the Conference on the
Law of the Sea, Seventh Session: March 28 - May 19, 1978.
(2)   See Document A/AC 105/C.2/SR 290, 23 March 1978.
(3)   See Amilcar O. Herrera et. al., *Catastrophe or New Socie-*
ty:A Latin American World Model, International Development Research Centre, Ottawa, 1976.
(4)   Ibid., p. 26
(5)   See Elisabeth Mann Borgese and Arvid Pardo, 'Ocean Management' in Jan Tinbergen (Coordinator), *Reshaping the Interna-*
tional Order:A Report to the Club of Rome, E.P. Dutton, New
York, 1976, pp. 305-317.
(6)   See Statement by Ambassador Wolf of Austria, *Note by the*
Secretariat, 28 April 1977, Enclosure 6 and informal working
papers.
(7)   Some countries, especially among the industrialized ones,

consider 'revenue sharing' as an adequate interpretation of
'benefit sharing', and 'benefit sharing' as the only corolla-
ry of the Common Heritage concept. The majority of countries,
however, interpret 'common heritage' in the wider sense, at-
tributed to it in our definition above. 'Benefit sharing' here
includes benefits other than financial, such as sharing in management prerogatives and technology.
(8)   See Elisabeth Mann Borgese, 'The Age of Aquarius' in A.J.
Dolman and J. van Ettinger (editors), *Partners in Tomorrow:
Strategies for a New International Order*, E.P. Dutton, New
York, 1978.
(9)   See Elisabeth Mann Borgese and Arvid Pardo, *The New International Order and the Law of the Sea*, Occasional Paper no.
V, International Ocean Institute, Malta University Press,
Malta, 1976.
(10) The principle of regional representation, which is becoming increasingly important in the United Nations system,
ought to be elaborated and refined. The four 'regions' - Asia,
Africa, Latin America and 'Western Europe and others', are
clearly inadequate as a basis for equitable regional representation. The concept of 'region' has many meanings and is no-
where clearly defined. As a basis of equitable representation,
the 15 regions established in the *Leontief Report* might offer
a fair, balanced, and workable solution: e.g. in a Council of
36 members, at least two members would have to be chosen from
each of these 15 regions, while six might be chosen at large,
to have more flexibility. See Wassily Leontief, *The Future of
the World Economy*, Oxford University Press, New York, 1977.

Building the
New International Order:
The Need for a
Framework Treaty
Arvid Pardo

INTRODUCTION; THE LEGAL CHALLENGE

In this paper some of the legal aspects of the new international order will be discussed. The discussion constitutes
an elaboration of some of the ideas and proposals contained in
the RIO Report where it was argued that if a new international
order is to be established which effectively extends equality
of opportunity, then the aims, means and institutions of the
new order must eventually be laid down in legal rules and standards which govern the behavior of States, international organizations, transnational corporations and other subjects of law.
(1) Without such provision, the new international order is likely to remain a slogan and global planning and resource management institutions will be little more than instruments of convenience.

International law is the body of rules and practices which
are binding upon States in their relations with each other.
Present international law developed in the XVI and XVII centuries as the law governing relations between States in Western
Europe. International law has passed through different phases
but until recently all, or nearly all, subjects of the law were
imbued with the Western European legal tradition.

A major contemporary challenge is the transformation of a
body of law that governed relations between a restricted number
of States into a law which can be accepted without reservations
by the expanded international political community regardless of
race or ideology. This can take place only if accepted international law serves not merely the interests of the nations that
developed it, but also the economic and social needs of the present world community as a whole. These needs may be defined

succinctly as, on the one hand, the need of rich countries for
the maintenance of high material standards of living and for
security of expectations in their economic relations with the
Third World and, on the other hand, the need of poor countries
to achieve both meaningful participation in economic decision-
making at the global level and greatly improved standards of
living for their populations. Common prerequisites to the satisfaction of the needs both of rich and poor countries are the
maintenance of peace, cooperative promotion of equitable economic and social development and a recognition of economic interdependence.

SOURCES OF INTERNATIONAL LAW
AND THEIR LIMITATIONS

The present international legal order is based on the sovereignty and equality of States. As a consequence, no State
can be bound by obligations without its consent. Established
sources of international law, however, offer ample possibility
to develop present law and to establish an agreed basis for a
new international order.

Custom, that is the adoption by States of a uniform practice in the belief that it should be legally binding, is an ancient source of international law. Although no State can be
bound against its will, it is generally recognized that the
adoption of a uniform practice on the part of the great majority of significant States in all geographical regions without
the active dissent of those which have not accepted the practice
can create new law. Thus, a new international order could be
developed through the operation of custom alone. Customary law,
however, is, for obvious reasons, an uncertain means for effective broad change in existing law. Hence other methods are commonly followed.

International Conventions, whether general or particular,
are now perhaps the predominant source of international law and
they supersede, as between the parties, customary law in effect.
The number, variety and complexity of international conventions
or treaties has increased considerably in recent years. Multilateral conventions in particular have multiplied. But negotiation of multilateral treaties is difficult, as demonstrated for
instance by the Conference on the Law of the Sea, when their
scope is global and their purpose is not to codify but fundamentally to change existing law.

Furthermore the processes of ratification and amendment
can be lengthy; treaties do not bind States which do not accept
them and as the number of potential participants to a convention
increases, the number of reservations also tends to increase
causing uncertainly with respect to the legal content of the

convention. (2) It is not surprising, therefore, that the negotiation of multilateral treaties which are global in scope is usually undertaken only after general acceptance of change in a particular field of international law.

The last thirty years have seen the establishment and remarkable expansion of the United Nations, its family of Specialized Agencies and of regional organizations. These organizations, but principally the United Nations, have come increasingly to occupy a central position in the declaration of new principles of international law. According to the United Nations Charter, resolutions of the United Nations General Assembly are not binding on member States, but when they are concerned with general norms of international law their adoption constitutes evidence of the opinions and practice of Governments. When resolutions enunciate general legal principles, they can also provide the basis for progressive development of international law. Because of this, States desirous of promoting the translation of moral precepts into legal principles governing the conduct of States have found it useful to submit their proposals initially to the United Nations General Assembly in order to obtain in this global forum a sense of the opinion of the world community. If the proposals receive wide support, negotiations are initiated to prepare the basis for additional United Nations General Assembly resolutions on the subject often culminating in a comprehensive resolution having the form of a Declaration, Charter or similar. Here the matter may rest. Should, however, substantial international consensus appear to develop, a general international convention may be negotiated.

This is the procedure which was followed in the case of the New International Economic Order. The proposal was submitted initially to a Special Session of the United Nations General Assembly where it received widespread support: a 'Plan of Action' was adopted. (3) A Charter of Economic Rights and Duties of States was subsequently elaborated and adopted by the General Assembly over the opposition of a minority of Western industrialized countries. (4) Adoption of the Charter was followed by a series of discussions and negotiations between rich and poor countries both within and outside the United Nations framework with the object of initiating implementation of some of its provisions. These negotiations, however, do not appear to have produced up to the present significant concrete results: certainly there is no sign of a sufficient international consensus to justify an effort to embody the principles contained in the Charter of Economic Rights and Duties of States in an international convention which would constitute the legal basis governing future international economic relations.

The tendency, particularly on the part of the Third World countries, to submit proposals for broad changes in some aspects of international economic relations to the consideration of the United Nations General Assembly is understandable: the proposals

obtain an immediate world-wide audience; a majority in the
Assembly is likely to be sympathetic; and initial General Assembly resolutions can be followed by a wide variety of political and other steps which can facilitate attainment of the ultimate goal. Finally, United Nations resolutions, while they may
not be binding upon States, offer evidence of the opinion of
States and can influence the climate within which the development of law takes places. On the other hand, there are some
dangers. Comprehensive General Assembly resolutions, such as
the Charter of Economic Rights and Duties of States, prescri-
bing broad principles of State conduct,lack any mechanism for
objective interpretation and application: interpretation is a
matter for individual States and practical implementation is
left to subsequent negotiations and eventual conventions.

Thus, resolutions, which are not supported by the political weight of major States, may receive only marginal acknowledgement in the practice of States. If effective implementation is desired, 'lawmaking' General Assembly resolutions must
in due course be followed by an effort to given precise content
to principles of conduct prescribed by the United Nations. This
is also required in the case of the concept of the New International Economic Order and of the Charter of Economic Rights
and Duties of States if both are not to suffer from the dangers
of uncertainty, and from prolonged controversy as to the obligations involved.

THE NEED FOR A FRAMEWORK TREATY

We have seen that a comprehensive convention to govern
economic relationships between States does not appear feasible
in the immediate future. This, however, does not exclude the
possibility of attempting to incorporate the fundamental points
contained in the Charter of Economic Rights and Duties of States
into a *framework treaty,* the provisions of which could in turn
be developed, when a greater degree of international consensus
has been reached, into more detailed treaties in the context of
action programs in the economic and social fields. Such an attempt can, and should, be designed in such a manner as not to
interfere in any way with the continuing discussions between
Western market economy countries and the Third World.

A framework treaty would not attempt to legislate a new
world order. Its basic purpose would be only to take an unmistakable initial step toward international economic - and social
- solidarity, and hence towards a world order based on cooperation rather than competition between States. In this sense it
would seek to give certainly and binding legal force under international law to those fundamental principles contained in
the Charter of Economic Rights and Duties of States as are im-

mediately acceptable both to rich and to poor countries.

This basic core of a framework treaty should be completed by provisions on three major subjects. First, definition of the procedures on the basis of which substantive issues could be progressively negotiated. Secondly, establishment of a flexible but also comprehensive, compulsory and binding system for the settlement of disputes arising from the interpretation or application of the treaty. (5) Thirdly, the framework treaty could contain provisions acceptable to States Parties, on matters directly affecting international economic relations which are not mentioned in the Charter of Economic Rights and Duties of States. Such provisions could relate, for instance, to facilitating scientific research and the interchange of its results in all fields and ensuring prompt access by all countries to appropriate technologies on fair and reasonable terms. Science and technology are the keys to the future of poor countries and access to them is indispensable for economic development. If acceptable to the parties to the framework treaty, other provisions could establish rights and duties of States with regard to certain global problems, such as expansion of international trade, energy, food and the flow of real resources to poor countries. Once ratified by a nation, the treaty would, in accordance with the legal principle *pacta sunt servanda,* be legally binding. (6)

The concept of a New International Economic Order postulates the willingness of States to accept international obligations constraining their sovereignty in various ways, yet sovereignty and the independence of States is the basis of the present international system, a basis which it would be futile to attempt to change in the foreseeable future. Apart from their participation in different international fora, States have not practiced the economic cooperation which is necessary for the achievement of the goals of the New International Order. It is vital, therefore, to introduce the habit of effective cooperation in the practice of States. One way of taking an effective step in this direction would be for the framework treaty to provide that outer space and celestial bodies and ocean space, beyond the limits of national jurisdiction, as determined by the Law of the Sea Conference, have a special legal status as a common heritage of mankind; as such they are not subject to appropriation by any State and should be used and administered exclusively for peaceful purposes through international mechanisms with the participation of all States. (7) The resources of these areas would be exploited with particular regard to the needs of poor countries. Such a provision would not only give access to technologically less advanced countries to areas otherwise inaccessible having great future potential, but it would also introduce into international practice a measure of the effective cooperation in political, economic, technological and scientific matters which is indispensable for the implementation of the New

International Economic Order.

Negotiation of a framework treaty in the early future,
therefore, appears to have few, if any, disadvantages; it need
not obstruct present negotiations in the framework of the United Nations or in other fora. On the other hand, the advantages,
political and other, are many: it would constitute the legal
foundation of the future world order and would represent a binding commitment to peaceful structural change and to the elaboration of a law of nations that serves the interests of all
peoples, poor as well as rich.

CONCLUDING NOTE

It may be appropriate to conclude with a warning. While
the present international economic order is being progressively
eroded by the forces of change, there is no certainty that it
will be succeeded by a new order. The concept of the New International Economic Order is based on two assumptions: (a) that
there will be peace in the world for the foreseeable future;
and (b) that all significant States, regardless of ideology,
are willing to cooperate on an equitable basis and will closely
coordinate economic and social objectives, policies and priorities in a manner which may sometimes even constrain perceived
immediate national interests. It is not yet evident that these
assumptions correspond to reality.

If the assumptions on which the concept of the New International Economic Order is based are not fulfilled, if the international atmosphere continues.to deteriorate, if States omit
to implement stated principles through effective coordination
of economic policies, not only will it become impossible to negotiate a framework treaty but ongoing negotiations at the United Nations and in other international fora will not be succesful. And a New International Economic Order will not be established in the world.

NOTES AND REFERENCES

(1) See Jan Tinbergen (coordinator), *Reshaping the International
Order: A Report to the Club of Rome*, E.P. Dutton, New York, 1976,
pp. 114-117.

(2) Reservations should be compatible with 'the object and purpose' of a convention, but application of the criterion of com-
patibility is a matter of appreciation.

(3) Resolution 3201 (S-VI), Declaration on the Establishment
of a New International Economic Order; and Resolution 3202 (S-

VI), Programme of Action on the Establishment of a New International Economic Order, adopted at the 6th special session of the U.N. General Assembly, 1 May 1974.

(4) The Charter was adopted by the General Assembly on 12 December 1974 at its XXIX session. The Charter seeks to establish "generally accepted norms to govern international economic relations systematically" and to promote the creation of a New International Economic Order. Of the industrialized market economy nations, only Sweden adopted the Charter; the United States, the Federal Republic of Germany, the United Kingdom, Belgium, Denmark and Luxemburg voted against it; most other Western industrialized nations abstained.

(5) Dispute settlement procedures might be modelled on the lines of Part IV of the Single Negotiating Text of the Law of the Sea Conference.

(6) In that it would lay down the 'rules of the international game', the framework treaty might resemble an international Treaty of Rome, although inevitably much less detailed.

(7) On 3 July 1979 the U.N. Committee on the Peaceful Uses of Outer Space approved a draft international agreement which declared the moon, the planets and other celestial bodies the common heritage of mankind. The draft agreement is expected to be approved by the XXXIV session of the U.N. General Assembly at the end of 1979.

Toward a Regime Governing International Public Property

Christopher Pinto

COMMUNITY INTEREST IN THE CONSERVATION
OF RESOURCES

The twentieth century has seen international law develop into a regulatory system of comprehensive scope. No longer concerned primarily with the prevention of aggression, it seeks the peaceful ordering of broad areas of relations within the community of States, and strives toward the establishment and maintenance of equity and fair dealing among them for the ultimate benefit of all. To fulfill this high purpose within a community which today comprises some 150 States with diverse social and economic systems, at varying stages of economic development, the law has had to acquire a capacity for ordered change, continually in search of the balance between new manifestations of interests and the *status quo*, between justice and mere stability. International law has proved, in the event, even more sensitive and responsive in this respect than its domestic counterpart.

Among the most vital community interests to be demonstrated since the second world war is that in vast areas which technology has only recently brought within range of human use and exploitation: outer space, the deep sea-bed and the Antarctic continent. The technique for the development of legal principles in each case has been substantially different. A regime for outer space began with the initiative of the technologically advanced countries in the United Nations General Assembly in securing the adoption of the Declaration of Legal Principles Governing the Activities of States in the Exploration and Use of Outer Space, resolution 1962 (XVIII) of 13 December 1963. This was followed by the conclusion, under the auspices of the United Nations, of the 1967 Treaty on Principles Governing the

202

Activities of States in the Exploration and Use of Outer Space,
including the Moon and Other Celestial Bodies, the 1968 Agreement on the Rescue of Astronauts .... and the 1974 Convention
on International Liability for Damage caused by Space Objects.
    The foundations for a treaty on the exploration and exploi-
tation of the deep sea-bed were laid in United Nations General
Assembly resolution 2749 (XXV): Declaration of Principles Governing the Sea-bed and the Ocean Floor, and the Subsoil Thereof, Beyond the Limits of National Jurisdiction 17 December 1970,
while the text of a Treaty on the Prohibition of the Emplace-
ment of Nuclear Weapons and Other Weapons of Mass Destruction
on the Sea-bed and Ocean Floor and in the Subsoil Thereof, prepared by the Conference of the Committee on Disarmament, was
adopted by the United Nations General Assembly on 7 December
1970. (Resolution 2660 (XXV)).
    The principles governing the Antarctic continent have yet
to be enunciated and to receive the approval of the community
through a diplomatic conference, or the United Nations. While
the Antarctic Treaty of 1959 may be of some assistance in such
a task, restrictive membership provisions and unrecognized and
conflicting territorial claims to portions of the area may encourage the community to look to more reliable sources in the
elaboration of a comprehensive treaty regime which would govern
that area. (1)
    The essence of the community's interest in these areas and
their resources (and particularly the last two) was foreseen
by Roscoe Pound who spoke of:

    ....the social interest in conservation of social resourc-
    es, that is, the claim or want or demand involved in so-
    cial life in civilized society that the goods of existence
    shall not be wasted; that where all human claims or wants
    or desires may not be satisfied, in view of infinite indi-
    vidual desires and limited natural means of satisfying
    them, the latter be made to go as far as possible; and to
    that end, that acts or courses of conduct which tend need-
    lessly to destroy or impair these goods shall be restrain-
    ed. In its simplest form this is an interest in the use
    and conservation of natural resources, and is recognized
    in the doctrines as to res communis, which may be used but
    not owned... (2)

Translated from the domestic to the international context,
this means that these areas and their resources must not be
wasted or selfishly exploited to the detriment of the interests
of the world community; they must be treated as the property
of all mankind, as international public property, to be cooper-
atively managed according to principles that would secure from
them the greatest benefit for the greatest number over the
longest period of time. No part of them can become the property

of any State, nor the subject of exclusive or uncontrolled use
or exploitation by those who might, at any given period, possess the technology needed to enable them to do so.

The outlines of a legal framework to give effect to this
interest of the community has developed in the last decade,
principally through the activities of United Nations organs
and conferences that have facilitated the development of relevant principles of customary international law with unprecedented rapidity and precision.

CUSTOMARY INTERNATIONAL LAW

The term 'customary international law' is generally interpreted to mean the established usages, the established practices of States, which have come to be regarded as obligatory
in character. (3) Recognition of the legal character of a practice was deduced from repeated acts and professions over a
long period, although no specific duration has been laid down.
In the early development of international law, the practice of
even a single State powerful enough to impose its will, say in
matters of maritime warfare, might have established a practice
which then came to be accepted by others through acquiescence.
More often a group of such powerful States might similarly establish and enforce a common practice.

The essence of customary law is the general acceptance of
a practice as obligatory. At a time when power lay in the hands
of a few States, when the international community lacked institutions or regular procedures for ascertaining opinion as to the
obligatory nature of a particular practice, and when communications were slow, evidence of a practice or the acceptance of
it was hard to isolate and formulation of rules based upon it
was fraught with difficulty. Principle had to be garnered in
the archives of Foreign Offices of the handful of States which
competed continually with one another to extend their commercial
and political influence, and whose records abounded in self-
serving interpretations, factual inaccuracies, subtlety and so-
phistry. Its essence had to be distilled by scholars who often
felt obliged - as did Grotius himself- to sift out the wholly
uncertain and the unjust, and to lay down better rules of conduct based upon inferences which, in their personal view, accorded more with morality and common sense. (4) Viewed against
the background of these beginnings, custom has, for all its du-
rability as a source of law, earned a reputation for vagueness,
and of being unsuited to the demands of modern international relations.

This view cannot be held of modern customary law. While the
beginnings of a custom will perhaps always be discovered in the
conduct of one State or a few, the speed of communications and

the development of representative institutional forums for the
orderly and regular expression of opinion have greatly enhanc-
ed the ability of the community to examine, discuss, and accept
or reject a new practice. Writing of the development of the
Law of the Sea, Professor Lauterpacht, as he then was, has this
to say:

> However, assuming.... that the emergence of the doctrine
> of sovereignty over the adjacent areas constituted a radi-
> cal change in pre-existing international law, the length
> of time within which the customary rule of international
> law comes to fruition is irrelevant. For customary inter-
> national law is not yet another expression for prescrip-
> tion. A "consistent or uniform usage practiced by the
> States in question" - to use the language of the Interna-
> tional Court of Justice in the *Asylum Case* (I.C.J. Reports,
> 1950, p. 276) - can be packed within a short space of
> years. The "evidence of a general practice as law" - in
> the words of Article 38 of the Statute - need not be
> spread over decades. Any tendency to exact a prolonged pe-
> riod for the crystallization of custom must be proportio-
> nate to the degree and the intensity of the change that it
> purports, or is asserted, to effect. (5)

Evidence of the acceptance or rejection of a practice is
now available through modern mechanisms with comparative speed
and accuracy, through the institutional maintenance of impartial
records of formal pronouncements, as well as of formal affirmation or denial through the voting process. These records lend
to the evidence a dimension unknown in former times: the democratization of modern international institutions has given new
strength and validity and offers a foundation of unprecedented
firmness to the formal expressions of collective will that bear
witness to the opinion of the generality of States as to what
is to be regarded as a practice that has become obligatory.
It follows that the existence of new institutions has to
a great extent removed the uncertainties often associated with
customary law in the past, as well as the delays that used to
attend its formation. Through machinery established by the
United Nations - the 1958 Conference on the Law of the Sea -
it was possible to develop President Truman's declaration in
1945 claiming the continental shelf of the United States, from
unilateral act to acceptance and incorporation in the Geneva
Convention on the Continental Shelf in just thirteen years. (6)
Not quite as smooth, but perhaps just as sure, has been the development of the exclusive economic zone as an institution of
customary international law. Beginning with the Declaration of
Santiago of 18 August 1952 by Chile, Ecuador and Peru, claiming
"sole sovereignty and jurisdiction" over the sea and seabed adjacent to their coasts up to a distance of "not less than 200

nautical miles", the sovereign right of every coastal State to
establish a corresponding zone for the purpose of exploiting
its resources is now widely accepted and generally acquiesced
in. The fact that there may not as yet be complete agreement
on some of the components of coastal State jurisdiction in the
zone, *cannot be allowed to call in question the fact of the
general recognition of the resource-related central core of
the concept.* This development has been brought about through
another forum established by the United Nations: The Third Conference on the Law of the Sea, where exchanges of view, canvas-
sing of opinion and an assessment of general trends can take
place with regularity, rapidity and thoroughness, replacing
with relative efficiency the labored and uncertain search for
repeated acts and forbearances by States that were formerly the
only means of determining the emergence of a customary rule.

It has been said that, in order to apply to the family of
nations as a whole, a customary rule must be universally accepted. But even in its pristine form this principle was qualified
in its application by the principle of acquiescence. (7) Given
the lack until very recently of developed institutional structures that might have facilitated the expression of the views
of States, the development of the law through custom might have
been seriously hampered had it been otherwise, i.e. if it had
been necessary to prove the negative (non-objection), or wait
until every country had expressed itself. Common sense demands
that the absence of protest while in possession of full knowledge of the facts should, unless circumstances indicate the
contrary, be interpreted as acquiescence or tacit recognition
of a particular practice.

Translated into modern institutional terms, abstention in
a regular vote on a decision declaratory of principle, carried
out in a broadly representative and fully informed forum following extensive debate and negotiation, must be interpreted
as acquiescence, in the absence of indications to the contrary.

In the light of the foregoing, we may assume that: certain
regularly maintained and uniformly publicised records of the
General Assembly and its bodies are, in general, impartially
compiled, and accurate; they embody the opinions of States as
to the binding (i.e. legal) character of certain rules, and
therefore are clear evidence of the existence of customary rules
of law; and that when they take the form of resolutions, decisions or other texts couched in reasonably precise and mandatory
terms, have received a wide degree of publicity and extensive
discussion and negotiation, then if they have been accepted or
not objected to by all or the overwhelming majority of members,
they must be taken to reflect rules of customary international
law, unless circumstances indicate the contrary.

This is not, and should not be confused with, an assertion
as to the legal effect of General Assembly resolutions. (8) This
is an affirmation that there exist in the practice of United

Nations organs, notably the General Assembly, its committees,
specialized organs and conferences, records and decisions that
are clear and unequivocal evidence of contemporary customary
rules of international law, and this is particularly true of
formal instruments like resolutions. (9) *Such resolutions embody, not create the law.* Vagueness of language may result in
a text being less readily applied in a given case, but it cannot weaken essentially the binding force of the rule of law
it reflects. On the other hand, the rules embodied in the text,
even though they have an independent life derived from the common belief of States in the existence of a legal rule, nevertheless are *reinforced as to their validity and contemporary
significance by the obligations of their membership of the
United Nations, which imparts to them the very character of
the Charter of the United Nations itself.*
     There are a number of relevant United Nations decisions
that are vehicles for affirming the existence of customary
rules of international law and are thereby reinforced by the
obligations of membership. (10) On the basis of principles contained in these decisions, viewed as principles of customary
international law, it is possible to formulate the elements
of an equitable regime that would apply in areas recognized by
the community as having the character of international public
property, and function with overall social efficiency in safeguarding and giving effect to the community's interest in the
natural resources of these areas.

INTERNATIONAL PUBLIC PROPERTY

     The foundation and source of these principles is a declar-
ed social interest in certain areas and their resources that
has emerged as a by-product of the recognition of the fact of
the economic interdependence of nations, and the establishment
of international economic cooperation as a principle of the
Law of Peace.(11) The Treaty on Outer Space speaks of the
"province of all mankind" (12); the Antarctic Treaty contem-
plates that activities under it must be peaceful "in the interest of all mankind" (13); the informal composite negotiating
text (ICNT) of the Conference on the Law of the Sea, echoing
the Declaration on the Sea-bed, declares that area and its
resources to be the "common heritage of mankind".(14) Declaration by the community of nations that an area and its resources
has an international social or public character, confirms that
its members believe that the area has such a character. (15)
Where there is no dissent, and acquiescence by all, that character must be regarded as thereafter sustained and strengthened
by the entirety of the legal rules which govern the community.
(16)

What is the relationship between States (as representing
groups of mankind as currently organized) and their nationals
on the one hand, and these areas and their resources on the
other? Do they possess rights? Are those rights rights in property i.e. of ownership, possession, or use? Of the expressions
referred to, the 'common heritage' is the most mature, and the
most fertile for deriving legal principle expressive and protective of the community's social interest in the use and exploitation of an area and its resources. 'Common heritage',
while used in a poetic and metaphorical sense (to the extent
that there is no real passing of property on death) does nevertheless, through the idea of 'inheritance' that it conveys,
clearly import the idea of rights in property commonly held.
What is the nature of those rights?

Early, and admittedly not fully developed, excursions in
search of conceptual antecedents were in the direction of the
Roman law concepts of *res nullius* and *res communis omnium*. The
first was rejected, since the sea-bed and its resources were
not the property of no one: on the contrary, they had solemnly
been declared to belong to 'all mankind', and 'all mankind'
must therefore have some legal relationship to them. Nor were
the seabed and its resources, as were *res nullius*, to be had
by any individual for the taking. On the contrary, according
to the Declaration, such taking was to be strictly controlled
and circumscribed: it had to be in conformity with an international regime of a specific kind. (17) That regime had yet to
be evolved, so that it followed that any prior taking could not
be countenanced at all since it would be *per se* contrary to community interests.

Res communis omnium, on the other hand, showed greater af-
finity and promise. The 'common' (i.e. popular) enjoyment aspect of the 'common heritage' certainly came very close to the
Roman concept, which, according to some writers, covered such
things as parks and rivers. The similarity was heightened in
that *res communis omnium* could not, in its original form, be
reduced to individual ownership. The thing was thought of as
being commonly and collectively held in undivided and indivis-
able shares, as was the case,it seemed, with the common heritage. (18)

But in the case of the 'common heritage of mankind' - at
least that part of it that comprised the seabed and its resources - the situation was compounded by the nature of the use
to which the thing was to be put. *Res communis* sufficed so long
there was no exploitative use, so long as no part of the thing
was to be taken, transformed or converted by some individual
and thereby placed permanently outside the reach of the other
members of the community who were entitled equally to profit
from it. If resource exploitation was to be permitted, then
clearly *res communis* was an inadequate concept for comparison,
lacking the means to ensure compensatory benefits for all.

The Declaration of 1970 seemed to contain a more elaborate concept, contemplating as it did, 'international machinery' which would, *inter alia*, give effect to provisions requiring "rational management of the area and its resources" and the "equitable sharing" of benefits. (19) This led some to seek comparison with the 'Trust' known to some jurisdictions, where property might be 'legally' owned by one person who was nevertheless under a duty to deal with it for the benefit of another, or others, who had 'equitable' ownership of the property. The 'international machinery' was seen as the 'trustee', charged with regulating all activities and channelling all benefits to the beneficiaries, i.e. all States, as representing mankind. (20) But nothing in the Declaration distinguishes 'legal' and 'beneficial' ownership in the seabed an its resources. Indeed, nothing is said of 'ownership' at all, and the idea of property is itself derived from the reference to 'heritage' which calls to mind the more legal form 'inheritance'.

Perhaps the closest to the 'common heritage' as it has evolved in some ten years of intensive negotiations at the Conference on the Law of the Sea is to be found in a Roman concept much less expounded and analysed by the early writers than the others which have been mentioned: *res publicae*. In that category of things were placed public baths, arenas, roads, (21) and (by some) the sea and the sea shore. (22) These were things, as another writer implies, *"quae publico usui destinatae sunt"* (23) a phrase which seems almost identical in meaning to 'common heritage'. According to the applicable rules, such things were not, in their original form, capable of individual ownership, but were subject permanently to the collective ownership of the community: *"....quae (res) publicae sunt, nullius videntur in bonis esse, ipsius enim universitatis esse creduntur"*. They had to be transformed or converted in some way before they could become the object of individual ownership. Over that process, the State, as the agent of the people or the public ('populus', 'poplicus', 'publicus'), kept careful control, to ensure that through it the potential for use by every other person was not impaired, or if impaired, was appropriately compensated for through taxation of one kind or another. (25)

The suppression of individual ownership, and the permanent merger of rights in collective ownership implied by the 'common heritage' concept, may suggest that a concept of rights in property has no relevance in this context and should be substituted by a right of common use that is *sui generis* and unrelated to a 'property' relationship. It would seem premature, at any rate today, to take such a position. Recognition of a right of property, albeit a collective or 'common' one, is a traditional and well-understood way of defining an interest so as to protect it. *Ubi jus, ibi remedium,* and a right of property, of ownership, may be a more familiar and firmer basis for action in the event of infringement of this social interest, than any

evolving and relatively vague concept of 'common use'. For the
overwhelming majority of States who adopt the collective approach, the concept of commonly held rights of property could
be of greater efficacy and value.

Thus when an area and its resources have been declared by
the community to be 'the common heritage of mankind', or to
have a comparable status, whatever the precise term used, they
assume the character of things *in patrimonio populi*; they become international public property, and collective rights of
ownership must be recognized in every State of the community
and their nationals, as well as in other groups of mankind,
such as peoples who have not yet exercised their right of self-
determination. The fact of collective ownership is thereby recognized as a part of customary international law. The rights
of ownership are protected from that moment on, and even while
the superstructure of a detailed regime and machinery are being
negotiated. (26)

THE SEABED BEYOND NATIONAL JURISDICTION AS INTERNA-
TIONAL PUBLIC PROPERTY; NEGOTIATION AND FORMU-
LATION OF PRINCIPLES

'The common heritage of mankind' was the most mature and
comprehensive concept of its type to come before the United
Nations and be made the subject of detailed elaboration and
intensive and prolonged negotiation by all countries. For the
reasons as set forth earlier in this paper, the Declaration
of 1970 must be regarded as containing principles of customary
law relating to the seabed and the ocean floor beyond the limits of national jurisdiction, and the resources of that area.
In the view of the overwhelming majority of States, the seabed
and its wealth had not previously been subject to an international regime: the remoteness of the area, and the absence of
the requisite technology for its exploration, had placed such
activities beyond the scope of contemporary human endeavor,
and therefore outside the contemplation of regulatory norms.
The matter simply had not occurred to the community, much less
had the community given its collective sanction to any applicable rules. The Declaration of 1970 demonstrated for the first
time that the community now recognized that there were certain
general principles of customary international law that were
applicable in respect of the area and its resources. Even if,
as has sometimes been argued, the principle of the 'freedom of
the seas' has been previously extended by analogy to the ocean
floor and its resources, such a view could not continue to be
valid in the face of the unequivocal evidence of the contrary
opinio juris sive necessitatis contained in the Declaration of
Principles of 1970.

The essentials of the Declaration - collective ownership of the resource *in situ*, collective benefit from its exploitation and collective management through a central regulatory authority - bear a striking resemblance to the Roman rules on public property, which, it will be recalled, could not accept individual rights of ownership in such property until something was done to 'convert' it; in that event, required compensation of the rest of the public (the collective owners) through State intervention; and posited the State as regulatory authority on behalf of the community. The idea of State intervention to spread the benefits derived from individual mining initiatives and to regulate such activities, is not, of course, peculiar to Roman law. For example, the *Arthasastra*, the ancient Indian treatise on the art of government written by Kautilya, Counsellor to the Kings of the Maurya dynasty who ruled India in the fourth century before Christ, recounts in detail rules dealing with the government's monopoly of mining and commerce in minerals, and in particular with the collection of some ten categories of revenue from those engaged in mining activities. (27)

Rejecting the idea that a single State could or should regulate exploitation of the sea-bed beyond national jurisdiction, the Declaration requires, as an integral part of the international regime for exploration and exploitation of that area, the establishment of 'international machinery' to administer collective ownership and ensure collective benefit. (28)

The 'common heritage' concept, which now forms part of the customary international law relating to the deep sea-bed, has a basis and a precedent in the general legal rules prevalent in several jurisdictions from ancient times. As developed in the Third United Nations Conference on the Law of the Sea, in which virtually all States and peoples participate, the principles and 'machinery' of the evolving regime have a universal character and are indicative of the rules that may be applicable, with appropriate modifications, to all areas and resources declared by the community to be in the nature of international public property.

In the following section a regime applicable to international public property is outlined. Before presenting this regime, however, it is necessary to first note a legislative principle which must be placed on a par with the most fundamental of rules of substantive international law: universal participation in the negotiation of a regime applicable to international public property.

As essential prerequisite to the adoption of principles governing areas which are recognized as objects of community interest is their negotiation and formulation through a procedure in which all States have the opportunity to participate fully on the basis of sovereign equality. Paragraph 4(c) of the Declaration on the Establishment of a New International

Economic Order requires:

> Full and effective participation on the basis of equality
> of all countries in the solving of world economic problems
> in the common interest of all countries, bearing in mind
> the necessity to ensure the accelerated development of all
> the developing countries.....

The establishment of regimes for these areas involves the
discussion of a variety of economic problems arising in connection with the exploitation of their resources. No restricted
group may assume the responsibility for formulating the relevant principles or for devising management systems for such
areas.

The need to afford the opportunity for universal participation derives from the nature of international law, as law
which is observed because of its essential rationality, simply
because it *ought* to be, and *must* be observed if disorder is to
be avoided. It follows that the wider the group that participates in its formulation the better their needs will be served
by the final product, the wider the recognition of the law's
applicability, and the greater its effectiveness and stability.

It is generally agreed that procedures within the forum
should provide for maximum efforts to secure consensus regarding each formulation. Minority positions must be fully represented and given due weight through such devices as postpone-
ment of voting to allow further efforts to reconcile views, and
requiring relatively high majorities for the final adoption of
a text. However, the basic democratic procedure of adoption
through a one-State-one-vote majority decision cannot be modified, or too long delayed.

Democratic procedures must similarly be provided to enable
development of the regime through amendment of the texts adopted and periodic overall review of the working of the regime,
leading to revision where necessary.

A REGIME FOR INTERNATIONAL PUBLIC
PROPERTY

In this section, a regime for international public property is outlined. Its main provisions are presented under the
following headings: general principles; principles of resource
management policy; the development authority; operational principles; responsibility to ensure compliance and liability for
damage; reservations; and amendment and revision. The suggested
regime is based upon the several documents referred to above
and on the clear trend of negotiations at the Conference on
the Law of the Sea.

I. General Principles

Legal status

1.1 The Area and its resources, whether living or non-living, renewable or non-renewable, are international public property (*res publicae*). All rights in the Area and in those resources while in their original location are vested in mankind as a whole, and cannot be alienated. (29)

1.2 No State may claim sovereignty or exercise sovereign rights over any part of the Area, or over any part of its resources in their original location, nor may any State or person become the owner thereof, or acquire any other proprietary richts therein. (30)

1.3 However, minerals and living organisms may be taken from their original location, and may then become subject to ownership or other proprietary rights, but only in accordance with this international regime, including any rules and regulations adopted, and any binding decisions rendered in accordance with it. (31)

1.4 No State or person may acquire or exercise rights with respect to the minerals or living organisms of the Area except in accordance with the provisions of this international regime. In particular, no such rights may be established or recognized until this regime has entered into force in accordance with its terms. (32)

1.5 All activities in the Area shall be carried out, organized and controlled by an international Authority (part II below) in which all States, as representing organized groups of mankind, shall participate on the basis of sovereign equality. The Authority shall act as the agent of mankind as a whole. (33)

General conduct of States in the Area

2.   The Area shall be open to use by all States without discrimination. The general conduct of States in, and in relation to, the Area shall be in accordance with this regime and other applicable rules of international law, including the Charter of the United Nations, in the interests of maintaining international peace and security and promoting international cooperation and mutual understanding.(34)

Benefit of mankind as a whole

3.   Activities in the Area shall be carried out for the benefit of mankind as a whole, irrespective of the geographical location of States, taking into particular consideration the interests and needs of the developing countries as provided for herein. (35)

Use of the Area exclusively for peaceful purposes

4.   The Area shall be used exclusively for peaceful purposes.
(36)

Participation of developing countries

5.   The effective participation of the developing countries
in the Area shall be promoted. In the sharing of benefits derived from the Area, particular consideration shall be given
to the needs and interests of the developing countries including the special needs and interests of the poorest among them;
of countries which, by reason of their geographical location,
are subject to any special disadvantages in relation to the
Area; and of countries which have not yet attained independence
or other self-governing status. (37)

Objects of archeological or historical interest

6.   All objects of archeological or historical interest found
in the Area shall be preserved or disposed of for the benefit
of mankind as a whole. Where a State of origin of such an object can be determined, that State shall have a preferential
right with respect to it. (38)

Settlement of disputes

7.   The parties to any dispute relating to the Area and its
resources shall resolve such dispute by the measures listed in
article 33 of the Charter of the United Nations. A procedure
leading to the compulsory settlement of the dispute shall form
an integral part of this regime. (39)

                        II. Principles of Resource Management
                                       Policy

8.   Management of all activities relevant to all resources of
the Area shall be governed by the principles which follow. All
such activities shall be carried out in such a manner as to
foster healthy development of the world economy and the balanced growth of international trade, to promote international
cooperation for the rapid over-all development of all countries
and the developing countries in particular, and specifically
with a view to ensuring:

(i)   orderly and safe development and rational management of
these resources, i.e. the conduct of all activities of exploration for and exploitation of the resources, in accordance with
sound principles of conservation, and the avoidance of waste;

(ii) expanding opportunities for all countries, irrespective
of level of economic development, social and economic system,
or geographical location, to participate in the development of
the resources of the Area, and the prevention of monopolization
of such activities;
(iii)generation of revenues for distribution to all countries;
(iv) just, stable and remunerative prices for commodities originating in the Area which are also produced outside the Area,
and increasing availability of those commodities so as to promote equilibrium between supply and demand;
(v)   security of supplies to consumers of commodities originating in the Area which are also produced outside the Area;
(vi) protection of developing countries from any adverse effects on their economies or on their export earnings resulting
from a reduction in the price of an affected commodity, or in
the volume of that commodity exported by it, to the extent that
such reduction results from activities in the Area, through
such measures as (a) promoting the establishment of, and participation in, commodity arrangements with balanced representation and decision-making as between producers and consumers,
and regulation of production of commodities from the Area until
such arrangements are operational; (b) establishment of a system of compensation for developing countries which suffer adverse effects on their economies or their export earnings as
foreseen above. (40)

III. The Development Authority

9.   There shall be established an international Development
Authority (the "Authority") which shall be responsible for carrying out, organizing and controlling all activities in the
Area in accordance with this regime, on behalf of mankind as a
whole. (41)
9.1 The Authority shall be empowered to carry out all activities in the Area and all related activities such as processing
and marketing, which may take place outside the Area. Its members shall contribute, according to their capacity, the finance,
equipment and personnel to enable it to do so.
9.2 So long as its members shall so decide, corporate entities
of member States shall have the right to carry out all such activities in the Area under negotiated contractual relationships
with the Authority. The Authority shall encourage and promote
such activities, which shall be organized by the Authority and
subject to its control (including the right of inspection) for
the purpose of ensuring compliance with the policies set forth
in paragraph 8, the operational rules and regulations of the
Authority, and the binding decisions of its organs in accordance with this regime.
9.3 The Authority shall adopt and apply standards, criteria,

rules and regulations for the safe and efficient conduct of all
such activities. (42)

9.4 The Authority shall ensure that all rights granted in accordance with this regime, and in particular, all rights under
contractual relationships with the Authority, are fully safeguarded and not subject to amendment, suspension or termination
except by agreement of the parties or by a binding decision
rendered pursuant to a dispute settlement procedure referred
to in paragraph 7, to which the parties are subject. (43)

9.5 The contractual relationships entered into by the Authority pursuant to paragraph 9.3 shall provide for sharing of production or proceeds as between the Authority and the Contractor, or payment by the contractor to the Authority of fees or
other charges, or both, sufficient to provide the Authority
with revenues which when taken together with other sources of
financing, will enable the Authority to carry out all of the
functions required of it pursuant to this regime. The Authority's income shall either be immune from taxation, or shall be
subject to taxes that will not be inconsistent with the aims
set forth in this paragraph. Schemes for apportioning production or proceeds, and levels of fees or other charges established by the Authority in relation to contractual arrangements under paragraph 9.2 shall be fair, and shall be applied
in a non-discriminatory manner. (44)

9.6 Any excess of revenues of the Authority over its expenses
and costs shall, to an extent determined by the Authority, be
set aside for distribution to its membership, all in accordance
with sound business and accounting practices. The sum so set
aside shall be apportioned equitably according to an index derived by the Authority from time to time by reference to criteria chosen as demonstrating the relative levels of basic
needs within the countries concerned.(45)

9.7 The principal organs of the Authority shall be (a) an Assembly, the plenary or supreme policy-making organ on which
all of its members are represented, meeting at intervals of
one or two years; (b) a Council or the executive organ, of limited membership, responsible on a permanent basis for ensuring
that the policies laid down by the Assembly are consistently
and efficiently implemented; and (c) a Secretariat of an international character, i.e. which "shall not seek or receive instructions from any government or from any other authority external to the Organization". Subsidiary organs of a technical
character responsible to the Council shall be established in
order to formulate, keep under review, and advise the Council
concerning the uniform application of, operational rules of a
scientific, economic or legal nature. (46)

9.8 There shall be an operational arm of the Authority, responsible for carrying out the Authority's functions under paragraph 9.1. Whether or not it is constituted as an integral part
or organ of the Authority, in its operational aspect it shall

be capable of functioning autonomously, and independent of the
Authority. Its assets, while initially provided in part by the
Authority must be kept separate from those of the Authority
and its members. (47)
9.9 Any organ of limited membership, e.g. the Council, should
not exceed one fourth of the total number of potential members
of the Authority elected on the basis of equitable geographical
representation. As an organization which must be of universal
membership, the optimum figure for such organs would currently
be about 40.
9.9.1 In the case of the Council, membership shall also reflect
numerically the current balance of economic (e.g. producers,
consumers), political (e.g. different social and economic systems) and other (e.g. level of technological capacity to develop resources) interests, as far as possible. (48)
9.9.2 In the case of organs with technical functions, the members must possess the qualifications necessary to contribute to
arriving at informed, expeditious and fair decisions on the
particular subjects for which they are responsible. (49)
9.10 Decisions in all organs shall be on a one-State-one-vote
basis, by the majority of votes cast. As the functioning of the
Authority is to reflect international cooperation for development, rather than confrontation among competing ideologies,
the decision-making process shall incorporate devices for safeguarding the positions of minority interests. Thus, important
decisions are to be taken by a qualified majority of, say, two-
thirds or three-fourths of the membership; any such decisions
shall be preceded by periods during which every effort will be
made to secure a consensus, or the acquiescence of the generality of membership; that there shall be opportunities to can-
vass the constitutionality of a proposal, and of the decision
when adopted, before a judicial tribunal. There shall be no
system of weighted voting or veto for a State, or group of
States. (50)
9.11 The Authority, including its operational arm, as an international public corporation representing mankind as a whole
shall have international legal personality and be entitled to
appropriate privileges and immunities, with respect to its
property, assets and transactions. (51) The operational arm of
the Authority, however, may be liable to suit in the course of
its activities, but shall remain immune from execution unless
specifically agreed to by the Assembly.

IV. Operational Principles

10.   The resources of the Area to which this regime applies include living and non-living resources of every description.
11.1 Activities shall be conducted in the Area in such a manner
that:

(i)   no danger shall be caused to human life and health;
(ii) the Area and any contiguous or neighbouring areas shall
be kept free from pollution and contamination that are liable
to create hazards to human health, harm to animal and plant
life and to the ecological system, damage to amenities or interference with other legitimate uses of any such area. (52)
11.2 In particular, the discharge or disposal of toxic or radioactive substances in the Area is prohibited. (53)
12.1 Scientific research in the Area shall be carried out exclusively for peaceful purposes. All programs for scientific
research shall be notified in advance to the Authority. The
results of such research and the analysis thereof shall be effectively disseminated through the Authority or other appropriate international channels. (54)
12.2 All States shall promote international cooperation in
scientific research in the Area for the benefit of mankind as
a whole, and of the developing countries in particular, by initiating, and participating in, international research programs
which have as their purpose the training of personnel of different countries and of the Authority. (55)
13.   Technologies and scientific knowledge used in the Area
shall, upon request, be made available to the Authority, and
to the developing countries, on fair and reasonable commercial
terms and conditions.(56)
14.1 An activity shall be carried out in the Area with due regard to the right of another or others to carry out authorized
activities in the Area. (57)
14.2 Activities in the Area shall not interfere with the exercise of rights outside the Area. There shall be prior notifica-
tion and consultation with a view to avoiding interference with
such rights.
14.3 Activities in the Area with respect to resource deposits
which extend from within the Area across its limits into another area, shall only be conducted with due regard to the
rights and legitimate interests created and subsisting under
the jurisdiction to which such other area is subject. (58)
14.4 Nothing herein shall affect the right of any State to take
such measures as may be necessary to prevent, mitigate, or eliminate grave and imminent danger to areas within its jurisdiction, or related interests, from pollution or the threat thereof, or from hazardous occurrences resulting from, or caused
by, activities in the Area. (59)

V. Responsibility to Ensure Compliance;
Liability for Damage

15.   States shall have the responsibility to ensure that all
activities in the Area whether undertaken by States themselves
or by their nationals under contracts with the Authority shall

be carried out in conformity with this regime. The same responsibility shall attach to intergovernmental organizations
and to the Authority in respect of its activities in the Area.
Without prejudice to the rules of international law applicable
in determining responsibility, damage caused by the failure of
a State or the Authority to carry out its obligations under
this paragraph shall entail liability. (60)

VI. Reservations

16.   The subject of reservation to this regime shall be governed by Section 2 of the Vienna Convention on the Law of Treaties.
Any reservation shall require the acceptance of the Assembly.
Acceptance shall be determined by the procedure prescribed for
important decisions pursuant to paragraph 9.10.

VII. Amendments and Revision

17.   This regime shall be subject to amendment at any time by
a procedure requiring adoption by the Assembly by the procedure
prescribed for important decisions pursuant to paragraph 9.10
and to periodic review. Any amendment or revision shall become
effective and binding upon all parties upon its circulation
to them and ratification by a majority of States prescribed
pursuant to paragraph 9.10.

NOTES AND REFERENCES

(1)   On the question of the legal regime for Antarctica see
University of Miami Law Review, vol. 33, no. 2, 1978, and the
authorities there cited.
(2)   Roscoe Pound, 'A survey of social interests', *Harvard Law
Review*, 57, 1943, p. 17. See also *Declaration of the United
Nations Conference on the Human Environment*. Principle 5 of
the Declaration states: "The non-renewable resources of the
earth must be employed in such a way as to guard against the
damages of their future exhaustion and to ensure that benefits
from such employment are shared by all mankind".
(3)   L. Oppenheim, *International Law*, Vol. 1, (8th Edn.), Long-
mans, London, 1955, speaks of a "clear and continuous habit of
doing certain actions (that) has grown up under the aegis of
the conviction that these actions are, according to International Law, obligatory or right", p. 26.
(4)   Speaking of Grotius, Fenwick notes that "The urgent task,
as he felt, was not to set forth the uncertain and unjust usages of the time, but to lay down better rules of conduct based

upon inferences from moral principles acknowledged in the abstract but consistently violated; and his appeal from existing
practice to the ideal conduct was so forcible that his words
became authoritative and statesmen relied upon his judgement
as the correct inference from accepted general principles".
Charles G. Fenwick, *International Law*, Indian Edition, 1967, p.
90.
(5) H. Lauterpacht, 'Sovereignty over the submarine areas',
British Yearbook of International Law, Vol. 27, 1960, p. 393.
(6) "The development of a new international legal order is no
longer characterised by the steady, time-consuming procedure
of traditional customary law-making where larger States usually
play a substantial role. It is not a coincidence that the observers of the evolution of international relations have witnessed the fast-growing process of the development of new customary law. The law of the continental shelf was one of the
first examples of a fast-growing custom, and the international
law of space has developed even faster". Eric Suy, 'Innovations
in the international law-making process', in MacDonald, Johnston and Morris (eds.), *The International Law and Policy of
Human Welfare*, 1978, p. 189.
(7) See generally on 'lack of opposition', 'tolerance', and
'silence' as implying 'consent' or 'acquiescence'; *The Fisheries Case* (United Kingdom v. Norway), *I.C.J. Reports*, 1951,
pp. 136-9; and Sir Gerald Fitzmaurice, 'The Law and Procedure
of the International Court of Justice 1951-4: General Principles and Sources of Law, *British Yearbook of International Law*,
1953.
(8) See on this Jorge Castaneda, *Legal Effects of United Nations Resolutions*, Columbia University Press, New York, 1969.
(9) For a cautious acknowledgement that certain U.N. resolutions are evidence of customary international law which "the
Court...may not ignore", see *The Legal Consequences for States
of the Continued Presence of South Africa in Namibia (South
West Africa) notwithstanding Security Council Resolution 276
(1970)*, Advisory Opinion, *I.C.J. Reports*, 1971, p. 16 and pp.
31,32. On this point, the view of Legal Counsel of the United
Nations appears to be that: "The most one could say is that
overwhelming (or even unanimous) approval is an indication of
opinio juris sive necessitatis; but this does not create law
without any concommitant practice, and that practice will not
be brought about until States modify their national policies
and legislation". See Eric Suy, *op.cit.*p. 190. The present paper proceeds on the basis that statements by the accredited
representatives of States in United Nations forums, supported
by their votes, clearly and expressly reflect the national policies of States on any given subject. States would not normal-
ly enact legislation on matters which do not require regulation
at the national level, and the absence of such legislation
should not be seen as weakening formal expressions of policy.

(10) Such relevant decisions include: the Declaration on the
Granting of Independence to Colonial Countries and Peoples.
(Res. 1514 (XV)); the Declaration of Principles governing the
Seabed and the Ocean Floor, and the Subsoil thereof, beyond
the Limits of National Jurisdiction (Res. 2749 (XXV)); the
Charter of Economic Rights and Duties of States (Res. 3281
(XXIX)); the Declaration on principles of international law
concerning friendly relations and cooperation among States in
accordance with the Charter of the United Nations (Res. 2625
(XXV)); the Declaration on the Establishment of a New International Economic Order (Res. 3201, Sixth Special Session); the
Declaration on Permanent Sovereignty over Natural Resources
(Res. 1803 (XVII)) and successive declarations under the same
title, such as Res. 2158 (XXI), 2692 (XXV), 3016 (XXVII) and
3171 (XXVIII); the Declaration of the United Nations Conference
on the Human Environment (Stockholm, 16 June 1972); and certain
records of the Third United Nations Conference on the Law of
the Sea.
(11) The Declaration on the Establishment of a New International Economic Order asserts that "International cooperation for
development is the shared goal and common duty of all countries.
Thus, the political, economic and social well-being of present
and future generations depends more than ever on cooperation
between all the members of the international community on the
basis of sovereign equality and the removal of the disequili-
brium that exists between them". Introductory paragraph 3. See
also Wolfgang G. Friedmann, *The Changing Structure of International Law*, Columbia University Press, New York, 1964, pp. 61-
62.
(12) Treaty on Outer Space, article 1.
(13) Antarctic Treaty, Preamble, first paragraph.
(14) Revised ICNT, A/CONF.62/WP.10/Rev. 1 Article 136.
Declaration of Principles, paragraph 1.
(15) As the representative of El Salvador (Chairman of the Legal Sub Committee of the Seabed Committee) declared at the time
of the adoption of the Declaration: "That principle endows the
international area with a peculiar character, and with this
Declaration the United Nations is now changing international
law". A/C.1/PV.1781, p. 17. The representative of Norway said:
"The fifteen broad principles here laid down are indications...
of the rules and provisions of international law, present and
future, applicable to the domain of the ocean floor and its
subsoil". A/C.1/PV.1774, pp. 18-20.
(16) The Declaration of Principles was adopted by a vote of 108
in favor, none against, with 14 abstentions.
(17) Paragraph 4 read with paragraph 9 of the Declaration of
Principles. Compare Revised ICNT articles 138, 139, 150, 153.
(18) Compare the statement of the representative of Yugoslavia
referring to "The concept of 'the common heritage of mankind'
with its three vital elements, common wealth, common management

and common benefits...." A/C.1/PV.1784, p. 28.
(19) Declaration of Principles, paragraph 9; Revised ICNT, Part
XI, section 5.
(20) Compare Revised ICNT, article 157(1); article 137 (2).
(21) See Max Kaiser: *Das Roemische Privatrecht*, München, 1971,
p. 381.
(22) See Mommsen (ed.), *Corpus Juris Civilis*, Berlin, 1905,
Vol., I, Book II, paragraphs 1-4: "..... proprietas autom corum
potest, intellegi nullius esse, sed eiusdem juris esse, cuius
et mare et quae subiacent mari, terra vel harena".
(23) See Vicenzo Arangio-Ruiz, *Instituzioni di Diritto Romano*,
Naples, 1927, p. 155.
(24) *Corpus Juris Civilis*, Vol. XXXI, 1, p. 14, a view attri-
buted to Neratius.
(25) For a discussion of the collective ownership and the regulation of individual appropriation of things conceived of as
res publicae, see Giuseppe Branca, 'Le cose extra patrimonium
humani juris', *Annali Triestini di Diritto Economica e Politi-
ca*, Vol. XII, 1941, 209 et seq.
(26) See U.N. General Assembly resolution 2574 (XXIV),sometimes
called the 'moratorium resolution', which declares that, pending the establishment of the international regime, States and
persons are "bound to refrain from all activities of exploitation of the resources of the area....", and that "No claim to
any part of that area or its resources shall be recognized".
See, in the same sense, resolution 176 (XVIII) adopted by the
Trade and Development Board of UNCTAD at its 510th meeting,
17 September 1978; the statement of the Chairman of the Group
of 77 of the Conference on the Law of the Sea (1978), Ambassador Nandan in A/CONF. 62/SR.109, the statement of the Chairman
of the Group of 77 of the Conference (1979) Ambassador Carias
on 19 March 1979. As one writer observes: "(The developed
countries) accepted that all exploration and exploitation
should be 'governed by the international regime to be established'; and even though they still maintained that the regime itself would have to be agreed among States, this made it considerably more difficult for them to initiate, or even to con-
done, activities by their own companies within the sea-bed
which were not in accordance with an agreed regime...." Evan
Luard, *The Control of the Sea-bed*, Heinemann, London, 1974, pp.
133-4.
(27) Kautilya, *The Arthasastra*, Trans. R. Shamasastry, Fifth
Edn., Mysore, 1956, Chapter XII 'On conducting mining operations and manufacture'. The work provides, *inter alia*, for the
office of 'Superintendent of Ocean Mines' (Khanyadhyaksha).
(28) Declaration of Principles, paragraph 9.
(29) Cf. RICNT, articles 136, 137 (2).
(30) Cf. RICNT, article 137 (1) read with article ,133 (b).
(31) Cf. RICNT, article 137 (3)
(32) Cf. RICNT, article 137 (3); Declaration of Principles, pa-

ragraph 4 read with paragraph 9.
(33) Cf. RICNT, articles 137(2), 153, 157.
(34) Cf. RICNT, article 138 read with article 141.
(35) Cf. RICNT, article 140 (1).
(36) Cf. RICNT, article 141.
(37) Cf. RICNT, article 148, 152.
(38) Cf. RICNT, article 149.
(39) Cf. Declaration of Principles,paragraph, as elaborated in section 6 of Part XI of the RICNT.
(40) Cf. RICNT, articles 150,151.
(41) Cf. RICNT, articles 153, 157.
(42) Cf. RICNT, articles 160 (2)(n), 162 (2)(n), and article 16 of Annex II.
(43) Cf. RICNT, article 153 (6).
(44) Cf. RICNT, article 12 of Annex II.
(45) Cf. RICNT, articles 140 (2), 160 (2)(j), 173 (2)(a).
(46) Cf. RICNT, Part XI, section 5.
(47) Cf. RICNT, Part XI, section 5, sub section E, and Annex III.
(48) Cf. RICNT, article 161...The emphasis accorded to technical capability throught the voting strength on the Council acquired by the countries possessing it, (generally speaking a matter of numerical strength,since any weighted voting system would be contrary to principle) would reflect the extent to which the membership is persuaded that production from the Area is needed for the general welfare of the community, and, therefore, whether the regime for the Area is to function along production oriented rather than restrictive lines. To judge from the existing examples of areas for which international regimes have been contemplated, e.g. the deep sea-bed, Antarctica, the 'activities' often considered relate to mining, and the 'production' is of minerals vital to the industries of the technologically advanced countries. The industrialized countries have insisted that unrestricted mineral production from the sea-bed's resources, for example, would benefit all mankind. However, when the food resources of the Antarctic's waters are discussed, the dominant theme is 'conservation'.
(49) Cf. RICNT, article 164 (1), 165 (1).
(50) Cf. RICNT, article 159, paragraphs 5-10.
(51) Cf. RICNT, part XI, section 5, sub-section G, article 170(2) and Annex III, article 12.
(52) Cf. RICNT, articles 145, 146, 208-210.
(53) Cf. RICNT, articles 145, 208-10; Declaration of the United Nations Conference on the Human Environment (1972), Principles 6 and 7.
(54) Cf. RICNT, article 143.
(55) Cf. RICNT, article 144 and Annex II, article 5.
(56) Cf. RICNT, article 147 and Annex II, article 15.
(57) Cf. RICNT, article 147.
(58) Cf. RICNT, article 142, paragraphs (1) and (2).

(59) Cf. RICNT, article 142 (3).
(60) Cf. RICNT, article 139. The principles governing 'liability' and 'responsibility' (treated often as the broader term, in debates at the Conference on the Law of the Sea) and the distinction between the two concepts, has not been adequately discussed. The current texts seem to leave open the possibility that certain damage caused by operators might give rise to 'absolute' liability such as is provided for in article II of the Convention on International Liability for Damage caused by Space Objects. See also RICNT, part XII;

International Responses to Technological Innovations
Bert V.A. Röling

TECHNOLOGICAL INNOVATION: EXPECTATIONS AND THREATS

Technological innovations are the direct consequence of the natural sciences and their foundation in empiricism. Empiricism started, centuries ago, as something quite revolutionary, being a reaction against the Greek and especially the scholastic tradition. It is in this context that Bertrand Russell calls Francis Bacon "the founder of modern inductive method and the pioneer in the attempt at logical systematization of scientific procedure". (1)

One wonders what it was that gave the impulse to this revolution and provided the power and the zest to find out about 'things'. The motives may well have originated from religious convictions and beliefs. It appears, for example, that Bacon hoped, through his empirical investigations, to discover the artlessness and innocence which Adam is supposed to have had before the Fall. Greek and scholastic philosophy had, according to Bacon, been a continuation of Adam's sin of Pride. Thus Bacon wrote: "We clearly empress the stamp of our own image on the creation and works of God, instead of carefully examining and recognizing in them the stamp of the Creator himself". (2)

It is important that we should realize that empirical science, and the technology derived from it, were originally seen as a means of retrieving the innocence and the artless power which man possessed before he was driven from the Garden of Eden. When compared to the situation that we are in today, the distance is indeed considerable. Today, we worry about the threatening implications of science and technology. We have grown to realize that our civilization could founder as a result of the knowledge and science acquired; that human knowledge can go too far and that it is possible for mankind to

know more and to do more than it can cope with. In the arms
race, for example, we justifiably speak of a 'race to oblivion'. (3)

History has known scientists, like Archimedes, Leonardo
da Vinci and Napier, who kept secret the knowledge of the
weapons of mass destruction which they had invented. That was
then possible for they lived at a time when inventions were
the work of a single man and when the inventor had and retain-
ed a say in their application. Leonardo wrote in his secret
diary about his "under-waterboat". Napier invented a mysterious
machine which, according to testimony, "could clear a field of
four miles circumference of all the living creatures exceeding
a foot of height". The danger of a Spanish invasion circumven-
ted, Napier decided that, given "the malice and rancour rooted
in the heart of mankind", (4) he could better take his secret
with him to the grave.

The realization that science and knowledge are not always
a blessing is quite old, possibly as old as history. Rabelais
has Gargantua write to his son: "Science sans conscience n'est
que ruine de l'âme". And the Dutch historian Johan Huizinga
referred some forty years ago to the necessity of asceticism
of thought to further worldly wisdom. When we worry about
science and technology today our anxiety is not in the first
place concerned with furthering worldly wisdom, but rather
with ensuring worldly survival.

The problem of 'survival' is a modern problem. In the past
it was barely a consideration since technology did not possess
today's terrible destructive capacity and military minds were
not preoccupied with the capture of technological innovations.
Certainly, there have been many wars in the past: an American
historian has calculated - goodness knows how! - that out of
3,400 years of recorded history, only 234 have been free from
war. (5) We can attribute the fact that we are alive today,
not to the wisdom of our forefathers, but to their ignorance
of destructive technology.

This ignorance no longer exists. The technology of this
century is characterized by its 'destructive ingenuity'. (6)
The real turning point was the Second World War. It provided
an enormous stimulus to the technological development of arms:
it gave the world German V1s and V2s and it culminated in the
atom bomb which although too late to be used against Hitler,
destroyed two Japanese cities. The exertions of the scientists
and the preoccupations of the generals can no doubt be explained by the fear of defeat. But whatever the explanation, it contributed to the recognition that arms are more important than
men. Today's world is a world of 'manned arms' rather than
of 'armed men'.

Today's world is also a world in which the quality of
weapons is frequently considered more important than their quantity. The process of innovation, rooted in the Second World War,

continues today, feeding upon its own technological 'successes'.
Hedley Bull has correctly observed that it is "this tendency
to continuous innovation (and not 'the atom bomb', or any particular weapon or weapon system) that is the most destructive
feature of the modern armaments race and the chief theme of
strategic studies". (7) Corbett similarly refers to "systematic innovation" and to the "powerful institutions at the center of society, commanding legions of trained minds and vast
economic resources". (8)

All this has led to the tendency to exploit each new invention to the utmost. Politicians have become convinced that
the power of their country is determined by its technology.
They are inclined to declare, over and over again, that they
consider the possession of certain new weapons essential for
security. Western 'spokesmen', as well as official NATO-state-
ments, have repeatedly stressed that Western security can only
be safeguarded by the possession of tactical and strategic nuclear weapons (and by being prepared to be the first to use
them!). It is understandable and inevitable that other states
conclude that what is good for the NATO countries is equally
good for us. The consequence is of course the proliferation
of nuclear weapons (to mention but one example of the spread
of military technology). And this proliferation will continue
until such time as the world's leading powers no longer see
such weapons as a condition for their independence and security.

We are of course a very long way off from such a situation. Indeed, all the evidence suggests increasing escalation
and increasingly sophisticated weapons and weapon systems, a
process which has led many polemologists to conclude that a
major war must be the inevitable outcome. (9) It is worth reminding ourselves that it was 'The New Learning', 'The Great
Instauration', with its origins in the desire to recapture
lost innocence, which has led to the arms dilemma; to a world
of science in which one of its most prominent practitioners
has admitted that "we have known sin" (Oppenheimer) and to a
world of states in which the super-powers maintain the means
for mutual genocide for the purposes of peace and security.

THE DIVIDED WORLD:
EAST-WEST AND NORTH-SOUTH

What sort of world was it to which technology bestowed
nuclear arms and missiles. It seems to me that this world could
be (and indeed still can be) characterized by two main features.
The first of these is the emergence, following the Second World
War, of the United States and the Soviet Union as super-powers
and the decline of the power of Western European nations. These

super-powers, like all super-powers before them are suspicious
of each other. Their situation, however, is marked by two important peculiarities: their respective spheres of influence
have not yet been defined, and probably never will be; and
they adhere to different, and hardly compatible, ideologies.
They both strive for real power. Although the atmosphere is
competitive, the original idea that the two systems could not
possibly co-exist has largely disappeared.

But they also share common interests. Not the least of
these - and this is the second feature characterizing today's
world order - is that they cannot become entangled in a direct
military confrontation. Given the destructive power of their
weapons, against which neither side has any sort of remedy,
this figures as an absolute priority.

Both are thus bent on political gains yet both are united
in their determination to avoid a direct military confrontation which might arise from their offensive policies and post-
ures.

The destructive capacity of their arsenals has compelled
the super-powers to negotiate bilateral agreements which aim
at minimizing the possibility of war - 'deliberate' or 'acci-
dental' - between them. (10) These agreements generally set
out to limit the freedom of action of both parties. In the
1973 Treaty both sides accept "that each Party will refrain
from the threat or use of force against the other Party, a-
gainst the allies of the other Party and against other countries, in circumstances which may endanger international peace
and security" (art. II). (11)

As far as arms negotiations are concerned there is absolutely no indication that either super-power will be able
to develop the attitude required to come to grips with the
extraordinary problem presented by the technological development of arms. Alva Myrdal has quite rightly concluded that
"disarmament negotiations have been used by the super-powers
for balancing each other and not for planning disarmament".(12)
Or, to put it in different terms, the super-powers are guided
in their arms control efforts by considerations of their reci-
procal relations in the balance of power. Considerations such
as these are in themselves not unreasonable given the important role which the balance of power plays in geopolitics. But
this 'rationality' is only a partial rationality since it considers but one aspect i.e. the mutual relationship whilst
leaving entirely unconsidered the consequences of super-power
behaviour for the rest of the world. In short, the East-West
relation leads the nuclear powers to respond in totally inadequate ways to the technological challenge posed by nuclear
arms.

In addition to the East-West division, there is the division between North and South; between old and young states,
between rich and poor, between a technically highly developed

world and a world in which technology has played only a modest
role. Decolonization has brought with it the emancipation of
the Third World; a political emancipation which has virtually
been completed; and an economic emancipation which has only
just begun. The Third World seeks the establishment of a New
International Economic Order which provides the weak with protection and support in their struggle for self-reliance and
well-being.

At present we live in a period of transition from European International Law to Universal International Law. The international community has become a community in which the poor
'have nots' are in the majority. And states such as these request and need a different legal order from the one required
by the rich nations to look after and to promote their interests. (13) A small and select group of European states created
traditional international law long ago. The validity of this
system of law, however, is now being questioned and new principles - of social justice - are in the course of being introduced. The process is characterized by a gradual change in
mentality and in starting points, *Entscheidungsprämissen*. (14)
We are in the middle of a *Kampf ums Recht* which will have far-
reaching consequences for the world of old states, with their
age-old privileges. Decolonization and the acknowledgement
of racial equality were the start. They were the natural consequences of the Universal Declaration of Human Rights. The
demand for a more equitable international order and for a
fairer distribution of scarce resources is in fact directly
supported by the Declaration. Article 25 affirms the right of
everyone "to a social and international order in which the
rights and freedoms set forth in this Declaration can be fully
realized".

All this has set the world in motion. Old values are being challenged and new ones proposed. Technology, aided by industrialization and communication, has added new forces to
this whirlpool. The limits of what is considered humanly possible have been shifted, new relations between powers have been
established, and conflicts of interest have given birth to new
ideas and values. The changes are of paradigmatic dimensions
and the emancipation of the Third World and the process of
technological innovation have been of decisive importance in
bringing them about.

Technology has helped to bring about a second and related
change in the foundation of opinion and approval. Haas had
rightly concluded that technology, "breaking upon the world
when it did, compounded the feeling of our being developed in
a massive 'collective situation' to which there can only be a
'collective response' if any one is to attain his objectives.
In this sense we are really embarked for the first time in
world history, on Spaceship Earth". (15) Some years earlier
Skolnikoff had pointed to what he called the side-effects of

technology, the first of which he refers to as being "the dramatic growth of the interdependence and interpenetration of
societies". (16) Because of the pervasive influence of technology, 'the world' can no longer be regarded as 'a family of
nations' (which has been used to justify dependent relations),
nor as a society of nations (which has emphasized members' independence). A percept has gradually developed which finally
found expression in the 'spaceship earth' concept (marked by
the interdependence of all concerned). It also encompassed the
feeling of solidarity between mankind and nature and it gave
expression to an ecological conscience, a feeling of respect
for nature and a profound bond with the biosphere.

The challenge of technology thus takes place in a divided
world, in a period of fundamental change, at a time in which
the main demand of two-thirds of mankind can be summarized as
'equality' and 'independence' (freedom). The challenge of
technology must also be faced in a world committed to the nation-state and the notion of national sovereignty. The developing nations especially, conscious of their new found and
often hard won freedom, have displayed a real distrust for supranational organizations vested with real responsibility.
This distrust is in part based on a real fear that such organizations serve the interests of the status quo and give greater
articulation to the needs and concerns of the rich and powerful nations.

In many of the UN megaconferences held in the past decade
the final declarations have emphasized that the solution to
problems must first be sought within the framework of the nation-state: cases in point are the Stockholm environment conference (1972) and the Bucharest population conference (1975).
Even the Declaration on the Establishment of a New International Economic Order advocates the adoption of an essentially
national approach to the problem of international equity. Only
occasionally is there a reluctant - almost grudging - recognition of the need for 'appropriate international machinery', as
in the case of the exploitation of the deep sea-bed. (17)

Clearly, many of the problems posed by new technologies
(concerning, for example, armaments, environment, population
and welfare) defy purely national solutions. To be tackled effectively, regional and global bodies will prove indispensable.
An optimum approach may well call for limitations on the exercise of sovereignty and of national prerogatives.

THE NATURE OF INTERNATIONAL RESPONSES

In discussing possible international responses to technological challenges it is thus essential to recognize the primacy of the nation-state. The nation-state is and is likely to

remain the most important unit of decision-making. It is nation-states which draw up the mandate for international organizations and which define the role they are to play in coming
to terms with international problems. It is usually up to the
nation-state to decide whether it will accept and act upon
the recommendations which emanate from international bodies.

We are concerned, however, with international responses.
It is perhaps useful to start by distinguishing between what
we need (what is necessary) and what we are capable of providing (given our opinions and views of the world). (18) Our
view of what is needed is conditioned by our understanding of
the 'things' we seek to control, our view of what can be done
is conditioned not by the 'things' but rather by our understanding of what is possible given the fact that decisions
must be taken by human beings and, in a democracy, supported
by 'the public'. This distinction has become confused with the
one between idealists and realists. *Idealists* are often seen
as being guided by their attitude towards the 'things' and by
what these 'things' require of us. Those who base their prescriptions on the opinions, ideas and prejudices assumed to
exist among 'the public' are commonly referred to as *realists*.

Obviously, to reach decisions which are realistic it is
necessary to consider both the nature of things and the ideas
current among the public. The approach to be adopted can perhaps be formulated as follows: the nature of things determines
the ultimate aim; public opinion determines what is politically possible ('feasible') and what could be made politically
possible and 'feasible' by information and education. It will
frequently be impossible to attain that which is demanded by
the nature of things without an intensive process of information and evaluation. Unless one were to yield all power to a
small, select group, or if this group were to seize the power
required to realize that which the thing - the technology -
demands.

In discussing how the technological challenge might be
met, it is not the intention to review every existing type of
response. We are more concerned with indicating broader possibilities. In this respect, I would specifically refer to the
character of the technology and to the size and nature of the
body which is to respond to it.

Character of the Technology. A distinction must first be
made between responses geared towards dealing with the peaceful use and the hostile use of modern technology. Peaceful use
can necessitate international cooperation, both in order to
maximize the benefits and to effect a fair distribution of the
output. Peaceful applications, however, may also carry certain
risks, which make international regulation necessary. The
peaceful use of nuclear energy, for example, carries with it
the danger of the proliferation of nuclear weapons as well as
threats to the environment. Similarly, there is the problem

of pollution from pesticides and from artificial fertilizers, from the waste generated by chemical industries, and there are problems associated with the transport of oil in giant tankers. The less spectacular and sometimes barely perceptible threat hidden in many peaceful uses could well prove to be as fatal for the world as the obvious danger of the hostile use of the new technologies.

Size and Nature of the Organization. The *size* of the body which is to formulate the response to the problem is obviously important. In some case the most appropriate response might be regional, as in the case of a group of nations which come together to plan and manage the water basin of a river. Often, however, the problem may require an organization which is global in scale, as is required in the case of the maintenance of peace, the exploitation of the sea-bed and the management of energy resources. The challenge is to find an optimum whereby all those affected by the effects of decisions are involved in the making of the decisions.

The *nature* of the organization which is to deal with problems of technology is also an important consideration. Here the basic distinction is between international governmental organizations (IGOs) and international non-governmental organizations (INGOs). The former are commonly divided in supranational and strictly international organizations, depending on whether or not they are vested with the authority to take binding decisions on a majority vote. Supranational organizations are practically non-existent: the E.E.C. (the European Economic Community) is the closest we have come to building one with effective powers. Usually, then, we will be dealing with international organizations in which the minority cannot be bound by the majority. In this case we are concerned with institutionalized forms of cooperation in which supranational elements may be present. The clearest example is the United Nations. Its General Assembly can adopt resolutions by majority vote, although they have only the legal power of recommendations. Because of this weak power the significance of these resolutions is frequently underestimated. They have, however, the important function of contributing to changes in attitude and mentality. They lead to the emergence and subsequent adoption of new viewpoints, they point to the direction in which law may develop, they are an important factor in that development, and they lay the foundation for the formulation of a more effective international response.

The INGOs are usually even further removed from binding decisions. For this reason they usually have greater freedom to formulate and to express their views and opinion. It is frequently their task to launch initiatives, to inform public opinion, and to prepare the way for possible solutions. Some international professional societies are also able to take decisions which are able to influence the conduct of their

members. The Pugwash Group, for example, was able to formulate
the 'Pledge for Scientists' (Oxford 1972) modelled after the
Hippocratic Oath sworn by physicians. (19)

In summary we can observe that we are dealing with a wide
range of international organizations some of which are close
to and others distant from actual decision-making. If we take
the ratification of an international treaty as the moment that
the international community takes a decision, then we can dis-
tinguish all kinds of preparatory bodies the influence of
which is generally in inverse proportion to their distance
from the decisions: as distance increases responsibility de-
creases and it becomes easier to hold and to advocate a position.

The role of IGOs is not restricted to formal decision-
making. They also play important roles in preparatory processes, the traditional realm of the INGOs. The UN is particularly prominent in this respect. General Assembly resolutions
are, as noted earlier, nothing more than resolutions. Even
where they refer to norms, the norms have only weak legal
power. They are often, however, a necessary intermediate phase
which precedes an effective ruling. Thus the 'Declaration of
Legal Principles Governing the Activities of States in the Exploration and Use of Outer Space' (20) preceded the Outer
Space Treaty of 1967. Obviously, governments are more prepared
to accept general principles in a non-binding Declaration than
they are to submit themselves to enforceable rules of conduct.
This is why C. Wilfred Jenks proposed over ten years ago that
the international community adopt a General Assembly resolution comprising 'A Declaration of General Principles Dedicat-
ing Science and Technology to the Service of Man' in preparation for an eventual World Science Treaty. (21) One of the
principles to be accepted was "that science is the common heritage of mankind". The Declaration also called for continuous
care to ensure that neither technology nor research inflict
damage upon the environment. Not until 1975 - 7 years after
Jenks' proposal - did the General Assembly accept a resolution
in this field: the 'Declaration on the Use of Scientific and
Technological Progress in the Interests of Peace and for the
Benefit of Mankind'. (22)

REGULATION OR ORGANIZATION

Regulations aimed at controlling the development and use
of technology will fall into one of three broad categories:
those which set out to maximize benefits; those which seek to
minimize disadvantages, following, where necessary, an assessment of pros and cons; and those which aim to ensure a fairer
distribution of advantages and disadvantages, and of partici-

pation and control.

The international response to a new technology is often
the creation of a new organization with a multipurpose function, i.e. one with a reasonably broad mandate. Since the
technology is 'new', knowledge as to its potential advantages
and disadvantages may be inadequate, and the organization will
probably give first priority to the collection of data and
their subsequent publication. This will usually be accompanied
by an evaluation of the data relative to interests which are
perceived to be threatened by the technology. Where the organization is vested with responsibility for formulating rules
for the use of the technology, the next step is traditionally
one of organizing conferences and symposia, stimulating investigation and coordinating ongoing and new activities. Where
the organization has the responsibility for monitoring the observance of rules, tasks will be expanded to include such activities as the collection and analysis of national reports
and the documentation, analysis and possibly resolution of
conflicts arising from the observance or non-observance of
obligations

As a general rule it is desirable that a body (secretariat, office) be involved in a succession of interrelated activities rather than be confined to isolated and singular
tasks. This helps guarantee responsiveness.

The sequence of tasks to be undertaken can be broadly
summarized as follows:

Orientation	Collection of data
Information	Publication of data
Evaluation	Assessment of data
Education	Stimulating the adoption of a point of view
Policy preparation	Advocating courses of action, such as acceptance of rules of conduct, forms of cooperation
Policy implementation	Execution of specific tasks such as the provision of assistance, inspection and the settlement of disputes
Decision-making	To the extent made possible by the authority vested in the organization

A clear example is given by UNEP (United Nations Environment
Programme), established as a result of the 1972 Stockholm Conference. It is a relatively small organization responsible for
essentially preparatory work. Its first director, Maurice F.
Strong, declared in the General Assembly of the United Nations
on 20 October 1975 that "UNEP has particular responsibility

for watching over the environment of the global commons and
these responsibilities provide the focus of UNEP's programme".
The Dutch delegate, Dr. Kaufmann, pointed in his intervention
of 21 October 1975 to the coordinating and policy-guiding task
of UNEP (in relation to both UN and non-UN initiated activities) and also noted that UNEP should aim "to intensify public
awareness and appreciation of environmental issues by stimulating the flow of relevant information, through appropriate
media and methods. Coordination of environmental action should
go hand in hand with efforts to improve environmental education and training". Dr. Kaufmann shared the opinion "that UNEP
must continue to give high priority to the consolidated development and improvement of Earth Watch Programmes...".

The example of UNEP serves to show that if an organization is to have an impact it should form the focal point of
continuous attention and action. The statements made with respect of UNEP also suggest that an organization should be vested with different responsibilities - investigation, policy-
formulation, education, monitoring and evaluation, and so on -
as a condition for effective action and as a basis for a real
international response.

No less an essential condition for the effective regulation of technology is the readiness and willingness to see and
to know the facts with respect to that which is to be controlled. In other words, dangers should be squarely faced. We
know, however, that those who are opposed to change and who
prefer to turn their backs on danger traditionally fear information and tend to resist any kind of action, even the most
rudimentary analysis of the most basic kinds of data. They realize, quite rightly, that 'facts' or 'things', to say nothing
of opinions, can constitute a powerful force, especially if
there is a consensus as to ultimate goals. We know too that
such consensus is a fragile commodity which can easily evaporate in the process of translating goals into strategies. It
is one thing, for example, to agree on the need to conserve
fish stocks and to know all there is to know about the ecological conditions required for the conservation of stocks. It
is quite another matter to put theory into practice for this
might require the imposition of limitations on fish catches
and this could result in unemployment among fishermen. The
question of which is the most important - fish stocks or employment - is obviously a political question where answers will
vary according to whether 'public' or 'private' interests are
afforded priority and to the time-frame employed. Obviously,
then, when it comes to deciding among the alternatives for regulation, the main question is not one of physical and technological determinants but rather of social choice. (23)

Even where a fragile consensus does exist, the defenders
of the status quo may fear - and thus resist attempts to gather
- more knowledge. The governments at the diplomatic conferences

on the law of war, for example, where 'dubious weapons' (24)
were discussed, were not prepared to allow the World Health
Organization to collect medical evidence on the effects of
such weapons, even though all parties were in basic agreement
that the weapons were undesirable and a precedent for such an
exercise already existed. (25)

In times of danger - and it is clear that a great number
of technologies does involve very considerable dangers - it is
of the utmost importance that the danger be acknowledged and
understood. Collecting and interpreting the facts can thus be
seen as an essential starting point for regulation and it constitutes an important area of responsibility for international
organizations.

TECHNOLOGICAL INNOVATIONS: THE FIELDS

A distinction has already been made between constructive
and destructive technology, between technological means of destruction and technology in the service of mankind. It has been
noted that civil technology may involve insidious, although
less obvious, dangers and thus may also require regulation. It
is to the problems associated with both types of technology
that we will now briefly turn.

Arms Technology

In this field a distinction needs to be made between the
prohibition of the use of certain weapons and the prohibition
of the possession of certain weapons. The former is laid down
in the law of war, the latter in the laws on arms control and
disarmament. It strikes many as odd that whereas the possession of certain kinds of weapons is permitted, their use is
prohibited. We are concerned here with cases where inspection
is barely possible. The possession of these weapons may involve
reprisals in kind should the opposing party break the usage
prohibition. Thus, no poison-gas was used in the Second World
War, not only because it was prohibited by the Geneva Protocol
of 1925, but because it was known for a fact that the enemy
would retaliate with the use of C-weapons.

The one and only instance of the prohibition of the possession of arms is the Biological Weapons Convention of 1972,
which remains the only true disarmament treaty. (26) Many
treaties exist which prohibit the presence of certain arms in
certain places: The Antarctic Treaty (1959); the Outer Space
Treaty (1967); the Treaty of Tlatelolco, concerning the denu-
clearization of Latin America (1968); and the Sea-Bed Treaty
(1970). The Non-Proliferation Treaty (1968) forbids the nuclear

'have-nots' from ever acquiring nuclear arms. Similarly, there
are treaties which limit the amount of weapons a nation is
allowed to possess, such as SALT I and SALT II, concluded between the United States and the Soviet Union, whereby both
parties commit themselves to abstaining from building an effective ABM system and accept a ceiling on the number of offensive missiles.

Arms control negotiations are presently underway in a
number of places and between different parties. There are
talks, for example, between East and West on Mutual (Balanced)
Force Reduction in central Europe (in Vienna) and involving
a larger number of nations at the Conference of the Committee
on Disarmament (CCD in Geneva). In 1979 a Special Session of
the United Nations General Assembly was devoted exclusively
to the subject of disarmament, although it failed to yield,
as could have been expected, concrete results.

Arms control and disarmament (arms reduction) negotiations are frequently confused as being synonymous whereas they
certainly are not. Arms control ensures the maintenance of the
present system of peace by deterrence or "to save the system
by adapting it to new conditions".(27) They do not constitute
steps in the direction of a new order. Disarmament or arms
reduction negotiations do or at least should.

Arms control negotiations are usually concerned with peripheral changes and leave the main issues - overarmament and
the deterrence system - untouched. Hence the increasing criticism of an activity which the public at large is supposed
to believe is important. Long ago, Dr. Johnson spoke of "nationalism as the last refuge of the scoundrel". Given the
hawk-mentality that is frequently behind the interest in arms
control, it could also be argued that arms control is 'the
last refuge of the scoundrel'.

At present, a great deal of attention is being paid to
the possible development of geophysical and environmental
weapons; i.e. weapons that make use of the forces of nature
causing earthquakes, hurricanes, climatic changes, solar ra-
diation through gaps in the ozone layer. A treaty aimed at
prohibiting the development of 'environment modification techniques' was drawn up in the CCD and subsequently adopted by
the UN General Assembly. The treaty, however, does not prohibit scientific research (an original proposal of the American
Senate had included research in the proposed prohibition).(28)
An interesting new aspect of the treaty is that suspected in-
fringements during peace time can be brought before a Consul-
tative Experts Commission (art. V). This could serve as an important means of acquainting governments and the public with
the facts.

In June 1975 Mr. Brezhnev spoke of the "serious danger
that still more frightful weapons than even nuclear ones may
be developed". In the same year the Soviet Union presented a

new draft treaty to the CCD 'On the Prohibition of the Development and Manufacture of New Types of Weapons of Mass Destruction and of New Systems of such Weapons'. (29) One cannot
be quite sure which weapons the Russians had in mind. The
first to suggest themselves are techniques relating to genetic engineering, i.e. manipulating genetic factors by way of
'recombinant DNA'. A positive aspect of the proposal is that
it suggests measures to prohibit atrocious weapons, not only
before they have been deployed by military powers, but also
before they have been 'invented'. The uncomfortable feeling
remains, however, that whereas our attention is being demanded for future arms development, precious little is being done
to come to terms with existing stock-piles of nuclear arms,
the use of which could spell the end, not only of our civilization, but of all of humanity. Is it all seriously meant,
or is it nothing more than a smoke-screen aimed at conceiling
a basic unwillingness to address really important issues? (30)

Peaceful Technology

Which of the technologies likely to be used for peaceful
purposes appear most in need of regulation? Some years ago
Jenks suggested that special attention needed to be given to
"the international control of nuclear energy, the innumerable
problems arising from activities in space (beginning with liability for damage by space vehicles and contamination of and
from space), environmental pollution in all its forms, the
regime of the ocean depths, new developments in the polar regions, and the regulation of supersonic flight and boom". He
went on to note that "weather and climate modification schemes,
earthprobing operations and control of certain cybernetic developments may soon be major additions to the list". (31)
In his *This Endangered Planet*, Richard Falk approaches the
problem from the perspective of the interest threatened by the
development of technology. He lists four areas where the
threats are planetary in their dimensions: the war system, the
pressure of population growth, the scarcity of goods, and 'environmental overload'. He notes that in all these areas developments are taking place which demand an adequate international response, arguing that "only new organizational forms with
a planetary scope that corresponds to the planetary dimension
of the situation can offer any prospect of a timely, corrective and adequate response". (32)
If we consider what has so far been accomplished in these
fields we can only conclude that the responses fall very far
short of what is required. Take, for example, the comparative-
ly straightforward case of the pollution of the oceans. Some
treaties have been concluded concerning the giant oil-tankers
which constitute an obvious threat. (34) There are also va-

rious treaties concerning the dumping of oil and other dangerous matter, in which a role was reluctantly assigned to the
coastal nations and to nations other than the flag nation.
Despite these agreements, the oceans continue to be dumping
grounds for all manner of refuse, including highly toxic atomic waste. And still the rivers are sewers which pour their
chemical effluent into the seas.

Organizations founded to deal with a new type of technology may have all kinds of functions in addition to those mentioned in section 4, i.e. maximizing benefits, minimizing losses and ensuring that benefits and losses are equitably distributed. The ITU (International Telecommunications Union),
for example, is concerned not only with ensuring equitable access to the frequency range but also with rendering assistance
to the states in need of help. But even in technically oriented organizations like the ITU, the division between old and
young states is evident, as it most certainly was at the World
Administrative Radio Conference (WARC) held in Geneva in September 1979. (35) Whereas the old states wish to adhere to the
rule 'first come, first served' as a legal principle for the
distribution of frequencies, the new states, noting that 10
per cent of the world's population has access to 90 per cent
of the radio spectrum, stress the fairer distribution of a
scarce resource.

The development of technology has led not only to communication satellites but also to observation satellites which
utilize remote sensing to detect the presence of natural resources. A monopoly on such satellites implies a monopoly on
another important source of power: information. The holders
of such information obviously possess a major advantage in
such matters as negotiations on raw material and commodity
agreements.

It is probably safe to assume that there is not a single
problem in either East-West or North-South relations which can
be characterized as being merely 'technical' or 'functional'.
In designing international responses to technologies and to
technological problems, it is thus essential to recognize that
if they are not already 'political', problems can easily be
'politicized'.

It will also be necessary to constantly keep in mind that
even the most well-meant treaty can have adverse effects, even
lead to situations which it was designed to prevent. The Non-
Proliferation Treaty is a case in point. (36) Similarly, it
can be shown that the Treaty of Versailles (1919) and the requirement of German disarmament was instrumental in the development of rockets in Germany, and that SALT I contributed to
feverish U.S. efforts to advance development of the cruise
missile.

Experience with treaties suggests that whilst it might
be possible to prohibit or at least hinder the development,

testing, manufacture and use of certain technologies, attempts
to legislate research on technologies are unlikely to be very
successful. This would certainly apply to weapon technologies,
although it is likely to prove just as difficult to isolate
other fields from their technological milieu. The only way to
put a stop to all military and to other areas of technological
innovation would be, as Hedley Bull has observed, "a reversal
of the general social trend to innovation; but this is something against which the most powerful ideological, social, political and industrial forces in modern society are arrayed".
(37)

CONCLUSIONS

We can conclude that the international response to technological innovation has generally been inadequate in every field.
The primacy of the nation-state and preoccupations with national sovereignty - sovereignty which sometimes exists more in
theory than in practice - has no doubt contributed to the lack
of effective decision-making. An adequate response may call for
comprehensive approaches involving strong international bodies
representing those affected by the technology. The process of
technological innovation can thus be seen to demand new forms
of organization involving choices with respect to the territorial size of the area they are to cover, the precise problems
they are to address, the functions they are to perform, and
the power they are to have at their disposal (are they to formulate 'recommendations' or are they to take decisions which
bind their members).
The formulation of an adequate response will thus depend
upon our ability to create the structures which make the response possible. The question, as always, is whether we really
want to build such structures, whether there is the political
will to do so. At present that will is soured by mutual mistrust and by the fundamental differences which divide East and
West and North and South.
Our failure must also be explained in terms of inability
to identify factual developments and to assess their long-term
significance, by our unwillingness to face these facts when we
are confronted with them, and by the deeply-rooted tendency to
adhere to all that is known and established. Hence the enormous
importance of information, investigation and evaluation. The
'things' we are concerned with determine that which is required,
but 'the people', 'the public' with its attitudes and opinions
rooted in experience and the past determine what is possible.
The gap between the 'things' and 'the people' can only be
bridged by knowledge of the facts. In a process of political
change, information and education thus play a decisive role.

The changes brought about by technology are likely to be so radical that even cursory knowledge of them is likely to lead to changes of mind and a reorientation of values. As Richard Falk has observed, "the facts and values that endanger our future are capable of their own somber eloquence". When these become known there will be "no need to cram a creed down resistant throats". (38)

Technology has power for good and for bad, for better and for worse. As John Kennedy observed, "Man holds in his mortal hands the power to abolish all forms of human poverty, and all forms of human life". What matters most of course is how this power will be used in what Brezinski has called the 'technetronic age'. (39) Von Weizsäcker spoke in this context of the adolescence of our technical culture in which we are ready to use all that science can provide us, in which we have not yet learned to apply moderation and restriction, in which daring and recklesness have not yet been tempered by insight. A more adult attitude will not manifest itself until we have gained real insights into the consequences of the technological route along which we stumble - the consequences for rich and for poor and in the short- and long-term.

And this brings us back to our starting point when we observed that 'science sans conscience' can lead not only to the destruction of the human soul but to the destruction of the human race. Is it to this conscience that our hopes are ultimately pinned? Hamlet is in world literature the man incapable of action, the man aware of the complexities of human situations and of the consequences of human action. In despair, he reproaches himself for not being like Fortinbras who was readily prepared to go to war:

> to gain a little patch of ground
> that has in it no profit but the name (IV,4,19);

or in Hamlet's own words

> a plot which is not tomb enough and
> continent to hide the slain (IV, 4, 73).

There, to Hamlet's way of thinking, lies the true greatness of the man of action:

> to find quarrel in a straw
> when honour's at the stake.

On the other hand there is the thoughtful man, the observer, the *Betrachtende*, who must weigh all the consequences of action, who knows nothing of 'blind involvement', but who is hampered is his actions by insights into the facts and a knowledge of their consequences.

>   Thus conscience does make cowards of us all

cries Hamlet in bitter self-reproach.

Cowards? Given the situation in which we find ourselves,
the threatening dangers with which we are confronted, would it
not be appropriate should we aspire to this cowardice? For "it
is something if conscience makes cowards of men, even if it
does not make saints". (40)

Perhaps we should avoid the word 'cowardice' in this context. It is more natural to expect that with more information
more knowledge about what is really at stake, more insights
into the madness of the present situation, something may emerge
which if not wisdom may be worthy of the word 'prudence'.

And thus we return to Francis Bacon. Only this time our
hopes are no longer set on the natural sciences but on the social sciences.

NOTES AND REFERENCES

(1)   Bertrand Russell, *History of Western Philosophy*, George
Allen and Unwin, London, 1946, p. 563. Ernst Cassirer in his
The Myth of State, Yale University Press, New Haven, Conn.,
1946, p. 294 also refers to Bacon as "one of the pioneers of
modern empirical thought". This view, however, is not generally
shared. Paoli Rossi in his *Francis Bacon, From Magic to Science*,
University of Chicago Press, Chicago, Ill., 1948 observes:
"Bacon should certainly not be seen as the inventor of modern
science on the grounds that he discovered the inductive method.
Such a view, though dear to the founders of the Royal Society
and to the Encyclopedists, has long been superseded". (p.138)
Rossi does, however, list various reasons why Bacon should be
afforded "a place in the history of philosophy and science".
(2)   This extract from Bacon's *Historia Naturalis* is quoted by
Rossi, op. cit., p. 129. Rossi notes (p. 130) that it was Bacon's motive and purpose "to redeem man from original sin and
reinstate him in his prelapsarian power over all created
things". In similar vein Frances Yates has written: "Bacon's
'Great Instauration' of learning was an attempt to return to
the pure state of Adam before the Fall, when, in close contact
with God and nature, he had insight into all truth and power
over the created world". Frances Yates, 'Science, salvation
and the cabbala', *New York Review of Books*, 27 May 1976, pp.
27-29.
(3)   Herbert York, *Race to Oblivion. A Participant's View of
the Arms Race*, Simon and Schuster, New York, 1971.
(4)   See John U. Nef, *Western Civilization Since the Renais-
sance. Peace, War, Industry and the Arts*, Harper Torchbooks,
New York, 1963, p. 122ff.

(5)   More reliable are the figures for more recent times. Istvar Kende has calculated that between 1945 and 1965 some 25
wars and some 100 civil wars have been fought. See Istvar Kende, *Local Wars in Asia, Africa and Latin America 1945-1969*,
Academy of Science, Budapest, 1972.
(6)   John U. Nef, op.cit., p. 377: "During the first half of
the nineteenth century destructive lagged behind constructive
ingenuity; during the first half of the twentieth destructive
forged ahead of constructive ingenuity. The industrial state,
which Comte and Spencer regarded as incompatible with the military state, was transformed into an engine of war".
(7)   Hedley Bull, *The Control of the Arms Race*, Weidenfeld and
Nicholson, London, 1961, p. 195.
(8)   J.P. Corbett, *Europe and the Social Order*, The Hague,
1959, as quoted in Hedley Bull, op.cit.
(9)   For such a view see SIPRI, *Armament and Disarmament in
the Nuclear Age,* viz.Alva Myrdal's conclusions 'The Game of
Disarmament', Pantheon Books, New York, 1976; and C.F. von
Weizsäcker, *Wege in der Gefahr*, Hanser Verlag, Munich, 1976.
(10) Reference can be made, for example, to agreements concerning the 'hot line' (1963, 1971), measures designed to reduce the risk of the outbreak of nuclear war (1971), the SALT
agreements (1972, 1979), the agreement concerning incidents at
sea (1972, 1973), and the prevention of nuclear war (1973).
(11) Nevertheless, it remains, juridically speaking, odd that
the threat or use of force is prohibited only under certain
circumstances, viz. "in circumstances which may endanger international peace and security", whereas Art. 2 sub 4 of the
U.N. Charter prohibits any threat of force and all use of
force. It must be said that in practice little has come of
the prohibition of the threats of the use of force. It is obviously not taken very seriously. Do the super-powers really
mean it? Subsequent practice, as during the oilcrisis, would
seem to indicate that they might not.
(12) Alva Myrdal in SIPRI, *Armament and Disarmament in the
Nuclear Age. A Handbook*, Stockholm-New York, 1976, p. 227.
Alva Myrdal also points out that the negotiations and the
treaties also serve "by a conscious design on their part" to
keep the smaller states at the desired distance.
(13) See on this point Bert V.A. Röling, *International Law in
an Expanded World*, Djambatan, Amsterdam, 1960.
(14) See Karl. W. Deutsch, 'Der Stand der Kriegsursachenforsch-
ung', *DGKF Hefte*, no. 2, Bonn, 1973, p. 16; and also Bert V.A.
Röling, 'International law and the maintenance of peace',
Netherlands International Law Review, 1973. pp. 1-102, p. 43ff.
(15) Ernest B. Haas, 'Is there a hole in the whole? Knowledge,
technology, interdependence and the construction of international regimes', *International Organization*, 1975, pp. 827-876,
p. 875.
(16) Eugene B. Skolnikoff, 'Science and technology: The impli-

cations for international institutions, *International Organization*, 1971, pp. 759-775, p. 761ff.

(17) See article 29 of the Charter of Economic Rights and Duties of States, resolution 3281 XXIX, 12 December, 1974.

(18) See on this William Fulbright, *Prospects for the West*, Harvard University Press, Cambridge, 1963, viz. p. 43. The distinction suggested has been of considerable importance among lawyers, in the conflict between natural law and positive law. Emeric de Vattel called natural law *jus necessarium*, the law that rational thinking suggests is ideally required and which society requires to attain its objectives (but the rules of which have no legal power) and called positive law *jus voluntarium*, the law that admittedly falls short of the objectives set by society but is the one desired and therefore possesses legal power.

(19) see SIPRI, op.cit., p. 282. The pledge states: "I will not use my scientific training for any purpose which I believe is intended to harm human beings. I shall in my work strive for peace, justice and the betterment of the human condition".

(20) General Assembly resolution 1963 XVIII, 13 December 1963.

(21) C. Wilfred Jenks, 'The new science and the law of nations', *International and Comparative Law Review*, 1968, pp. 327-345, p. 339.

(22) General Assembly resolution 3384 XXX, 10 November 1975. It should be noted, however, that this resolution was prompted more by an anxiety concerning human rights than a concern for the evil and destructive aspects of technology. It calls for international cooperation so as to ensure that technological developments serve peace, social welfare and the realization of human rights. Given its content, its title appears unnecessarily grand.

(23) See on this John G. Ruggie, 'International responses to technology: Concepts and trends', *International Organization*, vol 23, 1975, pp. 558-583.

(24) 'Dubious weapons' are new weapons (such as incendiary weapons, high speed munition, fragmentation bullets or bombs, delayed action weapons) which may contravene the principles of the laws of war. These laws of war stipulate that weapons can be prohibited because of their inhuman effects, even if they are considered to be of military necessity. It is a matter of weighing 'inhumanity' against 'military necessity'. See SIPRI, *The Law of War and Dubious Weapons*, Stockholm, 1976.

(25) In 1969 the WHO had reported on *Health Effects of Possible Use of Chemical and Biological Weapons*, document EB 45/18 Add. I, Geneva.

(26) On 28 July 1976 the United Kingdom submitted a draft treaty on Chemical Weapons to the CCD. The text is reprinted in *Survival*, November-December, 1976, pp. 272-275.

(27) Richard A. Falk, *The Endangered Planet, Prospects and Proposals for Human Survival*, Random House, New York, 1971,p.62.

(28) Senate Resolution 71, of 22 February 1973. In 1975 a
joint US-USSR draft was submitted to the CCD. An amended version was submitted to the UN General Assembly in 1976.
(29) The text was included as an annex in the General Assembly
resolution 3479 XXX of 11 December 1975.
(30) It should always be kept in mind in this respect that the
Soviet Union has always declared itself in favor of nuclear
disarmament and has in fact made far-reaching proposals towards this end. It will be recalled that in 1976 the Warsaw
Pact proposed an agreement concerning the prohibition of the
first use of nuclear weapons. This proposal was rejected virtually out of hand by NATO!
(31) C. Wilfred Jenks, op.cit., p. 328. Later, when summing up
the treaties which he considers to be desirable, he also refers to "a Molecular Biology Treaty formulating a code of
protective measures against the use of depraved biological and
psychological skill for purposes prescribed by the law as inhuman". (p. 339)
(32) Falk, op.cit., p. 97.
(33) The Public and Private Law Conventions, Brussels, 1969,
on dangers caused by accidents. The Private Law Convention's
objective is the prevention of accidents by making it possible
to limit the amount of the damages claimed (art. V) and by
making insurance obligatory (art. VII). The insurers are relied upon to take care that only ships in a sound condition
will be put to sea. The Public Law Convention gives the threatened coastal state the right to take such actions, as, for
instance, shooting at and so setting fire to a stranded tanker
in order to limit the damage (art. I).
(34) See James Barros and Douglas M. Johnston, *The International Law of Pollution*, Free Press-Macmillan, New York-London,
1974. On rivers, p. 83ff, air, p.174ff; oceans, p.22ff. They
conclude that "it is generally agreed that the existing principles of international law, as described by the leading ju-
rists, provide an inadequate legal basis for the effective
treatment of international pollution problems" (p. 69). From
the treaties dealt with, the inadequacy of the special agreements so far made is shown.
(35) WARC, attended by 140 nations, was held to decide how the
world's radio broadcasting frequencies should be allocated for
the remainder of the century. The conflict between the old and
new nations was well in evidence. The *New York Times*' page 1
story on the conference was appropriately entitled 'Rich and
poor clash, delaying world talks on radio frequencies'.
(36) See Richard A. Falk, 'Beyond internationalism', *Foreign
Policy*, vol. 24, 1976, pp. 65-113.
(37) Hedley Bull, op.cit., pp. 197-198. Whereas it might be
possible for individual nations to regulate the flow of research
funds for military purposes, supervision at the international
level cannot at present be considered.

(38) Falk, *The Endangered Planet*, p. 445.
(39) Zbigniew Brezinski, *Between Two Ages:America's Role in the Technetronic Age*, Vintage Press, New York, 1971. It relates to the age in which technology and electronics introduce the new 'things'.
(40) See John U. Neff, op.cit., p. 385.

Index

About the Contributors

EDITOR

Antony J.Dolman (United Kingdom): Senior Fellow, Foundation
Reshaping the International Order (RIO), Rotterdam. Trained
first as a city planner and then as an environmental planner,
he practiced and taught planning in Europe and developing countries. Growing interest in international relations led him to
abandon city planning and to take up the development problematique. In 1975 he became associated with the RIO Project and
edited the *RIO Report* (1976) which has now been translated into
12 languages. He has been involved in various capacities with
the programs of UNIDO, UNESCO and UNEP and has served as a consultant to a number of international non-governmental organizations. The author of several volumes on planning, he edited
Partners in Tomorrow: Strategies for a New International Order
(with Jan van Ettinger, 1978). His book *Managing the World's
Resources* (1980) is published as a complementary volume to
Toward Global Planning and Resource Management.

CONTRIBUTORS

Silviu Brucan (Romania): Professor of Political Science, University of Bucharest. His former public appointments have included the posts of Permanent Representative to the United Nations, New York, and Ambassador to the United States. He has
also headed the Romanian broadcasting system and edited a national newspaper. His books include *The Dissolution of Power*
(1971) and *The Dialectic of World Politics* (1978).

Harlan Cleveland (U.S.A.): Director, Program in International
Affairs, Aspen Institute for Humanistic Studies, Princeton.

Starting August 1980: Director, Hubert H.Humphrey Institute of
Public Affairs, University of Minnesota, Minneapolis. His many
public appointments have included the posts of graduate school
dean (Maxwell School, Syracuse University), Assistant Secretary
of State, Ambassador to NATO and President of the University of
Hawaii. His most recent public service is as Chairman, U.S.
Weather Modification Board. His books include *The Obligations
of Power* (1966), *NATO: The Transatlantic Bargain* (1970), *The
Future Executive* (1972), *The Planetary Bargain* (1975), *The
Third Try at World Order* (1977) and *Humangrowth: An Essay on
Growth, Values and the Quality of Life* (1978).

Richard Falk (U.S.A.): Professor of International Law, Woodrow
Wilson School of Public and International Affairs, Princeton
University, and Senior Fellow, Institute for World Order, New
York. He has acted as director of the North American partici-
pation in the World Order Models Project since 1968. His books
include *Law, Morality and War in the Contemporary World* (1963),
Legal Order in a Violent World (1968), *The Status of Law in
International Society* (1969), *This Endangered Planet* (1971),
A Global Approach to National Policy (1975) and *A Study of Future Worlds* (1975). His forthcoming work includes an attempt to
write a history of the future from the viewpoint of oppressed
peoples, including those in the advanced industrial countries
who are "invisibly oppressed" by the threat of nuclear warfare
and by the prospects of ecological harm.

Johan Galtung (Norway): Institut d'Etudes du Développement,
Geneva, and Project Coordinator, Goals, Processes and Indicators of Development Project, United Nations University. Formerly, Professor of Conflict and Peace Research, University of
Oslo, and Director and Founder, International Peace Research
Institute, Oslo. His books include *The European Community: A
Superpower in the Making* (1973), *A Structural Theory of Revolution* (1974), and *The True Worlds: A Transnational Perspective*
(1980). Many of his papers have been grouped together in *Essays
in Methodology* (2 vols.; 1977, 1978) and *Essays in Peace Research* (5 vols. by 1980).

Johan Kaufmann (The Netherlands): at present Ambassador to Japan, was involved for more than 20 years in a large variety of
United Nations activities. His public appointments have included
those of Counsellor, Netherlands Permanent Mission to the United
Nations, New York (1956-1961), Permanent Representative to the
United Nations Office and other International Organizations,
Geneva (1961-1969), Permanent Representative to the Organization for Economic Cooperation and Development, Paris (1969-1974)
and Ambassador and Permanent Representative to the United Na-
tions, New York, (1974-1978). He has served as adviser to the
U.N. Secretariat and is at present a member of the Board of

Trustees of UNITAR. His books include *Conference Diplomacy*
(1968) and *United Nations Decision Making* (1980).

Stel Kefalas (Greece): Professor, College of Business Adminis-
tration, and Director, International Trade Development Center,
University of Georgia. He is a member of 14 professional societies and has been Management Development Instructor since
1970 for numerous academic and business organizations. He has
served as Academic Director of both the Annual Executive Program, University of Georgia (1972-1978) and the Venezuelan Advanced Management Development Program, IESA/INCE (1975-1977).
He has coauthored *Management Systems: Conceptual Considerations*
(1975), *Management: Making Organizations Perform* (1980) and
Making Organizations Work: Readings and Cases (1980). He contributed to the chapter 'Goals for Multinational Corporations'
in *Goals for Mankind* (1977).

Elisabeth Mann Borgese (U.S.A.): Killam Senior Fellow and Professor, Department of Political Science, Dalhousie University,
Canada, Chairman of the Planning Council, International Ocean
Institute, Malta, and adviser to the Delegation of Austria at
the Third United Nations Conference on the Law of the Sea. She
was formerly associated with the Center for the Study of Democratic Institutions, Santa Barbara. She has written extensively
on the oceans and marine resources; her books include *The Ocean
Regime* (1968), *The New International Economic Order and the Law
of the Sea* (with Arvid Pardo, 1976), and *Seafarm: The Story of
Aquaculture* (1980). She is joint editor of the *Ocean Yearbook*
and is currently researching a book on ocean mining.

Arvid Pardo (Malta): Senior Research Associate, Institute of
Marine and Coastal Studies, and Professor of Political Science,
University of Southern California. He has formerly held the
posts of Permanent Representative to the United Nations, New
York, High Commissioner in Canada, and Ambassador to the United
States and the USSR, posts which, for part of the time, he held
contemporaneously. He has also been a visiting fellow at the
Center for the Study of Democratic Institutions, Santa Barbara
and coordinator of marine programs at the Woodrow Wilson Inter-
national Center for Scholars. He has written extensively on
ocean law, politics and policy, his publications including *The
New International Economic Order and the Law of the Sea* (with
Elisabeth Mann Borgese, 1976).

Christopher Pinto (Sri Lanka): Special Ambassador relating to
questions on the Law of the Sea and the International Law Commission, Geneva, Attorney of the Supreme Court of Sri Lanka,
Barrister of the Inner Temple, and Chairman of the International
Law Commission. He held legal positions with the International

Atomic Energy Commission and the World Bank prior to becoming
legal adviser to the Ministry of Defence and Foreign Affairs
and, subsequently, Ambassador to the Federal Republic of Germany and Austria. He has been closely involved in the U.N. Law
of the Sea conference and is Chairman of the 50 nation negotiating group responsible for elaborating an international regime and machinery for the seabed beyond national jurisdiction.
He has written extensively on international law and ocean space
problems.

Bert V.A.Röling (The Netherlands): Emeritus Professor of International Law and Peace Research and former Director, Institute
of Polemology, University of Groningen. He began his career as
a judge in the Netherlands and became the Netherlands judge in
the International Military Tribunal for the Far East. His involvement in the Tribunal led him to take an increasing interest in international affairs and he went on to become one of
the founders as well as Secretary-General of the International
Peace Research Association. He has been an active member of
Pugwash and is a member of the Board of the Stockholm International Peace Research Institute. His books include *International
Law in an Expanded World* (1960), *Einfuhrung in die Wissenschaft
von Krieg und Frieden* (1970), *International Law and the Maintenance of Peace* (1973), and *The Law of War and Dubious Weapons*
(with Olga Suković, 1976).